International Perspectives on Educational Reform and Policy Implementation

International Perspectives on Educational Reform and Policy Implementation

Editors

David S.G. Carter and Marnie H. O'Neill

 The Falmer Press

(A member of the Taylor & Francis Group)
London • Washington, D.C.

UK   The Falmer Press, 4 John Street, London WC1N 2ET
USA   The Falmer Press, Taylor & Francis Inc., 1900 Frost Road, Suite 101, Bristol, PA 19007

First published in 1995

A catalogue record for this book is available from the British Library

Library of Congress Cataloging-in-Publication Data are available on request

ISBN 0 7507 0406 3 cased
ISBN 0 7507 0407 1 paper

Jacket design by Caroline Archer

Typeset in 10/12pt Bembo by
Graphicraft Typesetters Ltd., Hong Kong.

Printed in Great Britain by Burgess Science Press, Basingstoke on paper which has a specified pH value on final paper manufacture of not less than 7.5 and is therefore 'acid free'.

Contents

Contents

Preface

The inspiration for this work, presented as a two-volume companion set, was derived, initially from a period of study leave in 1985 and again in 1990 requiring protracted periods of residence in the USA and UK and resulting in our close involvement with academics, administrators and schools people in different education systems and at many levels. Contacts made then have been maintained and strengthened, and, for both of us, as we compared notes and experiences from attending a number of national, regional and international conferences, it became evident that educators appeared to be saying essentially similar things about the implementation of change — policies, programmes and practices — seemingly driven by external forces which had taken over the agenda from the profession. Somewhere in all this ferment was the exercise of the political will to govern in a directly interventionist fashion in education.

It was an intriguing thing to witness as we moved around the world, for example, gubernatorial elections being run on essentially education platforms especially after the publication of *A Nation at Risk*, the direct involvement of the Thatcher government in developing and imposing a National Curriculum in Britain, with the Education Portfolio becoming one of the hottest in Cabinet; a similar phenomenon in New Zealand and parallels in Australia, where numerous inquiries into education across the States and Territories, followed by radical revisions to curricula and organization took place throughout the 1980s continuing to the present. Those who believed in domino theory as this applied to education in Western society could have had a 'field day'. There appeared to be a set of forces at work which could only be worked out through the radical reform, restructuring, and/or transformation of education systems at all levels, although the work of schools was singled out for particular attention. The latter was motivated by a general dissatisfaction with the deficiencies in the perceived performance of schools and their failure to deliver value for money in terms of the dollar spent; the need to align schools more closely with economic reforms; and a view, prevalent at the time, of education in terms of human capital. In all the countries mentioned above, we were very aware that there was a common conception, at least by those outside of education (and some within it) that the transformation of schools and the reform of school systems would enable each country concerned to recapture its rightful share of the global market-place. It seemed rather bizarre to us that education, with its underlying moral imperative, was to be a major player for the exercise of market forces in realizing socio-economic goals in which the 'size of the global cake' was fixed.

In this volume, a number of educators and academics, selected because they were in a good position to bring their insights to the study of the historical, social and economic forces at work in the formulation and implementation of educational policy, try to understand the nature of a new educational reform era. Similarly in Volume 2 they were selected to represent the voices of people, teachers, administrators, academics and consultants who are immersed in, and keen observers of, the change process at work. The material they present is significant in its own right and should resonate with the experiences of many who have sought to manage and direct the process, and/or have been immersed in it themselves.

The perspectives offered are designed to capture different cross-cultural experiences of educational change and policy implementation; to contemplate and compare the collective experience represented in the following pages and thereby to enhance our understanding of the processes and forces involved. The various contributors to this volume have brought their unique insights into focus in order to analyse and exemplify the change process at work, for we would argue that there is such a thing, which is identifiable, has an air of predicability about it, and once recognized and understood can be directed and managed. That we have failed to do so on any grand scale to date is probably why the voluminous literature on change and the collective recorded experience of four decades of change management, on the whole, makes such dismal, yet fascinating, reading. We hope that the collective experience reflected in this and the companion volume will cause the serious reader to pause and reflect on this in some detail, for while we understand better the nature and complexity of implementation, as but one phase of the change process, we are perhaps a little less certain about the nature of change itself than we once were. It has become more highly differentiated from the tidal wave which tends to overwhelm us in its human dimensions, to the steady surf, and the ripples and currents all of which variously interplay to reinforce or work against human intents and agency in a given setting, at a given level and at a given scale.

In the chapters of this volume the various contributions have been grouped into three sections. Part 1 examines relationships between politics and educational reform, in which the myth that education is apolitical is exploded. Politics into policy and policy implementation is the main focus in Part 2, and in Part 3 selected education-reform phenomena addressed in the preceding sections are returned to, but examined from, quite specific and different perspectives. Finally, the Epilogue draws a number of themes together, locates them in chronological context and maps out an implementation research agenda for those interested in following up some much needed and potentially fruitful lines of inquiry.

Although the texts have been constructed as companion volumes, and should provide a more comprehensive reading if taken together, they are not mutually dependent. Each volume has been compiled to offer interesting comparative readings of similar education phenomena in different national settings.

We wish to thank the many people who have contributed to this volume, knowingly or unknowingly, in their interactions with us and with the contributors and for the many insightful comments about what we were trying to do. In particular we would like to thank Jane Piscioneri and Sheena Carter, at the University of Notre Dame Australia for their valuable secretarial and administrative support and encouragement in bringing this manuscript together. If the various studies presented in this volume present a mirror to others in similar settings facing the same sorts of challenges and in so doing helps them avoid the pitfalls inherent in Santayana's dictum, 'Those who ignore the lessons of history are condemned to repeat them', this project will have achieved its purpose.

David S.G. Carter   Marnie H. O'Neill
The University of Notre Dame Australia   *The University of Western Australia*

List of Acronyms

ACT	American College Test (program)
AEC	Australian Education Council
ATs	Attainment Targets
BRT	Building Resource Teacher
BSCS	Biological Sciences Curriculum Study
CBAM	Concerns Based Adoption Model
CDC	Curriculum Development Centre
CSE	Certificate of Secondary Education
CURASS	Curriculum and Assessment Committee (of the Australian Education Council)
DES	Department of Education and Science
DESSI	Dissemination Efforts Supporting School Improvement
DfE	Department for Education
EC	European Community
ERA	Education Reform Act
ERO	Education Review Office
ESEA	Elementary and Secondary Education Act
GCE	General Certificate of Education
GCSE	General Certificate of Secondary Education
LEAs	Local Education Authorities
GMS	Grant Maintained Schools
DfE	Department for Education
GNVQs	General National Vocational Qualification
HMI	Her Majesty's Inspectorate
HMSO	Her Majesty's Stationery Office
ILEA	Inner London Education Authority
KERA	Kentucky Education Reform Act
KS	Key Stages
LEA	Local Education Authority
LMS	Local Management of Schools
LOTE	Languages Other Than English
LoUs	Levels of Use
MAD	Multiple Adoption Design
MAVO	(Project) — A Dutch Secondary (General) Education Project
MOVEET	Ministers for Vocational Education Employment and Training

x

MSC	Manpower Services Commission
NASDC	National School Development Corporation
NASUWT	National Association of Schoolmasters/Union of Women Teachers
NC	National Curriculum
NDN	National Diffusion Network
NFER	National Foundation for Educational Research
NGA	National Governors' Association
NIE	Newly Industrialised Economies
NSTA	National Science Teachers Association
NVQs	National Vocational Qualifications
NZCER	New Zealand Council for Educational Research
NZQA	New Zealand Qualifications Authority
OBE	Outcomes-Based Education
OECD	Organisation for Economic Cooperation and Development
OHMCI	Office of Her Majesty's Chief Inspector
PAC	Parents Advisory Council
PM	Prime Minister
PPTA	Post Primary Teachers Association
QUERC	Quality of Education Review Committee
RoA	Records of Achievement
SAT	Scholastic Aptitude Test
SATs	Standard Assessment Tasks
SBM	Site-Based Management
SEAC	School Examinations and Assessment Council
SoA	Standards of Achievement
STs	Standard Tasks or Tests
TGAT	Task Group on Assessment and Testing
TOSA	Teacher on Special Assignment
TQM	Total Quality Management
TVEI	Technical and Vocational Education Initiative
UK	United Kingdom
WEAC	Wisconsin Education Association Council

Introduction

Marnie O'Neill

After death and taxes the only constant is change! The latter is a naturally occurring process reflected in the statement by the Greek Heraclitus that, 'everything is in a state of becoming'. This view of change is taken as a backdrop to the work reported in these pages. It is *not*, however, its focus and neither should it be equated with improvement, although the two appear to be used interchangeably — if not synonymously — in both theoretical discourse and practical endeavour.

An optimistic view of human nature subscribes to the position that it is possible to take control of change and direct it in order to realize an alternative future, such that when we actually arrive there it is not too different from the scenario which was originally envisioned. From this perspective we are dealing with planned or directed change which *is* the focus for the work undertaken in this project.

As is frequently the case in education, the concept of reform is not so clear as it once was and now subsumes other concepts such as school restructuring, transformation and systemic reform. Frequently these become metaphors or slogans for change and, over time, come to mean different things to different people and groups. The collective experience of reform in education is replete with examples of this phenomenon and it is selectively captured in the various chapters of this book and its companion volume.

In a similar vein, the complexities inherent in implementation have become more highly differentiated as our understanding of this phenomenon has increased — especially over the course of the last two decades. Apart from it becoming a major research focus for policy implementation and curriculum reform, it has become 'sloganized' as a banner for school and curriculum improvement having a life of its own.

Stenhouse (1975) in discussing curriculum development and reform, distinguishes between social movements and social trends. Drawing on Heberle (1951) and Gusfield (1968), he argues that a movement has a doctrine, and an educational movement has convictions or beliefs about an educational doctrine which it attempts to put into place, using any available evidence to support it, rather than to modify it. A trend, on the other hand is the result of similar but uncoordinated actions of many individuals. The distinction may offer a useful point of reference in reading the various contributions presented in these two volumes.

Sources of Curriculum

Sources of curriculum policy and content are drawn from what it is thought desirable or necessary to be learned from the available body of knowledge — the cultural content — and the perceived needs of the learner and the society. The nature of the decisions taken inevitably depends a good deal on who is doing the perceiving, and what ends will be served. Although there is a tendency for educators to write as if curriculum change (whether movement or trend) is 'pure', it is not, and there will be positions that are residual, emergent or resistant, in relation to the dominant trend.

An 'academic rationalist' orientation to curriculum design emphasized scholastic rigour in science and mathematics and transmission and preservation of the cultural heritage in literary arts and humanities, partly because this high culture knowledge was regarded as being of intrinsic worth, and partly for its virtues in providing intellectual training, albeit to an intellectual elite, in the English Grammar School tradition. In the instrumentalist values of the modern world, a 'knowledge for itself' approach can be defended if the recipients are likely to have any use for it subsequent to schooling. 'Education as intellectual training' might be worthy if that training were appropriate to the abilities of the learners and the vocations to be pursued. The logic of these defences became strained by the impact of comprehensive compulsory education policies.

An emergent trend of giving more weight to the perceived needs, interests and characteristics of the learner informed the British version of child-centred education, prevalent in the 1960s and 1970s. Documents such as The Plowden Report and The Bullock Report, originating in Britain but exerting a pervasive influence elsewhere, became key influences in educational change in Australian and New Zealand curriculum developments in the 1970s. What is now sometimes regarded as a romantic view of the child as an eager participant in education tailored to suit the specific needs and interests of the individual and relevant to the lived experience formed the basis for school- and even classroom-based curriculum development.

Client-centred approaches to psychology transferred to education (Rogers, 1969) on the theory that self-actualization and maximum fulfilment of individual potential would have a pay-off for society at large by producing happy, fulfilled, productive individuals with the desire, initiative and capacity to achieve. Such an individualized approach to curriculum is not compatible with meeting societal needs for some kind of comparable assessment system for among other things, the selection of students for further education, training or employment. Neither is it easy, from this perspective, to hold schools or systems accountable for financial expenditure involved in terms of the quality or quantity of educational outcomes actually achieved.

Shifting Values

From the mid-1980s, there was a shift away from cherishing the needs and desires of the individual to addressing the needs of society. Although Hirsch (1988) and Bloom (1987) are occasionally referenced as the catalysts for this change, residual criticism of child-centred approaches had been evident in the Black Papers in the United Kingdom (Cox and Boyson, 1975) and in various back-to-basics lobbies in Australia. Kerry Kennedy, in his chapter analysing the policy contexts of curriculum reform in Australia, Great Britain and the United States identifies as a common element, a crisis of confidence in education itself. As is illustrated in several cases in the companion volume, existing curricula and the ways in which they were operationalized in schools had been perceived, at one level or another, to be inadequate. Education was reclaimed by various governments as an instrument to advance the national (economic) good, rather than as a means of realizing personal development and fostering individual achievement that could be claimed, only in the aggregate and then indirectly, to contribute to national advancement.

The conceptualization of societal needs changed as well. Earlier analyses, such as that advanced by Berger and Luckman in 1967, for example, emphasized the production of cultural cohesion through promotion of a cultural canon viz. every child had to be told the same story, whether literary or historical. According to Reynolds and Skilbeck (1976), however, simple reproduction is insufficient, even if it were possible; instead, the curriculum should offer students the opportunity to interpret and reinterpret culture, viewed dynamically, in order to develop the necessary intellectual and social skills to resolve broad cultural problems. In the context of the early 1990s, the cultural cohesion components of societal needs are being replaced. Contemporary societal needs have been redefined within the framework of monetarist policy, with education being regarded as an instrument for the correction of economic ills and governments assuming new market-orientated corporate identities. The effects of this phenomenon on emerging curriculum trends is discussed by David Carter in Chapter 2 with specific reference to the Australian scene. In this discourse, societal needs are increasingly accepted as:

- production of greater economic good, promoting national interest through more favourable participation in international trade;
- tailoring outcomes of schooling more directly to employer needs to reduce costs and improve productivity; and
- establishing more overt, direct links between structure and outcomes of schooling and employment competencies to improve rates of youth employment.

An alternative construction of these goals, however, to be inferred from the economics of the post-October 1987 stock-market crash read as:

*   reducing educational costs by streamlining curricula and reducing options;
*   reducing drain on social welfare by keeping young people off the dole and in education and training programmes; and
*   improving standing on OECD tables for retention in post-compulsory schooling.

Kennedy's comparative analysis of reforms in the US, the UK and Australia considers them, at source, all to be politically driven. In the UK, unlike Australia or the US, reforms were nationally legislated, whereas in the US and Australia, they required something of a consensus between federal and state levels of government. Even so, in both countries there is an evident strengthening of the hand of central government in areas of education that traditionally were the preserve of the states.

With respect to the United Kingdom, in his chapter in this volume, Richard Aldrich asserts that the government made a unilateral attempt to regain control over an education system that had developed a momentum of its own, and in so doing set the agenda for the reorganization of comprehensive secondary schools according to its own priorities and values. In part, the Education Act of 1988 was expected to restore control of the system to the government in a highly direct and visible manner, and to reallocate control over the delivery of education away from producers to consumers. Ideologically, this was to be achieved by harnessing free-market forces in the operation of which parental choice was regarded as a primary mechanism for stimulating schools to perform. When allied to national assessment and the publication of 'league tables' positioning schools against each other on publicly verifiable criteria that could be understood by all — but particularly parents — educational standards would be raised. The difficulties and pitfalls attendant on this are addressed by both Denis Lawton and Richard Aldrich and analysed in detail by Caroline Gipps.

In a parallel situation in New Zealand, outlined by Michael Peters, where teachers have been accused of capturing the curriculum and constructing it to serve their own interests, the role of politicians was to reclaim the curriculum for those who are 'end-users' of the product, by applying public-choice theory to the delivery of education and the provision of educational services.

Peters' analysis of the politics of educational reform in New Zealand frames it in terms of a deliberate and sustained attempt at cultural reconstruction, in which the now clichéd objective is to deliver the necessary research, skills and attitudes required for New Zealanders to compete in an increasingly competitive international economy. According to Peters, the message underlying school reforms in his country is that in the past there was too much emphasis on social and cultural objectives and insufficient attention paid by educators to economic goals and realities. This theme is exemplified in Volume 2 where Roger Peddie illustrates the shift away from cultural inclusion and affirmation for language study to an instrumentalist position designed among other things to serve the economic interests of New Zealand in dealing with its trading partners. To realize this objective, space on the timetable, previously allocated to Maori language and culture as well as predominantly European languages other than English, was re-allocated to develop in students the languages of countries likely to be significant trading partners on the Asia–Pacific rim both now and in the future.

The Powerbrokers of Reform

In a number of the countries, the reform initiatives were seen by their respective governments to be so important to national policy interests that the prevailing strategies for bringing about educational change were by-passed or simply ignored. In England and Wales, the results appeared to be evidently draconian because of the high visibility with which policy decisions were put into effect, such as the abolition of the Inner London Education Authority (ILEA) accompanied by political wrangling conducted under the glare of the media. In virtually all of the countries represented in this book and its companion volume, business and commercial interests were consulted and represented in strategic forums more extensively than were those of educators and the lay public. In the UK, wresting control from the producers (teachers and LEAs) and placing it in the hands of consumers (parents and employers) was regarded as a prerequisite to promoting national efficiency and competitiveness.

Under the Australian Constitution, education remains a residual power of the states. A negotiated consensus at the Australian Education Council (AEC), an intergovernmental body (before its demise) consisting of federal and state education ministers, was used to arrive at a national approach to the development of policy for Australian schooling, and thereby to bypass the constitutional and financial constraints of Australian federalism. The Hobart Declaration of 1987, articulating, among other things, a common set of national goals for schooling in Australia, was part of a nationally negotiated agenda manifesting through its centrepiece the development of a national curriculum in eight areas of study. A series of national reports compiled by committees which notably eschewed educators set out employment-related competencies (Finn, 1991), a set of key competencies (Mayer, 1992) and a national framework for competency-based vocational training (Carmichael, 1992).

The desire for improved quality of student outcomes was compounded by demands to make school systems more accountable and more cost-efficient. Administration of education was restructured as an enterprise along corporate management lines described by David Carter in Chapter 2. Devolutionary procedures were initially packaged in the language of participatory democracy in the Australian states as well as New Zealand. Peters reports, however, that of the organizational innovations to be set in place in New Zealand — Parent Advocacy Council, Board of Trustees, Community Education Forums and the National Policy Council — only the Boards remain. Devolution of functions previously administered centrally offered some cost savings — in New Zealand the local boards comprised of volunteers inherited much of it — devolved a lot of central administrative responsibilities to the periphery, but without any significant increase of personnel (see both Angus and O'Neill, in Volume 2 in this regard). The centre also retained responsibilities for staffing, and left in place various budget and curriculum constraints which effectively prevented schools from any radical change. Hall (Chapter 7), also notes this tendency to leave in place many of the rules and regulations which constrain local decision-making when site-based management reforms are set in train.

Most of the instances of, and political arguments for, reform presented in these two volumes entailed cost reduction as at least part of the agenda. Steffy and English in Volume 2 report on one of the few cases in which *per capita* funding to education was actually increased. As a result of a class action equity suit, educational provision in Kentucky was found to be in violation of the Constitution, leading to the largest tax increase ever experienced in the state. The resulting Kentucky Education Reform Act (KERA) put in place an integrated comprehensive programme to produce change in curriculum, finance and governance. In spite of the comprehensiveness of the programme, and the support for schools built into the reform agenda, Steffy and English suggest that the reform is wobbly. Three years after the reform was initiated, less than half of the schools had established school councils; the teachers were unhappy about the additional workload imposed by the councils, and, at the elementary level, were frustrated and anxious about the mandated requirements to initiate multi-age and multi-ability grouped classes. At the macro level when a well-funded, carefully developed, comprehensive and integrated reform is at risk it is usually due to a complex of relationships and other interrelated factors which are likely to be conditioned at source by the interplay of both structural and human factors. These are carefully considered by Shirley Hord in Chapter 6.

Politics to Policy

Kingdon (1984), cited by Jim Lowham in Volume 2, argued that there are occasions when policy changes can be made readily, and others when the resistive factors will be too great. He identified three currents — 'political', 'problem' and 'alternative' — that must be moving in the same direction in order to create a 'window of opportunity' optimizing the implementation of policy in a given setting. Such windows tend to open rarely, and remain open for relatively short periods of time. On that basis, it would appear that policy reformers have to sit around waiting for such a window to open, but evidence offered by contributors in these two volumes indicate that some of the factors can be manipulated. Thus, in the context of national-curriculum reform in Britain, it is speculated that the open window resulted from a 'break-and-enter' action. The political will and the problem were both apparent to policy makers; and, in this instance the alternative or resistive current was simply neutralized by the Education Reform Act of 1988.

In Australia, the policy window was open between 1987 and 1992, when state and federal governments reached consensus on educational reform through the Australian Educational Council. By 1993, the window had closed. At the state level of government, changes in the ascendancy of political parties and ideological conflicts concerning the content of the emerging national-curriculum statements and profiles resulted in withdrawal of consensus. As a result, the national curriculum in Australia has not been taken up in the form originally envisaged by the AEC, but has been variously interpreted and modified to suit the needs of the states and territories and their prevailing political orthodoxies with respect to the provision of education services.

A retrospective account of a more successful exploitation of a 'window of opportunity' is given by Miriam Ben-Peretz in Volume 2. Working from a related notion of the need for synergy to accomplish major educational change, Ben-Peretz describes the ways in which intermediate school reform in Israel was accomplished. In so doing, she identifies three broad groups involved in effecting the restructuring of the system which had to be persuaded to act in concert to generate the synergy to produce a successful reform:

- central and local authorities (Ministry of Education, Parliament and local municipal authorities);
- stakeholders (teacher organizations, principals, teachers and parents); and
- external factors (political parties, Supreme Court, scientists, institutes of teacher education).

The Gap between Policy and Implementation

Symptomatic of many of the reforms reported by the contributors in these two companion volumes is a design–implementation gap between policy formulation and implementation of the proposed reform in its setting. Policy makers are frequently (even usually) a different group at a different level of governmental decision-making than those who will be responsible for implementing proposed changes. According to Gene Hall in this volume and Jim Lowham's case study in Volume 2, policy makers rarely develop a process for the implementation of their policy formulations — the people on the receiving end of the policy are simply expected to make it work in practice. Hall and Hord in their respective chapters in this volume suggest that this gap exists because, in spite of the experiences of the 1970s and 1980s policy makers still tend to act on the assumption that change is an event, not a process. Hall argues that for a reform to have a chance of successful institutionalization, implementation, like design, has to be planned and budgeted for over an extended period of time. Rather than the short-term expectations of many American innovations, Hall cites European exemplars with both longer time frames and more comprehensive support systems for maintenance of innovations to hold them in place until they become institutionalized. Both Hall and Hord make cases for multi-level involvement in implementation, so that participants at all levels of the system contribute to the day to day process of changing practices — whatever form these may take (i.e., administrative or pedagogical). Although Hord advocates a more collegial approach to implementation than the model of the 'hero principal', leadership is obviously a critical factor in managing change, as is evidenced in the instances presented by Carter and Walsh in Volume 2.

What does seem inescapable is that teachers who will be required to make changes to their classroom practices have to understand the proposed changes both at the ideational and the programmatic level, and to be convinced that both the human and material costs of the proposed change will be worthwhile in terms of improved outcomes for their students, however these may be conceived and measured.

Lawton, in Chapter 3, suggests that when Kenneth Baker announced his intention, in 1987, of introducing a national curriculum, there was a good deal of public support for it in principle, although there were some doubts expressed about the details of implementation. This assertion is subjected to further scrutiny, from an historian's perspective, by Richard Aldrich, who points out that assumptions surrounding control by the British government demonstrated how ill-equipped it was to implement its reforms. The quangos and working parties involved necessarily included large numbers of professional educators, (previously identified as being among the parties who had captured the curriculum!). Their attempts to turn legislation into curriculum were frequently rejected by the government which viewed them as being deliberately subversive. Aldrich is of the opinion that the likely outcome of the impasses is that professionals will be replaced by party *apparatchiks*.

In the UK the resistance by a majority of the teaching profession to national-assessment protocols (both their nature and form) became most evident during the early implementation phases of the national curriculum. Caroline Gipps examines the issues and practices of assessment attendant on the operation of the four key stages of the national curriculum, and their impact on teachers and schools. Some of the issues she deals with, from technical and political perspectives, include validity and reliability, manageability in relation to consumption of time and practicality. Teacher dissatisfaction with assessment procedures for 14-year-olds led to a boycott of the formal tests because of the extra workload; the boycott was upheld in court, and only 5 per cent of Key Stage 3 schools sent in their results. Difficulties with assessment procedures have had different effects at different levels. Gipps indicates that the assessment procedures for 7-year-olds have had a positive effect on teaching and assessment practices, and contributed in a positive way to teacher development. This is supported by the findings of the study reported by Neville Bennett and Clive Carré in Volume 2.

In the event, assessment at Key Stage 4 proved to be unworkable, and has led to changes in the structure of national curriculum. Instead of a full entitlement curriculum to the age of 16 years as intended, the 10-level scale was revised to finish at age 14 to allow opportunity for vocational options at ages 14 to 16. There are now in effect three national curricula at 16+: academic and general, vocational and occupational.

The New Orthodoxy

Evidence presented in these two volumes, albeit selective and necessarily constrained, indicates that a shift is taking place in the relationship between politics, government and education in complex Westernized post-industrialized countries at least. Government interventions appear to have been driven by a range of motives including:

- improving national economics by tightening a connection between schooling, employment, productivity and trade;
- enhancing student outcomes in employment related skills and competencies;
- attaining more direct control over curriculum content and assessment;
- reducing the costs to government of education; and
- increasing community input to education by more direct involvement in school decision-making and pressure of market choice.

There have been some seeming contradictions in attempts to decentralize power to schools which paradoxically require some centralized locus of control to accomplish and maintain the shift (see the exemplar provided by Betty Steffy and Fenwick English in Volume 2). Without deregulating at the same time, the capacity of schools to act on their supposed new powers may be inhibited by residual rules and regulations put in place under the old regime but still left in place under the new (Hall, Chapter 7). Reforms that centre on governance may have little to do with educational outcomes (Steffy and English). Devolution of responsibility to schools may apparently result in cost savings at the centre, but actually represent a transfer of costs to the periphery, where the burden has to be carried in terms of additional workload by teaching and administrative staff, or otherwise absorbed by voluntary community service such as is found on school boards. (Further exemplars are comprehensively documented by Peters, Chapter 4 in this volume, and by Angus, and O'Neill in Volume 2.)

The combined effects on curriculum policy-making appear to have been both instrumental and conservative. Aldrich, Kennedy and Lawton argue that, in the UK, conventional subject structures have been left in place, reinforcing old hierarchies and a 'back-to-the-future' mentality. In contrast, with respect to New Zealand, Peters argues that recasting knowledge and values as 'skills and competencies', not only circumscribes education in instrumental terms, but also contributes to the 'commodification' of education, and, because it is more readily related to trade competencies, makes it inherently more vocational.

Gipps' critique of the development and implementation of assessment procedures for national curriculum in the UK indicates that the trend is towards a narrower, more conservative, simplistic (and cheaper!) assessment framework. The continuing and seemingly heavy-handed political intervention in curriculum and assessment matters at an everyday level; has exacerbated teacher frustration because the changes have been so constant and pervasive, and conducted on such an impossibly short time scale, that there has never been an opportunity to stabilize a set of practices and then to evaluate them properly in terms of their efficacy in bringing about the desired learning in the students for which teachers are primarily responsible.

In spite of a voluminous literature on the subject, problems of implementing change and innovation continue to be intractable and recurrent in both problem-finding and problem-solving with respect to implementation. In both the UK and Australia, as elsewhere, the experience to date has been that governments expect and rely on professionals to translate proposed changes at the policy level into curriculum while excluding them from both policy-making bodies and curriculum design. In Australia, the combination of constitutional constraints, and lack of a coherent, coordinated and long-term implementation plan suggests that implementation of national curriculum will be at best piecemeal. Even where state governments are prepared to support it, its effects will be diluted, because it will be used alongside existing state curriculum documents, and adapted in a variety of ways. Ivan Snook, in New Zealand, where the reforms to date have been structural and concerned primarily with the administration of schools, is of the opinion that the battle of curriculum content is yet to come.

Chapters by Shirley Hord and by Gene Hall and David Carter argue that although there is a body of data available to guide and inform implementation strategies and attendant interventions, there are still research questions to be addressed and they provide suggestions for some research dimensions for the remainder of the 1990s. More worrying is the evidence that the information that is available is not being used effectively, by other researchers and practitioners. In part this appears to be because, at the levels of policy formulation and planning, the notion that change is a process which must be planned, budgeted for and supported over an appropriate time span has been given only tacit recognition, and is generally lacking in tangible support on the scale needed at the point of implementation. An evident gulf remains between what we know and what we do in this regard.

This chapter began with the question of whether what has been perceived in political terms as a shift to the right was a movement or a trend. In some contexts, such as the UK, New Zealand and Australia, the national curriculum initiatives might be seen as a movement — ideologically based, directed and organized by vested interests and powerful lobby groups armed with specific agendas, formal leadership and well-articulated objectives. In other settings, such as the US, it may have been more of a trend; or simply the result of muddling through on a large scale on the basis of the power plays of *Realpolitik* (see James Cibulka in Chapter 1 for an exposé of this). Despite the fact that some reforms have been enacted into law with the clear intent of improving the outcomes of schooling, the explicit intention for restructuring national culture and economic interests does not appear to have occupied the forefront of the initiatives undertaken to give them coherence on a systemic scale. Both movement and trend styles of reform tend to founder on a common rock — the seeming failure of change managers, broadly defined, to incorporate appropriately, funded, detailed coherent and internally consistent implementation procedures at all levels of the system. While we now have a much greater understanding of implementation and the change process *per se* than even a decade ago, the human tendency to reinvent the wheel still pertains in this area of endeavour. It is captured in all its rich complexity in the writings of eminent scholars and educational leaders who have contributed to these companion volumes.

Part 1

Politics

Chapter 1

The Evolution of Education Reform in the United States: Policy Ideals or *Realpolitik?*

James Cibulka

Educational reform in the United States has been under way officially since roughly the early 1980s. During this time it has evolved in a number of ways from the conceptions of reform which were prevalent at that time. The general direction of this evolution has been commented on widely — from programme-specific mandates to 'restructuring' and from largely a state role to a stronger role for the federal government.

This evolution, however, has been characterized by anything but a uniform much less coherent, set of developments. After more than a decade of activity, many reform nostrums continue to compete. Accordingly, it is by no means clear in which direction education reform is headed in the United States. Clune (1993) poses the choice in this way: What is the best path to systemic education policy, a standard/centralized model of policy or a differentiated/decentralized one? Boyd (1987) describes the confusion with the term 'schizophrenia'. As usual, many Americans are convinced that they can have it both ways!

In this chapter, I discuss a number of competing perspectives on education reform in the United States and examine the reasons for the incoherent, kaleidoscopic nature of reform activity in this country. The chapter begins with a brief discussion of the role of ideals in policy development versus policy based on power.

Education Reform Policy: Ideals or *Realpolitik*

To frame the analysis which follows it is useful to begin by sketching two quite different conceptions of public (governmental) policy which have wide following among academics and the general public: *policy as ideals* and *policy as Realpolitik.*

Policy as Ideals

When viewed as a set of ideals, policy is the attempt to specify the nature and cause of a social problem and the appropriate responses to that problem. This model of policy is often referred to as a rational model striving toward some optimal end. In fact, however, those who design the policy may be bounded in their understanding of the problem being addressed and the available responses to it. Indeed, they may frame the policy recognizing a host of constraints. Nonetheless, they strive for the best available policy under these circumstances. In this sense policy can be viewed as an analysis and discussion among policy analysts and policy makers concerning the best approach to a problem. Finding that ideal approach is the central problem in shaping public policy. The task is very much an intellectual one, and our approaches to policy reflect the evolution of our best thinking on the matter.

An example of this conception of education policy as a matter of striving for the ideal can be found in the debate over school-district consolidation and local control. In the 1930s and 1940s concern about the small size of many school districts and high schools in the United States led education reformers to advocate school-district consolidation. It was argued that larger districts and larger high schools would equalize educational opportunities through finding reforms and improved economies of scale, resulting in a wider range of courses from which students could choose, improved facilities, and other benefits. But in the 1960s this conception of reform began to be questioned. Critics charged that large schools and school districts had become too bureaucratic and removed from local community ties, including the influence of the family. Later, in a widely read book Powell *et al.* (1985) decried the 'shopping-mall high school' with its panoply of course offerings, while Coleman *et al.* (1982) argued that the achievement advantage of Catholic high schools could be explained by their narrower set of course offerings compared with those in a typical comprehensive public high school. The conception of the problem in other words, changed dramatically in the intervening period, and with it the policy prescriptions. Our ideas and thinking not only underwent an evolution; they came full circle.

Much educational policy can be understood as a search for the best approach to funding schools, helping students read better, making them more culturally literate, reducing inequality of educational opportunity, and a host of other 'policy problems'. What is recognized as a problem in one period of history may be totally ignored in another, or as in the example above, the same problem may be interpreted as requiring the opposite response. Some analysts (Guthrie *et al.*, 1987) have argued that policy reflects an attempt to choose among competing values such as choice, equality, and efficiency.

Policy as Realpolitik

Policy also manifests itself in another light. Many observers see policy as little more than an exercise in power among individuals and groups. According to this view, the content of policy more or less reflects the degree to which those with power are able to influence or coerce others to accept their view. In seeking to understand the driving force behind a policy, these analysts point to power relationships rather than ideals. (This view has been widely applied in analysis of foreign policy, (e.g., Kissinger, 1994; Morgenthau, 1956) but is less common as an approach to understanding domestic policy, at least in the United States). They argue that conceptions of problems and ideas about preferred solutions to those problems are at most handmaidens to this underlying concern for advancing or preserving power. Therefore, a policy cannot be understood solely according to its technical provisions embodied in statutes, regulations, and guidelines. Indeed, this palpable content may be misleading without an appreciation of the larger political context shaping the policy's enactment and implementation.

An example of this view of policy as power is the passage of the Elementary and Secondary Education Act (ESEA) of 1965, which greatly expanded the federal government's role in this domain (Bailey, 1970; Munger and Fenno, 1962). The new law was the successful culmination of decades of effort by various proponents of a more activist federal role in education. Three roadblocks had stood in the way — race, religion, and 'reds'. The race issue had been disposed of or at least neutralized by the passage of the Civil Rights Act of 1964. The religious issue stood in the way because the Catholic Church had long insisted that federal aid should benefit religious schools, a position that in turn attracted a great deal of opposition from various groups. Another obstacle was disagreement over whether federal aid would lead to federal control of schools, an anathema to many who saw local control of schools as essential to maintenance of American democracy and protecting it from the Soviet threat. Some proponents of federal aid argued for special provisions for cities, which had experienced a large influx of blacks from the rural South, while others insisted on aid which would benefit virtually all state and local jurisdictions. What resulted was a grand compromise. Each of the law's five titles was crafted to carefully placate groups with concerns on one or another of these issues. For instance, Title I of the law (known today as 'Chapter 1') was directed at the 'educationally disadvantaged' but broadly targeted so that it became in effect, general aid. Within low-income target areas, all children, not just the educationally disadvantaged, would be served. Eligibility criteria were written to ensure many jurisdictions would receive help. At the same time the pretext was maintained that Title I money was special aid to meet a particular need, not ongoing general aid. This was accomplished by insisting that federal aid was to supplement rather than supplant existing funding from state and local sources. As for the religious issue, religious schools within the eligible areas could receive services. A number of provisions were added to assure those worried about federal control that the new law would not intrude on state-local prerogatives. In other words, the new 'law of the land' was an elaborate labyrinth of skilfully crafted compromises meant to satisfy enough political interests to assure its passage. Anyone reading the law who lacked an understanding of these issues behind its passage might well dramatically misinterpret the provisions it contained or pass over the significance of its omissions. Like many laws, the successful passage of the Elementary and Secondary Education Act of 1965 was *Realpolitik* at work.

It bears mention that any policy is inevitably a mix of ideals and power considerations. To argue that policy is entirely one or the other would misstate what the models in fact are intended to convey, namely, that ideals of power drive the policy while the other is secondary in significance.

In the next section, these two models will be used to analyse American educational reform.

American Educational Reform as an Evolution of Ideals

In an important sense, education reform did not begin in 1984 or even the years immediately preceding the passage of the now well-known report *A Nation at Risk*. Reform has been a continuous process over many decades (Cuban, 1990) because American public-school officials have long viewed themselves as social reformers, at the same time that various segments of the American public have consistently sought to impose one or another reform on the public schools. Thus, the current period of reform is only the most recent in a long succession of efforts to remake the pubic schools in someone's image.

Moreover, until very recently those who have advocated reform of American public schools usually have embraced the view that the system's supposed problems could be remedied through the straightforward inclusion or exclusion of some component, such as vocational education, life adjustment, character education, special attention for the disadvantaged or gifted, and so on. The idea that the system should be radically transformed from top to bottom has been the exception. John Dewey's progressive education model may well be that exception, since it was to include a fundamental reorganization of curriculum and teaching methods, which also implied new teacher-training programmes, student assessment, and so on. In that respect progressive education was a precursor to the current efforts to 'restructure' American public schools.

The first-wave of educational reform in the 1980s began from simpler assumptions about the requirements for transforming the ailments of American public schools. Standards had fallen, it was alleged, to a dangerously low level of mediocrity. Hence, these standards could be raised by increasing graduation requirements, expanding the number of years of required subjects, lengthening the school day, mandating a specific number of minutes of instruction, etc.

Some business leaders and their allies also advocated paying teachers for performance (the long controversial concept of merit pay), rewarding successful schools, and punishing failing schools or school districts. A majority of states passed education-reform bills that included some combination of these as well as many other specific elements. An example is South Carolina, which included state-curriculum development, student-performance assessments, financial rewards to schools for improved performance, merit pay for teachers, state intervention in failing schools, and many other features (Cibulka, 1990).

In most states, the logic linking these particular elements together into a coherent, logically consistent strategy of reform was almost non-existent. One can, of course, cite exceptions like South Carolina, whose more-or-less comprehensive package of reforms was designed by the state's governor at the time, Richard Riley. For the most part, however, reform was envisioned as a series of specific changes in the operation of the educational system, which, when added together, would have a cumulative impact sufficient to reverse the decline of standards. Various interests pushed for their particular magic wand and frequently won its inclusion in the state's reform bill. This 'grab-bag' approach seldom troubled anyone, because of the widely shared premise that if enough 'fix-its' were applied, the system would undergo a transformation.

Where then, did the idea come from that the system should be 'restructured', not merely fixed? The idea came from several quite different sources, all of which embraced restructuring language, but in truth envisioned drastically different things by the terminology. First, there was the Reagan administration and its conservative allies, which continued to raise concerns about standards. Second, there was the growing concern from the nation's business community about child poverty and its implications for national productivity. Third, there were efforts from within the education establishment, particularly policy analysts in universities, to redefine the parameters of reform.

All three groups could point with alarm to the test results of the first-wave reform efforts. While many cautioned that drawing conclusions about success or failure of reform was premature, given that it was just being implemented and that the measures of reform often were flawed, there was nonetheless an irresistible tendency for the media and elected political officials to do so. Not surprisingly, these early indicators showed for the most part very little improvement in the performance of American schools. For example, scores on the Scholastic Aptitude Test (SAT) and its counterpart the ACT continued to decline or remain stable. Dropout and graduation rates showed little improvement. School officials occasionally could point to some promising development, but the overall news was quite bleak.

Thus, the idea that this incremental strategy of reform was not working gradually won acceptance in the late 1980s. However, the specific diagnosis of the system's ailments and its necessary remedy remained a matter of dispute — as it does today.

There were first of all the critics outside the school system who voiced the view that the American public-school system remained fundamentally unaccountable, that its spending continued to increase while its performance declined. The champion for this view was Ronald Reagan, whose popularity as President helped give this line of criticism legitimacy, even if the American public was not willing to buy entirely Reagan's prescriptions. Reagan advocated school choice as an example of restructuring which would work, and also championed such controversial nostrums as school prayer. He blamed some of the system's problems on excessive federal involvement, and he sought to reduce federal education spending as well as federal influence. During Reagan's second administration (1984–8) his controversial Secretary of Education William Bennett used the 'bully-pulpit' strategy of verbally criticizing public-school officials, particularly teachers' unions, for impeding reform. Reagan did not believe that government could or should be viewed as part of the solution; instead, government was, he was fond of saying, part of the problem.

While Reagan was viewed as a strongly pro-business president, his diagnosis was too simplistic for many business leaders. Reagan rarely was criticized directly by the business establishment, but the difference of direction became apparent by 1987. The Committee on Economic Development, whose members include the 'Fortune 500' business establishment of large companies, published a report entitled *Children in Need* (1987). The report cited the declining status of children in American society and argued for a human capital investment in children, particularly those in poverty. It was now evident to American business leaders that the decade of labour surpluses was coming to an end with the aging of the American population, a development which meant that American public schools could no longer afford to tolerate a large dropout rate.

Although the 'school-to-work' concept was only in the early stages of development at that time, within a matter of years this reform nostrum would provide the national business leadership with another important 're-structuring' strategy for addressing their concerns. By 1993 federal legislation intended to reorient the nation's schools to train more literate workers was passed.

According to one formulation of the school-to-work precepts, the majority of students who are not college-bound should be provided with work-related experiences as an integral component of their education. (Others see the school-to-work idea as equally applicable to students who wish to pursue higher education, on the premise that everyone will change careers with greater frequency in the future and will need a different set of skills from those provided to youth by the American schools in the past.) School-to-work advocates are quick to point out that their reform would be radically different from the old vocational education model and would touch virtually every school, every grade level, and every teacher.

This initial concern for children in poverty, and related concern about the decline of the American family, also led many in the business establishment (as well as a diverse group of other advocates) to embrace the idea that children's services should be better coordinated and more comprehensive. In the late 1980s prominent foundations began to find projects to promote experi-mentation, which included closer linkages between public schools and other private and public human-service providers. While not a new social-reform idea in American history (Crowson and Boyd, 1993), the concept of coordin-ated services for children is viewed once again by many as a key strategy for restructuring America's public schools and making them more accountable and effective. Like the school-to-work idea, the reform is seen as an appro-priate response to a changing set of external circumstances to which schools should respond more effectively, in the first case to a changing economy and in the second, to a changing world of childrearing.

During the late 1980s, partly in reaction to the apparent failure of 'first-wave' reforms, and partly as a function of their own ideology, American academics began to question whether the appropriate policy response had been made. Actually, much of the academic establishment had been extremely critical of *A Nation at Risk* soon after its publication. Only two years earlier James Coleman and colleagues (1982) had withstood a blistering academic attack on their study of pubic, private and Catholic high schools, for having concluded that Catholic high schools produce on average higher achievement for low-income youth than public comprehensive high schools. The attacks on Coleman's work were endless, as were *ad hominem* assaults. Thus, profes-sors in university schools of education had shown themselves to be quite defensive in protecting the legitimacy of the public schools, almost as assidu-ously as public-school teachers and administrators.

The initial attacks on *A Nation at Risk* by the academic establishment pointed to its alleged elitism (it denied that underachievers need special treat-ment) and its ostensible misplacement of blame on schools for problems of the economy.

Within a matter of years, however, some of the most perceptive aca-demic analyses of reform (e.g., Timar and Kirp, 1988; McDonnell and Elmore, 1987) discarded this defensive posture in favour of a new conception of the problem: the initial reforms had not gone far enough to alter the system. The notion that reform must be systemic (Smith and O'Day, 1990) eventually emerged from this analysis. Initially the critiques of first-wave reforms fo-cused on the need for greater attention to the conditions of work in schools. Teacher professionalism was said to suffer because of poor salaries, little opportunity for advancement, low entry standards, and little control by teachers over their work. Accordingly, a variety of reforms were advocated, e.g., career ladders, national licensure, and not least, site-based management.

The latter idea in particular, site-based management, was embraced quickly by academics, and especially school practitioners, in response to another allega-tion about round-one reforms: they had made the system more centralized and bureaucratic and actually reduced discretion for professional decision-making. It was alleged, moreover, that they had reduced the incentives for more than minimal compliance with the mandates imposed by state legisla-tures and local school boards. Some even saw in site-based management a way to borrow the best of private-school attributes without conceding ground to the advocates of privatization.

Smith and O'Day (1990) reframed the restructuring discussion, arguing that systemic reform required greater coherence in the policy system as a whole, thus state policies for curriculum assessment, teacher training and development, accountability, and employer hiring had to be dovetailed. Moreover, as the idea evolved, its achievement came to depend not solely on the states, but also on the federal government.

By the end of the 1980s this idea that reform required more federal involvement was winning acceptance among the nation's governors, not merely within the academic world. However, the exact nature of the federal role continued to be controversial, both within the academy and among governors. George Bush provided a new impetus for centralization of education policy when he convened the nation's governors in a highly symbolic 'Education Summit' in 1989. While it was ridiculed at the time as a public-relations gesture by the President, in retrospect the summit led to the development of national education goals and subsequently, efforts to establish standards for those goals. Thus, unlike his predecessor Reagan, Bush came to see federal involvement as a key to leveraging reform. While supporting public-school choice and the concept of federal assistance to 'merit schools', Bush also pushed for a national research and development effort, largely privately financed through a National School Development Corporation (NASDC). A National Education Goals Panel and a National Council for Education Standards and Testing were created by Congress at the President's urging. His 'Goals 2000' programme contained elements which were anathema to the Democratically-controlled Congress, but some of its precepts were adopted by his successor Bill Clinton and subsequently were passed by Congress in 1993. To be sure, Clinton adopted the specific label 'systemic reform', and brought into his administration some of its architects such as Marshall Smith. Still a Republican president had endorsed a stronger federal role prior to Clinton and had helped to make systemic reform an idea which was acceptable in the political mainstream not merely in the academy.

Thus it came to be that by 1994, fully a decade after the education-reform movement had been officially launched, most informed opinion acknowledged the need for the restructuring of American public schools. Even many school officials, while rejecting the 'education bashing' of their critics, acknowledged in general terms the need for restructuring, adopting this terminology loosely.

Despite the rhetorical symbiosis, however, consensus on restructuring disguised these several meanings of the idea just discussed. Is restructuring something as radical as a voucher system extending government aid to private schools, and should it permit other kinds of 'privatization' such as charter schools, wherein school boards can contract with private firms to operate schools? Alternatively, does restructuring amount to a shift in orientation toward some focal group (children in poverty) or programmatic focus (school-to-work, coordinated services)? Still further, does restructuring require, as some claim, systemic reform with its greater coherence at state and national levels?

Even these three conceptions of restructuring oversimplify the choices as various advocates see them. Some claim, for example, that the charter-school idea is too radical while others see it as too timid a response to the need for comprehensive structural reform. Some see privatization as the answer, while others argue that 'only for-profit' private schools would yield the necessary changes in schools. Therefore, while there has emerged a consensus that schools need to be restructured to respond to a problem, what this problem is one will find little consensus about, and even less commonality of opinion on how to remedy it.

To those not accustomed to observing American politics, this shallow consensus may well seem to be a curious, if not paradoxical, phenomenon. Behind a veneer of consensus, Americans march in an apparently common direction lacking any common roadmap, much less itinerary. And they are in fact walking in many directions at once, not unduly bothered that they will eventually arrive in the same place.

Part of the explanation for this confusion of ideals must well exist outside the ideas themselves. In fact, the explanation for a lack of clarity in the nation about which reform ideals to pursue may be discovered within the other conception of educational policy discussed earlier, 'policy as *Realpolitik*', which is discussed below.

Policy as *Realpolitik*: A Second Perspective on Education Reform

There are at least two rival political explanations for the confusing state of thinking about how to reform American schools, both of which are rooted in some alternative conception of power, and which both carry some plausibility, depending on which 'facts' you care to recognize and to which you are willing to give greatest credence. The first conception of policy as a manifestation of power is 'ideological hegemony', the second is 'pluralist and ideological bargaining'.

Ideological Hegemony

This occurs when one set of political actors is able to control the debate about policy alternatives, by proffering a dominant conception of a problem which requires attention, shaping the language of discourse within which people frame the problem, influencing the data they employ to understand the nature of the problem and setting forth a solution with a rationale for its preferability. The key actors need not be all of one political party, institutional affiliation, or even philosophy. A convergence of interests at the top of the system is sufficient to provide the necessary ideological rationale, incentives, and controls in the remainder of the political system so that a convergence of ideas will occur. The convergence may gloss over inconsistencies and contradictions within the policy and conflicts of interest.

This hegemonic perspective on policy is sometimes called elite theory (Dye, 1992), but in fact has a wide number of variants such as critical theory, neo-Marxist and so on. While the distinctions among these views is potentially important, we shall not attempt a full exposition and exegesis here, apart from offering some examples of the utility of this approach.

The arguments supporting this interpretation of education-reform developments in the United States go something like the following: the dominant theme of reform has been the declining competitiveness of the American economy. While this decline arguably is rooted in factors well outside the nation's school system such as the emergence of a global economy, and competing centres of wealth in other parts of the world, nonetheless the American school system undoubtedly is one piece in the puzzle of how to restore American competitiveness. For example, the flow of economic capital across national borders, as a function of the global trade and investment, mandates the need for a mobile, flexible workforce. This, in turn, dictates that schools should produce workers who are willing and able to be retrained and redeployed. Efforts to restructure schools so that they have strong early childhood programmes to remediate poverty or to coordinate services for children are consistent with the need for an activist state which supports economic development. While greater equality of educational opportunity is not an end in itself, it is instrumental to America's hegemony as a national economy, because it resolves potential labour shortages and reduces the risk of social unrest. In particular, the decline of manufacturing and the concomitant rise in the importance and complexity of technical jobs, requires a shift in the orientation of the nation's school system away from primary attention to the college-educated. Insofar as any hope of a new middle class is likely to emerge from within the ranks of this new technically literate and flexible part of the workforce, restructured schools are a vital institution for maintaining social mobility and the American dream of a better future.

Still working within this analytical frame, it can be said that restructuring is an idea which is flexible enough to move government in any number of directions as changing needs dictate, just as the same concept has been employed to make private firms more responsive to pressures from competitors in the market-place.

Accordingly, restructuring can encompass a mix of eclectic strategies, whatever works in particular circumstances. Just as restructuring in private firms is capable of including both decentralizing management strategies like site-based management alongside increasingly centralized ownership and control, the same pragmatism can be tolerated in school reform under a broad umbrella of restructuring.

A hegemonic model of policy development thus frames policy not so much as a contest of ideas as a reflection of efforts by elites to solve a common underlying problem. In America that problem remains one of economic development and the need to realign the system of schooling to serve a changing capitalist economy. It is in this sense that ideological hegemony can be said to occur, because once everyone accepts this conception of the problem a variety of solutions can be entertained and even tolerated.

A hegemonic model is capable of conceptualizing policy as an evolving phenomenon. A variety of factors such as unforeseen events, the complexity of schooling as an institution, and so on make it impossible for elites to anticipate or plan fully for the future. What merely is critical to the maintenance of a hegemonic perspective is that public opinion and policy initiatives remain focused on the need to reshape schools according to an economic imperative.

Pluralist and Ideological Bargaining

This is another way of explaining the inconsistent ideas within the education reform. This cacophony of voices advancing reform, and the resulting confusion, is little more than a reflection of interest-group liberalism at work — warts and all. In this system of governance, the public interest is seen as the by-product of competition among elites and interest groups, as well as political parties. Policies are amalgams and compromises, a blending of ideas intended to garner support. According to pluralist theory, the players in this game vary from issue to issue, depending on what interests them and what is at stake. Furthermore, the coalitions and cleavages are fluid, as are the winners and losers in a policy settlement. In such a system, policy will seldom meet any stringent test of substantive or instrumental rationality; its *raison d'être* is the maintenance of social and political consensus.

At the same time, pluralist bargaining works only insofar as the interests of the political players are widely shared and acknowledged. Where there are deeply rooted conflicts, such as class, race, ethnic, and gender strife, ideological bargaining tends to replace pluralist bargaining (Peterson, 1976). Face-to-face negotiation frequently is replaced by third-party negotiation through the media, in order to bolster public support for each position and to avoid personal friction among the players. As the number of mobilized interests expands, along with their claims to special treatment or privilege, it becomes harder to achieve compromise through relatively covert bargaining processes. The setting of policy becomes both more public and conflict-ridden.

In recent decades, educational governance in the United States has moved increasingly toward ideological bargaining, even though elements of the old pluralist system still prevail. What has emerged is an unstable system of education governance which mixes pluralist and ideological policy processes. This mixed system is apparent in many other areas of policy besides education, such as welfare policy, health policy, and even foreign policy. Nonetheless, its emergence in education policy carries a special irony, since the progressive tradition of reform which left such an indelible impact on American education established an ideology which eschewed political partisanship in favour of 'non-political' professional expertise. A system of pluralist bargaining, as long as it endured, did little to openly challenge this ideology, however far from the truth it swayed. But the increasingly acrimonious politics of the 1980s and 1990s has laid bare the pretence that education is apolitical. To remedy such defects, some critics such as Chubb and Moe (1990) call for market choices which allegedly bypass politics altogether.

There is much in the American education-reform movement which is consistent with the thesis that reform policies reflect pluralist and ideological bargaining. The relatively widespread adoption of site-based management by school districts, in the face of surprisingly sporadic opposition from teachers' unions, can be interpreted as pluralist bargaining at work, wherein school boards and teachers have agreed to make marginal changes in governance. So far there is little solid evidence that such reforms do lead to achievement improvements (Malen and Ogawa, 1988), although some experiments which combine site-management with public-school choice make this claim. Even the more ambitious experiment in Chicago with school-based councils, which has mixed elements of site-management and political decentralization, arguably is a pluralist compromise. It did not eliminate the central office and was incomplete in its delegation of enumerated powers to principals and local school councils. Not surprisingly, the reform likewise has failed to demonstrate solid achievement gains across the school system. Thus far, therefore, such experiments in site-based management and governance have led to symbolic gains for school authorities. They restore, for the short-term at least, a modicum of public confidence that American school officials are responding to the need for change.

At a national level, the emergence of a bipartisan consensus around national goals and standards also exemplifies that pluralist bargaining is possible. When George Bush advanced his 'Goals 2000' platform for reform, it was ridiculed by Democrats in Congress and pummelled by the educational establishment, including many professors. Yet shortly thereafter when Bill Clinton modestly changed the programme by dropping choice and merit schools and adding a few other provisions, 'Goals 2000' won accolades and was passed into law. Perhaps its most controversial feature, opportunity-to-learn standards for schools, was retained but made voluntary and left open to definition later. National standards and stronger national testing were likewise made voluntary for the states, alleviating old fears about federal control.

The Clinton administration's school-to-work and 'tech-prep' initiatives won even easier Congressional approval. Why is this so? Is it evidence that school officials and teachers' unions, which have been so defensive about much reform, have been converted? This is possible, but more likely they see an initiative like school-to-work as a kind of restructuring which is no basic threat to jobs and will bring much federal aid without the prospect of radical change. The long-term consequences of retooling the American school system to reflect career needs and shifts in the economy can only be speculated on at this time, but the politics separating this reform from other more radical versions of restructuring are self-evident.

Few attempts at restructuring have met such widespread opposition from providers of education as choice. Teachers' unions led well-financed campaigns to defeat state-wide voucher initiatives in Oregon, Colorado, and California, which took on the characteristics of ideological bargaining aimed at shaping voter opinion. (Because of controversial features in these various proposals, unions also garnered opposition from diverse other groups.) As a result, only a relatively small voucher programme exists in Milwaukee, Wisconsin, achieved despite strident opposition by the state's otherwise powerful teachers union, the Wisconsin Education Association Council (WEAC). Unions have been less adamant in opposing other forms of choice such as open enrolment, post-secondary options, and charter schools, but generally they have accepted such reforms only reluctantly in the face of insurmountable support from proponents of these reforms and have bargained to make such reforms as weak as possible.

What has emerged then, is a highly variegated and complex picture of restructuring reform as one moves among the nation's schools, school districts, and states. This uneven landscape of reform reflects, from one angle, what one can expect in a system of decentralized governance where states are the sovereigns responsible for public education, where local school districts were once delegated substantial local control, and where the federal government must exercise its authority and power within prescribed limits and often through monetary inducement. Such a system was designed by the nation's founders to facilitate pluralist bargaining. Accordingly, the fact that Americans have no one idea of restructuring but a number of competing conceptions, is a reflection of governance by bargaining.

Perhaps the only potential challenge to an economic imperative as a driving force to education restructuring (apart from political decentralization such as that in Chicago) is the call for coordinated services for children. Still its *raison d'être* is unclear (Cibulka and Kritek, in press). Should children's services be improved to bring the urban underclass into the economic mainstream or to save tax dollars (both economic considerations) or as a matter of fairness and equity in the distribution of societal benefits (a judicial, ethical consideration)? Supporters of coordinated services use both lines of logic, and the movement's allies are diverse. This is a pluralist conception of reform *par excellence*, but its staying power as a mandate for restructuring remains unclear. By 1994 some of the major foundation support for the reform had been withdrawn. Expanding children's services with new tax revenue in a period of fiscal conservatism will not prove easy, and simultaneously the problems of reorganizing government from Congress at the top through layers of bureaucracy in a federal system will be a formidable challenge. The gradualist ideas inherent in the coordinated services movement — built on the premise that the welfare state needs to be rethought and retooled — are the products of pluralist politics, but it is not clear that the implementation of the movement's ideas will be easily achieved within the constraints of the mixed system of pluralist-ideological governance characterizing the United States at this time. Moreover, even if coordinated services gain momentum as a major restructuring theme, it is by no means certain whether it will open the political system to the voices of parents and community who have felt excluded by the system or whether it will be merely another means for consolidating professional dominance of schooling.

Conclusion

In the mid-1990s, there is little serious debate in the United States over whether the American school system should be restructured. Even most 'diehard' defenders of the status quo have learned to adopt, at least rhetorically, the language of restructuring. As pointed out here, however, such convergence of language disguises deep fractures within the nation as to the precise kind of surgical procedure restructuring will require.

At one level, as has been shown, educational reform policies can be viewed as a problem of generating sound *ideas* about what and how to restructure America's schools. Such ideas have evolved in the most recent decade of frenzied reform efforts. But the evolution has been in the direction of embracing more alternatives, not fewer, despite efforts to bring it all together under a label like 'systemic reform'. Hence, political decentralization occurs at the same time that further centralization is envisioned through national goals, national standards, and national assessment. Many different conceptions of choice are offered, but few are adopted. School-to-work initiatives are widely discussed. The list goes on and is likely to grow more lengthy in the years ahead.

Some of this apparent confusion can be explained, it has been argued, by shifting our conception of education policy reform to *Realpolitik*. However, two very different political power interpretations of restructuring are possible. A hegemonic view stresses the common ideology of reform rooted in problems of the American capitalist economy. Using this perspective, the apparent contradictions within the restructuring movement become less significant because restructuring itself is an ideology the widespread acceptance of which signals a victory for the elites who have advanced it and stand to benefit most from its implementation.

The other interpretation of policy as *realpolitik* portrays the present moment of confusion as the logical upshot of the nation's system of pluralist and ideological bargaining. While less than fully rational by some objective standards of logic or theory, governance by incremental bargaining achieves a momentary consensus which can be expected to evolve still further over time as new developments dictate. This system of bargaining becomes problematic only to the extent that ideological bargaining rather than pluralist bargaining becomes so dominant that the nation's educational system is politically grid-locked among contending opponents.

If they were asked which of these competing models of policy is the most accurate, most Americans probably would not know which one to choose. Nor probably would most be willing to discard the American faith that with the right combination of ideals, politics aside, the nation's schools can be fixed. Faith in education as a route to social mobility remains a central feature of American culture, and government (read 'politics') as an instrument of social progress has been an enduring object of scepticism.

The gravity of the challenges facing the American people in the last decade of the twentieth century cannot be underestimated. The glue that has held the American polity together across many challenges has been a widely shared faith in the future and the hope of economic betterment for oneself and one's children. For the first time since the Great Depression of the 1930s, which posed the most recent major threat to the nation's political stability, Americans have cause to be deeply pessimistic about their economic future. As Robert Reich (1994), the Secretary of Labor acknowledged, the nation has divided itself into three economic classes — a well-educated middle (and upper) class which remains very secure; a sizeable urban underclass, primarily but not exclusively consisting of people of colour; and a marginal and shrinking mid-dle class which is greatly insecure. While the Clinton administration and many others are intent on reversing this trend, the outcome of this economic trans-formation is far from clear. For one, the politics of centralism have all but ruled out any major attention to the urban underclass, including the appalling condition of urban public schools.

How to generate a set of strategies to create a new middle class is perhaps the central economic and political problem confronting the Clinton adminis-tration, an agenda which almost totally escaped the attention of the President's two Republican predecessors. In this grand scheme, education reform, while it is important, is not the central pivot (Fowler, in press).

This larger policy problem is so formidable that it will summon the most creative thinking of the nation's intellectual and political leaders. The necessity for this national debate is only slowly occurring to the American people as the severity of their situation dawns more clearly upon them. The role of govern-ment in addressing this economic challenge will be at the centre of the debate. Those advocating a more activist political system in responding to the na-tion's economic challenges will have to overcome the legacy of Watergate, which reduced trust in government to an all-time low in modern American history.

Americans are accustomed to groping through their problems with little long-term foresight. The question they must ask themselves is whether this strategy of equivocation and denial, which has turned on remarkably good luck in the past, is a sufficient orientation for controlling their future. How-ever, Americans are also a remarkably self-critical people. It is this resource, if it can be directed toward generating new policy ideals rather than more of the self-destructive politics of recent years, which will help them reshape their key institutions, among them the nation's schools.

Note

1 The nation has had a national testing programme since the 1970s known as the National Assessment of Educational Progress (NAEP). It has been strengthened to permit comparisons of state-by-state performance. There has been much debate about whether to use NAEP or some other assessment as a national test, and if so in what way.

Chapter 2

Curriculum Reform and the Neo-corporatist State in Australia

David S.G. Carter

The economy of Australia, reflecting current difficulties evident in the operation of the global economy, is slowly and painfully moving out of recession — a trend for which the current Keating federal Labor government assumes full credit. Populist claims have been made in the media by the current Prime Minister that, in his previous role as Treasurer, recent economic improvements can be 'sheeted home' to the success of his economic restructuring policies of the 1980s. Basic to the latter has been a centralist and pervasive micro-economic reform agenda covering many areas of the economy including transport and 'the Waterfront', for example, and encompassing areas of schooling and workplace reform for teachers.

In the 1980s 'The Lucky Country' became 'The Unlucky Country', or so our politicians had us believe as they then sought to locate the origins of the country's economic malaise on global forces substantially outside the control of politicians and policy makers and their stewardship of the national economy. In endeavouring to address seemingly intractable economic difficulties a new form of federalism emerged, which was based on the principles of corporate management and known as 'corporate federalism' (Lingard, O'Brien and Knight, 1993). Lingard (1991) locates the rise of corporate federalism in the early beginnings of the previous Hawke Labor government, which first came to office in 1982 and especially during its post 1987 term, in which the states became more vulnerable to national policy developments by the federal government's ability increasingly to restrict state access to central sources of funding under the rubric of a national agenda for micro-economic reform. This policy continues to be asserted by Prime Minister Keating in the current term of Labor. In this regard, Lingard, O'Brien and Knight observe:

> It appears that, under corporate federalism, the Commonwealth Government wants to pull to the centre all those aspects of policy central to microeconomic reform and to devolve as far as possible other functions to the states. One result of this tendency has been the creation of national policies geared to the creation of a national economic infrastructure. (Lingard, O'Brien and Knight, 1993, p. 233)

Further, according to these scholars, what might be called a neo-corporatist, efficient state strategy has engendered a corporate managerialist reformation of the public service as well as a reformation of commonwealth-state relations in terms of corporate federalism. This internal restructuring of the agencies of the state are a tangible political manifestation of the need to solve Australia's current round of economic problems.

Notwithstanding a new found economic optimism, the natural resource endowments of Australia fuel the popular belief held by its citizenry that we should be doing a lot better with respect to the reduction of a large balance of payments deficit; reducing structural inefficiencies; becoming more competitive with our Asian neighbours; reversing trends in falling productivity and, until recently, arresting rising unemployment. The dilemma of fulfilling public expectations for the maintenance of high standards of living and adequate social-service provision, while concurrently reducing costs, places politicians and their economic advisers in a 'no win' position with the public at large. The largest budget allocations for provision of health, education and social-welfare services have evidently taken the brunt of the push for cost efficiencies and the pruning back of public expenditure under an economic reform agenda seeking 'more for less'. In vigorous pursuit of this agenda by the federal government, an efficiency imperative based on economic rationalist arguments, narrowly and naively interpreted with respect to the nature of education, has dominated national debate and the public-policy agenda. An offshoot of the redistribution of resources, in line with revamped federal policies, has been that associated responses in the contemporary social and economic climate have encouraged education to be redefined in essentialist and instrumental terms *inter alia* to better serve the needs of the labour market.

Following the exploration of some philosophical and conceptual issues surrounding the socio-political context of the work of schools in general, and associated curriculum issues in particular, the discussion moves to a consideration of recent changes in the Australian states and territories involving unprecedented collaboration between the federal and state governments in education. While certain collaborative aspects of a national-curriculum initiative are being maintained this, and cognate issues, are now interpreted and mediated differently by the states. The specific form it takes substantially depends on state-level political persuasions, affecting in turn the ideological response to developing further the emerging national-curriculum statements and profiles across eight learning areas.

Instrumentalist versus Liberal Perspectives on the Curriculum

The wholesale adoption of instrumentalist views by some opinion leaders, notably politicians, economic rationalists, corporate managers and trainers, has generally precipitated negative responses from educators. Skilbeck (1987), for example, has suggested that the liberal-humanistic tradition is being set aside in favour of technicist solutions to problems focused on matching the curriculum essentially to the needs of society as it now exists. The ascendancy of 'life adjustment' models of the curriculum, emphasizing practically oriented and personally relevant curricula for everyday living, are far removed from the reconstructionist ideals underpinning a core curriculum of common learnings for all the nation's children and youth. This, it was argued, would provide students with access to a common culture, viewed dynamically, and a common set of values within the traditions of mainstream society.

Social reconstructionist ideology was clearly articulated in a benchmark document under the auspices of the (then) national Curriculum Development Centre (CDC), in 1980, entitled *Core Curriculum for Australian Schools*. Significant within the prevailing political orthodoxy was the demise of the CDC and its resurrection as the Curriculum Corporation of Australia. The CDC document provoked widespread public discussion, as was its intention, but little apparent 'take up' of its ideas and ideology by the states and territories followed its publication and dissemination. It did, however, *indirectly* have an influence on subsequent curriculum activity via the actions of policy makers who incorporated aspects of the document into the reports and policy statements of a plethora of contemporary reviews and Committees of Inquiry. The latter have been relatively commonplace over the last decade in all state and territory education systems in turn, and were primarily concerned with structural reforms and curriculum revision. This has been a feature of the high-profile education and training received in Australia, as elsewhere, over the last decade.

Taking culture as the starting point for curriculum building stands in stark contrast to that which takes its inspiration and direction from the views of experts in the fields of science and technology, economics and management. The latter are of course more amenable to a public-policy agenda which views education as one means of revitalizing the economy and creating wealth for Australia. At an ideological level, the real issues centre around goal clarification involving values conflict and the nature and purpose(s) of education in a post-industrial state moving into an increasingly complex and uncertain future. A consideration of alternative futures in education requires informed public debate by a wide community of interest within a democratic framework that is truly participatory.

At a practical level there are also problems to be encountered in operationalizing the efficiency criterion. According to Beare (1986), wherever the efficiency approach has been tried in education, '. . . it has run up against an intractable problem, namely that some of the most highly valued outcomes of schooling are not measurable in this way.' It follows that there is always the danger lurking that only those outcomes which are measurable will come to be valued, thus, 'The problem has always been that economically driven objectives will overwhelm the delicate sensitively educational ones' (pp. 6–7).

National Concerns and Policy Initiatives

As mentioned earlier, the main feature of the Australian government's superordinate socio-economic reform policy has been to treat education overwhelmingly as a mechanism for economic development at the expense of something to be intrinsically valued for its own sake. In seeking to achieve national goals, the government has emphasized a number of priority areas including:

- increasing participation in education;
- an emphasis on skills training;
- involving the private sector and trade-union representatives in skills education;
- increasing school retention rates; and
- improving the overall quality of education.

The achievement of these goals places a heavy emphasis on secondary education, particularly in the later years of schooling, to counter national and personal disadvantage and give credence to educational outcomes now linked to national productivity in an explicit and direct manner.

Under the Australian federal system of government, education, constitutionally, is a residual power of the states and, as such, must be administered by the states. Notwithstanding this hitherto mutually understood arrangement, recently increased incursions into education at all levels by the federal government, in addition to forging closer links between education, the business sector, employment and training have become both a conspicuous and high-profile activity. Federal government intentions were signalled by the formation of a 'megaministry', The Department of Employment, Education and Training (DEET), in 1987, headed at that time by the federal Minister of Education, the Hon. J.S. Dawkins. On assuming office he quickly made his overall intention clear, which, starkly put, was to use the education system to create wealth for Australia. This he planned to achieve by intervening in education matters directly in a situation where central government would no longer simply be the states' banker, but would seek to give educational leadership, justified in terms of a central government role necessary to promote the national interest and requiring the effective allocation and use of national resources to meet national goals.

Skills for Australia (1987), which was the first of several policy documents to emerge in quick succession under his signature, made explicit his policy agenda for DEET with respect to national education and training policies. In this document the Federal Minister for Education asserted that:

A high-quality basic education is an essential prerequisite for a vocationally skilled and adaptable labour force. More needs to be known about the levels of competence achieved by our students at school, especially in the core disciplines of language, mathematics and science . . . We also need to examine new ways to impart less measurable skills on which future prosperity depends — life-time learning, enterprise and initiative, pursuit of excellence, communication skills, teamwork and responsibility. In other words, we need to lay the foundations of a productive culture. (Dawkins, 1987, pp. 8–9)

In a subsequent publication he focused more clearly on his objectives for schools in which education was couched in terms of economic rationalist values, framed by notions of a skilled workforce to make Australia 'The Clever Country', and countenanced by a view of education as human capital in which government should invest now in order to realize a return at a later date. This was expressed in the following terms:

Schools are the starting point of an integrated education and training structure in the economy. They provide the foundation on which a well-informed, compassionate and cohesive society is built. They also form the basis of a more highly skilled, adaptive and productive workforce. As skill upgrading and retraining of adults becomes more necessary, so will the quality and nature of schooling received by individuals need to change. It will need to be more adaptable and prepare for lifelong education. (Dawkins, 1988, p. 2)

The success of this policy during his term of office can be measured in terms of a more direct role for, and involvement by, central government in what had previously been essentially a states' and territories' responsibility under the Australian Constitution. It was realized in no small part because of the extant political climate of the late 1980s in which the federal Labor government shared its social democratic aspirations with a majority of Labor governments at the state level. Recent electoral changes have witnessed a backlash to what is seen as encroaching centralism by several conservative states in a number of policy areas, and especially in moves towards a national curriculum for schools.

The *zeitgist* for schools and the school curriculum has to be understood developmentally. As a multiplicity of new policies and new directions were being charted for schools over the decade of the 1980s, the curriculum was earmarked for special attention — especially by politicians, bureaucrats, economists and trainers. Professional educators in any significant numbers were largely excluded from the debates about 'ends'. Early in the decade there was a marked 'back to basics' movement in evidence. It was widely believed by vested interests in academia and business that increasing the rigour of curricula would arrest a much publicized seeming decline in academic standards, although the Quality of Education Review Committee (QUERC) (1985) was at pains to point out that in fact there was no evidence to show that cognitive outcomes had either improved or declined in the preceding fifteen years prior to the Committee's formation. Nevertheless education, and its critics, enjoyed a high public profile throughout the 1980s and beyond, manifesting a number of concerns and public disquiet regarding, in particular, its poor articulation with the world of work in a period of record high youth unemployment, and lack of value for its returns on the tax dollar spent.

Curriculum Concerns

Since the advent of the first Hawke Labor Ministry in 1982, the curriculum has been used increasingly to play a central role in furthering key social as well as economic policy objectives. In keeping with Labor's social policy, making the curriculum more sensitive to individual needs and more inclusive in its nature and scope was likely to provide a greater degree of equity for the socially disadvantaged and educationally deprived, while a more socially relevant curriculum would enhance national economic performance. New ways of thinking about the curriculum, paralleling similar social and economic trends in Britain, have been substantially brought about by increased student retention rates and fostered by lack of employment opportunities especially for youth. Between 1980 and 1987 the school retention rate went up dramatically from around 30 per cent to just over 50 per cent (see Commonwealth Schools Commission, 1987, p. 57). In *Skills for Australia* (1987) by the 1990s, a retention rate of 65 per cent in the post-compulsory years of schooling, was publicly reaffirmed.

In order to meet the needs of a broader range of students now completing the full six years of secondary education, a number of options have been provided. One effect of this was that choice in education has nowadays taken on a new meaning. It has become 'particularized' insofar as it is regarded as being specific to particular students choosing particular schools with a particular curriculum. In Western Australia, for example, a unit curriculum has been in place since 1986, marking one response to the accommodation of student choice (Carter, 1993a). At the senior secondary level, the solution in Tasmania was to provide for a range of courses and pathways leading to post-secondary vocational courses, tertiary studies or entry to the labour market. Similar trends in post-compulsory education occurred in Western Australia over the same time frame. Other state systems, where attempts have been made to match curricula to a wider range of ability, due to a more diverse population staying on at school in the later years, have addressed the problem through provision of broad groups of subjects. This allows for increased student choice of subject selection within the framework of a core of studies (McGaw, 1984; Andrich, 1989). The problem for curriculum directors has been to resolve the tensions between balance and coherence on the one hand and choice and diversity on the other. This is not readily achieved and seemingly has been accommodated via system adjustments rather than accomplished by trade-offs, thus, in effect, masking the underlying conflict of choice versus prescriptivity.

Curriculum Frameworks

Throughout the decade of the 1980s and culminating in the work undertaken under the auspices of the Australian Education Council (AEC) since 1986, a collaborative effort between the federal government and the states to frame national curriculum statements as frameworks has become pervasive across the various states and territories.

As a curriculum device, a framework can be conceived of as a structure employing principles of curriculum design, resulting in a particular pattern of curricular organization. The structure broadly circumscribes curriculum elements such as purposes, content outlines, learning activities and assessment, states relationships between them and gives criteria for their selection. Frameworks are usually accompanied by guidelines for the selection and sequence of elements, together with strategies for implementation. Provision is made for the incorporation of externally developed syllabus statements and curriculum packages within the structure, accompanied by details of course and instructional planning completed by teachers, within a school, to meet the needs of students in a specific local context. This structure allows for flexibility and choice while maintaining the integrity of the overarching design. To be effective these criteria do presuppose a good clear design at the system level allowing for, and facilitating, a range of legitimate interpretations in schools and classrooms. It also goes some way to ameliorating the tensions between prescriptivity for accountability, and choice for meeting individual needs and aspirations.

Among their other advantages, curriculum frameworks have been instrumental in allowing for more flexibility on the part of schools and teachers in their use of a range of different syllabuses and content areas, especially at the secondary level of schooling, to achieve certain types of student outcomes. These have emerged at the system level and their introduction, supported by centrally developed policy statements such as that incorporated on the 1985 Victorian Ministerial Review, has allowed for choice and localized decision-making, but within clearly defined and commonly understood boundaries.

The move towards system-level curriculum frameworks should, however, be seen within the overall trend towards core curricula at both state and national levels which has occurred over the course of the last decade. This movement in part can be referenced to the more subtle influences of the previously mentioned discussion document *Core Curriculum for Australian Schools*. While the notion of 'core' and 'electives' has been variously interpreted, the concept has been associated with moves to school-based decision-making and the devolution to schools of numbers of functions previously the concern of central office staff in a number of state and territory education systems. The move away from centrally determined largely prescriptive syllabuses to frameworks, with responsibility for the development of courses devolved to regions and schools, is now well established in states such as Queensland, Victoria and Western Australia. Intra-state harmonization of system-level frameworks converging with the AEC's thinking following *The Hobart Declaration on Schooling: Common and Agreed Goals for Schooling in Australia*, and AEC intentions (then) to move towards a national curriculum, facilitated a massive collaborative agenda between state and commonwealth governments crystallized by a nationally engineered curriculum mapping exercise (Australian Education Council, 1988).

Inclusive Curriculum

In addition to those common core and national curriculum concerns that acquired a prominent position in policy-making at both the federal and state levels of politics, there have been increased efforts to raise public consciousness regarding inclusive curriculum and in attempts to make curricula more inclusive of gender, ethnicity and disadvantaged groups generally. According to Kalantzis and Cope (1987), a crucial tool of social enablement is one of success in formal schooling. Multi-culturalism and non-sexism should not be soft options for building the self-esteem of the disadvantaged, but matters of intellectual validity and educational rigour for all students. As such they should be common inclusive processes supporting related objectives that are of prime importance.

The interaction especially of gender and ethnicity with SES, however, raises a number of complex issues and questions. To date the results have been rather mixed where practical attempts have been made to rework curriculum to make it more inclusive. Although the underlying principles of inclusivity have achieved wide acceptance in Australia much still remains to be done regarding their implementation to achieve system-wide impacts and national policy objectives (see Carter and Bednall, 1986, for example).

Under corporate federalism the micro-economic reform agenda has once again reasserted its dominance, thus diluting the impact of inclusivity by equating equity and efficiency in the readjustment of social policy as a response to economic imperatives. Even a cursory reading of a significant policy document such as *The National Policy for the Education of Girls in Australian Schools* (1987) focuses on what are at source essentially social-justice concerns but with their moral overtones reduced by couching them in terms of labour productivity and efficiency.

Assessment Issues

Another major shift in policy, nationally, has been in the areas of testing, public examinations and credentialling. In general, external summative assessment leading to certification in most, but not all, states, was applicable only to those students completing the full twelve years of schooling. This has included the final post-compulsory years of secondary education at the conclusion of which students graduate at about the age of 17 years. An internally assessed credential has been awarded to students completing their compulsory education, normally after ten years of schooling. There are no formal assessment criteria in the public-education sector for entry to primary (elementary) school, or for transition from primary to secondary school.

Differences occur both inter- and intra-state, serving to highlight some of the inadequacies of curriculum provision for the post-compulsory years. A consequence of higher retention rates and increased expectations for access to tertiary and/or further education has been to place enormous pressure on tertiary institutions to provide extra places for students when they are not adequately resourced to do so — a further consequence of a number of policy initiatives by the federal minister at other levels of the education system. Consequently, the innate conflict between Australian societal concerns for egalitarianism and the avoidance, or denigration, of elitism — the 'tall poppy' syndrome — is likely to be exposed if, based on the British experience of national curriculum implementation, national testing or simplistic assessment models for credentialling purposes are ever put in place in the middle school years (Bennett *et al.*, 1992). While pressure is being exerted in certain quarters of the education community to avoid standardized tests at all costs, their possibility is not lost on those swayed by market forces and a league table mind-set who wish to compare students and schools against nationally determined standards. These and cognate issues are taken up by Caroline Gipps and Denis Lawton, in the British context, in later chapters of this volume. In Australia, arguably, this platform simply complements the logic of moves towards a national curriculum — or at least the achievement of common and agreed national goals for education.

Initiatives for National Curriculum Reform

What is most remarkable about the policy initiatives that occurred from the federal minister's office, or otherwise under his aegis, was that he was able to have them taken up and implemented on a wide scale in an area for which he had no mandate or constitutional responsibility. In achieving large scale and pervasive structural and curricular reforms at just about every level of the education system Minister Dawkins engaged in a strategy which was itself essentially corporate in its *modus operandi*. Under the aegis of an intergovernmental committee in education, known (then) as the Australian Education Council (AEC), in which the Federal Minister for Education has only been a full member since 1972, he has met regularly with ministers and their advisers from each of the Australian states and territories as well as New Zealand. It is noteworthy that Spaull (1987), suggests that, increasingly the AEC, had become a forum in which the states responded to a federally driven education agenda. Under the Dawkins regime from 1987 to 1991 its hand was strengthened so that the power and influence of the AEC grew to make it an important policy-making instrument under the direction of the federal minister acting in consultation with his ministerial colleagues in the states. From 1988, until he became federal treasurer in 1991, John Dawkins used this forum to secure ministerial agreement with respect to the curriculum agenda he had outlined in his main policy blueprint for educational reform which was outlined in *Strengthening Australia's Schools*.

The role of the AEC in setting the policy framework for collaboration with the states in moving towards a national curriculum is summarized by Macpherson as follows:

> The AEC . . . took charge of national curriculum development, initially by identifying five learning areas (later eight) across the curriculum of the primary and secondary schools. They also agreed to develop, using an inter-state process, national curriculum framework statements and profiles in each area to guide planning by teachers and schools. The major vehicle for this process was the AEC's Curriculum and Assessment Committee (CURASS). (Macpherson, 1993, p. 32)

As an outcome of *The Hobart Declaration*, and in subsequent AEC deliberation and consultation with the states, John Dawkins was able to secure the agreement of his ministerial colleagues in the pursuit of a set of *Common and Agreed National Goals for Schooling in Australia*. This was mediated to the states and territories by the AEC as an agreement to develop in all students:

- the skills of English literacy;
- skills of numeracy, and other mathematical skills;
- skills of analysis and problem-solving;
- skills of information processing and computing;
- an understanding of the role of society and technology, together with scientific and technological skills;
- a knowledge of Australia's historical and geographic context;
- a knowledge of languages other than English;
- an appreciation and understanding of, and confidence to participate in, the creative arts;
- an understanding of, and concern for, balanced development and the global environment; and
- a capacity to exercise judgment in matters of morality, ethics and social justice.

The list is rather conservative in the curriculum policy that it portrays, but what is significant in the statement of *Common and Agreed National Goals for Schooling in Australia* (i.e., *The Hobart Declaration*), of which the listing above is but a part, is that mutual agreement was obtained between the federal Minister for Education and eight state and territory ministers for education in an area previously guarded jealously by them. It needs to be remembered though that the declaration was more a symbolic statement rather than constituting a blueprint for action.

A central feature of this activity at the policy level was, over a number of years and via a substantially enlarged educational bureaucracy, to evolve a national curriculum framework. In its documented form this consisted of two parts — a national statement for each of eight learning areas comprising English, mathematics, health and physical education, technology, studies of society and environment, national languages other than English (LOTE), science and the arts as well as a subject profile for each area. The latter provided an assessment framework in an 'outcomes-based education' environment (OBE) for the eight agreed areas each of which represent national curriculum priorities. The national profiles, and the behavioural pointers embedded in them which are indicators of student achievement referenced to prescribed educational outcomes, provide the mechanism for a more common approach to assessment across state borders than has been the case in Australia hitherto.

Embedded in the national curriculum statements and profiles are a number of employment-related key competencies (Finn, 1991; The Mayer Committee, 1992) responses to which have resulted in a most overt attempt to vocationalize the school curriculum and polarize debate in Australia concerning vocational versus liberal forms of education. At an eventful meeting of the AEC in Perth, Western Australia, in early July 1993, much of the developmental work leading to the formulation of the national curriculum statements and profiles came to an abrupt halt with the decision to put the concept of a national curriculum on hold, but to 'return the fruits of the collaborative activity, the student outcome statements, to the states and territories for further development' (McCreddin, 1993, p. 30).

Whether this was a major catastrophe in the light of subsequent collaborative activity or a blessing in disguise seems to be a matter of perspective. Prior to the meeting there was some apparent concern about the scale and pace of the intended reforms, and pressures being exerted by the federal minister without due regard to the sensitivities of 'states rights'. The latter were voiced especially by some of the newly elected conservative state governments apparently suspicious of, and opposed to, the centralist tendencies emerging from the exercise of federal power in Canberra. It may be premature to think that the intensive intra-state consultative and collaborative activity in evidence prior to the July meeting of the AEC had become habituated, but many of the states have continued with the further development of the national profiles across the eight learning areas in a mutually cooperative way transcending state borders in the process. This is a remarkable departure from the status quo in the Australian education context. Cooperative activity is occurring in a form in which the national agenda for curriculum and structural reform of education systems is held in view while being interpreted and mediated to schools through a process of trialling, review and further refinement conducted at state level. With twenty–twenty hindsight vision on the part of the states and territories implementation is now occurring on a time scale that is more acceptable to teachers and schools, and a marked departure from that originally envisaged by the AEC and its constituent committees. If this intensity of activity can be maintained it is still likely to yield many of the results intended by the signatories to *The Hobart Declaration*, but customized to the needs of individual states and territories.

Conclusion

What we have witnessed to date in a number of Australian state education systems as well as at the national level is what Broadfoot (1985) refers to as the ascendancy of a technicist administrative ideology which finds its expression in corporate management techniques. The move to corporate models of management in many spheres of public life has featured widely in contemporary Australia.

In the entrenched form of educational reform policy, that has been in place since the latter part of the 1980s, is the convergence of corporate federalism with economic rationalism allied with a view of students as human capital. Latterly this has occurred within an agenda of micro-economic reform which has tended to confine discussions about educational and curriculum reform at the ideological level to a restricted range of interest groups and power brokers. These are readily identifiable through statements made by high-profile public figures mainly in the fields of commerce, industry and the trade-union movement. At the federal level of politics it is noteworthy that originality in thought and action by a broadly based community of interest has been singularly lacking. According to Birch and Smart,

> Recent turbulence in the education policy-making area seems likely to accelerate as its professional ranks become increasingly influenced and infiltrated by 'outsiders' such as politicians employers and concerned community groups. In short, the politicisation of education policy seems likely to grow rather than diminish so long as widespread anxiety about the quality and direction of education persists in the community. (Birch and Smart, 1990, p. 150)

The interlocution of the lay public has been accompanied by a marked lack of sophistication in educational thinking. With this has come requirements for the widespread use of explicit benchmarks such as performance indicators, and measurable outcome statements. Skilling and multi-skilling are now by-words in the language of productivity, training and education. These trends are also likely to continue as long as a federal Labor government remains in office.

At the opposite end of a continuum starting with policy is that of practice (see Gene Hall's chapter in this volume and Jim Lowham's in Volume 2).

Those countries featured in these companion volumes have been faced with similar labour-market problems and stagnating industrial complexes and it is all too easy to blame the schools when things go wrong. In this vein, Carré and Carter (1990) document some of the difficulties encountered by teachers charged with implementing the British National Curriculum on an impossibly short time scale. In the Australian context, prior to the July 1993 meeting of the AEC, a similar power-coercive pattern of implementation was beginning to emerge. The backlash this provoked, particularly by the conservative states, resulted in polarizing opposing viewpoints in the Committee resulting in a backing away from the agenda for a national curriculum in the form which it had developmentally assumed.

Kennedy clearly points out that unless policy makers can convince teachers that the reforms they propose are in the best interests of students there will be little positive action and even positive resistance on the part of teachers and school administrators (1988, p. 372). A similar finding is also reported by Carter and Hacker (1988). There has been a radical and massive shift in thinking about the curriculum with huge policy implications also evident in many other parts of the world. For curriculum policies to translate into practice it takes teachers to make them work. If the Western Australian experience to date is taken as being representative of moves towards the implementation of national profiles, they have to be shown that they will work for the benefit of students if teachers are to be convinced of their value.

The present continuing activity of the states and territories, leading to the further refinement of national curriculum profiles and statements according to their perceived needs, appears to be geared towards this end. It is to be hoped that the collaborative and shared experiences that have occurred since 1986 will not founder on a narrow and parochial interpretation of states rights as the states and territories pursue their own agendas, but as Kevin Piper dryly notes, 'The colonial legacy dies hard in Australian education, and it does not roll over and expire gracefully. Not, at least, while there are empires to protect' (1989, p. 10).

Chapter 3

The National Curriculum in England Since 1988

Denis Lawton

I have been asked to discuss the national curriculum in England, which, I suggest, can only be understood in the context of the whole Education Reform Act (ERA), 1988 — a highly political document. The intention of the Act was to change the nature of the English education system by moving away from planning and cooperation between central and local government towards a market in which parents were promised the right to choose schools.

Education, and therefore the curriculum, is essentially a political matter — for several reasons. Education, which has almost unlimited capacity for spending money, has to contend with other claims on the Exchequer, and such decision-making is essentially political. In addition, education is a legitimate political concern because what is taught and other questions such as 'to whom?' are inevitably expressions of political values. For some years after the 1944 Act there was an assumption that education could be non-political, but by the end of the 1960s this was clearly seen to be a false assumption.

Even so, it is undesirable for education to be *used* for party political purposes. There is a difference between legitimate political concern and party political manipulation. The line may be a thin one, but educationists should guard the distinction carefully. Since 1979 — and especially since 1988 — I think politicians have crossed over the border between legitimate concern and political interference, motivated by political ideology — specifically by the activities of right-wing extremists whose influence is out of proportion to their numbers.

It may be helpful to describe very briefly the events which led up to the dramatic changes in 1988. The 1944 Education Act was a major landmark in English history: for the first time secondary education was free and compulsory for all. Unfortunately, the Act said nothing about the curriculum 5–16, and for some years after World War II the attention of planners was focused on the question of the organization of secondary schools (should there be one, comprehensive, school for all, or should there be three different kinds of school for supposed different types of ability?). Schools were generally left to their own devices in planning curricula, except that for the 20 per cent or so 'academic' students the school-leaving examinations (General Certificate of Education (GCE), Ordinary and Advanced Levels) provided syllabuses for examinations to be taken at age 16 and 18. The other 80 per cent were thought not to need examinations, which some educationists felt had a distorting effect on the curriculum.

Parents and employers, however, wanted to have some kind of school-leaving certificate, and in the 1960s official action was belatedly taken when a new examination — the Certificate of Secondary Education (CSE) — was established (for the 40 per cent below the top 20 per cent). This examination was a moderate success: it was more 'teacher-friendly', involving coursework and projects. Throughout the 1970s and 1980s there was a demand for a 'single examination at 16+' which, from the teachers' point of view would be more like CSE than GCE (Ordinary Level). Eventually, a new common format was invented — the General Certificate of Secondary Education (GCSE) and the first examinations took place, coincidentally, in 1988. It was generally regarded as a success, despite some right-wing mutterings about lower standards.

That brings us to another strand in the story 1944–88: standards. The 1944 Act was passed during World War II, as an all-party consensus measure — part of the general wish for a better post-war world with improved health services, housing and education — for all. But by the 1960s the consensus was wearing thin: the cost of the education service was increasing, and doubts were voiced about 'value for money'. Worse still, in the late 1960s, there was a group of right-wingers within the Conservative Party consistently criticizing education policies, not only on grounds of cost, but also for social and moral reasons: progressive education was allegedly encouraging undesirable attitudes in the young, such as lack of respect for authority, bad manners, and indiscipline, as well as sloppy standards in English, maths and other subjects. The events of 1968 in England and elsewhere seemed to confirm right-wing prejudices. *The Black Papers*, edited by Professor Brian Cox, (Cox and Dyson, 1969a; 1969b) articulated all that was wrong with modern education in a series which began in 1969 and continued until 1975 (Knight, 1990).

Throughout the 1970s there were Conservative demands for a return to selective secondary schools (grammar schools), traditional teaching methods, and the kind of curriculum content which would encourage greater regard for our cultural heritage and traditional values.

A third strand was the growing demand within the Conservative Party for parents to have greater influence over their children's schooling, including choice of school. This kind of consumerism in education was at first exemplified by various voucher schemes which were put forward, but when an experimental scheme was clearly unsuccessful, more general attacks on the state system, and the local education authorities (LEAs) that ran it, were mounted. By the time that a new Education Act was being discussed in 1988, the right-wing demand included ending the state monopoly in education, opening up education to market forces and creating new kinds of schools, which although receiving government finance, would be more independent than the maintained schools controlled by LEAs. In some respects a central-ized national curriculum ran counter to these ideas, but as we shall see, one powerful reason for a national curriculum was closely connected with market ideology.

Elsewhere (Lawton, 1992) I have argued that given ideological differ-ences between the parties, it is still important to find as much consensus as possible on a number of issues, including education. The national curriculum (1988) is a good example of an issue which began as a legitimate political concern, with the possibility of consensus, but the opportunity for consensus was lost when successive politicians allowed the national curriculum to be distorted for short-term political reasons.

When Kenneth Baker, in 1987, announced his intention of introducing a national curriculum, there was a good deal of support for the idea in principle, although some doubts were expressed about details of implementation.

The national curriculum has four components:

- subjects (three core plus seven other foundation subjects);
- attainment targets (objectives specified at ten levels of achievement);
- programmes of study (the subject syllabuses); and
- an assessment scheme (see below — TGAT).

Baker's interpretation of a national curriculum based on subjects was in itself political, but conflict might have been avoided had the rest of the model been allowed to survive.

Planning the assessment scheme for the curriculum was entrusted to the Task Group for Assessment and Testing (TGAT) under the Chairmanship of Professor Paul Black. The main achievements of the TGAT Report were to shift the emphasis of discussion:

- from summative testing to formative assessment (incorporating a major role for teacher assessment);
- from 'absolute standards' to criterion-referencing; and
- from fixed minimum standards (age-related benchmarks) to the flexibility of broadly defined attainment targets with ten levels (not rigidly age-related).

Professor Black's TGAT model was greeted by most educationists with some enthusiasm. It was the redeeming feature of an otherwise disappointing, backward-looking national curriculum. Unfortunately, since then the story of TGAT has been one of gradual dilution — largely as a result of political attacks and criticisms from reactionaries. In his Presidential Address to the Education Section of the British Association in August 1992, Paul Black complained about the 'demise of TGAT' (Black, 1992). A promising pro-fessional model has become more and more bureaucratic and political. Since then a number of other erstwhile supporters of the national curriculum have complained about the damaging increase in political interference (see Chitty and Simon, 1993).

Why was there this regression to ideology? I have elsewhere (Lawson, 1989) suggested that there are four (overlapping) ideological positions on education which are important for curriculum planning, at least three of which could be found in the Conservative Party during the period of the national curriculum debate:

- The Privatisers (who would prefer to abolish state schools and let people pay for what they want and can afford);
- Minimalists (who accept the need for state schooling but choose not to use it for their own children, and prefer the State to provide something less expensive — they tend to talk about 'the basics' and see schooling in terms of training for work rather than general education);
- Pluralists (who would like state education to be so good that there would be no motive for having private schools — nevertheless they argue in favour of the continued existence of independent schools on grounds of social diversity, freedom of choice and academic differentiation); and
- Comprehensive Planners (who would like to plan for a single system catering for all social and intellectual types of children). If there were any 'comprehensive planners' in the Conservative Party in the Thatcher years they kept very quiet.

The kind of national curriculum that Conservative politicians would have supported in 1988 depended mainly on their ideological position. Privatisers would have preferred no national curriculum (Sexton, 1988); minimalists wanted a concentration on basics (the three core subjects); pluralists preferred something like the HMI (Her Majesty's Inspectorate) Entitlement Curriculum for all. A compromise was needed, but compromises run the risk of incoherence.

The national curriculum in 1988 resembled an entitlement curriculum in some respects; but the unnecessary concept of 'core' was introduced presumably as a sop to the minimalists; and the idea of a national curriculum was made acceptable to some privatisers as an essential framework for the assessment figures which would be published in league-table form and used by parents to choose schools. Bad schools would close; the market would solve all problems of quality.

Since 1988 there have been several further moves to the right. For example, the innovatory Standard Assessment Tasks (SATs) have been replaced by unreliable short written tests; an entitlement curriculum has been diluted to a new hierarchy of Core–Extended Core–Options.

Moreover the national curriculum has to be seen in the light of other ERA (1988) changes, especially the policy of open enrolment and some aspects of Local Management of Schools (LMS). By attaching a cash value to each student and encouraging schools to compete for those students, in effect a voucher system has been created. What was the justification for sacrificing a planned system on the altar of market choice? The answer is to be found partly in powerful transatlantic right-wing links, and partly in the neo-liberal views of Hayek whose thinking dominated the Thatcher years.

On the particular issue of the market, a book by John Chubb and Terry Moe has been very influential. The two American authors have paid several visits to England to spread the gospel, and were invited by the *Sunday Times* to prescribe a solution for the English system. Their long article was published in the *Sunday Times Colour Supplement* (February 9, 1992). Their book *Politics, Markets and America's Schools* (1990) was based on the belief that replacing democratic control by parental choice would automatically solve institutional problems in US schools. On p. 217 they say '. . . we think reformers would do well to entertain the notion that choice is a panacea.' After a brief visit they came to the conclusion that the same magic formula would work in England: free all schools from Local Education Authorities (LEAs) and allow anyone to set up new schools to be paid for by the State. Unencumbered by 'democratic control' and pushed on by parental choice, schools will just improve! The hidden hand of the market sorts everything out — planning is completely unnecessary. Research shows, however, that the issue of choice is very complex, and unfortunately Chubb and Moe did not deal with some of the hard questions. For example, if choice is a panacea, why are there still some very bad private schools?

The influence of Chubb and Moe does not, however, explain why such dramatic changes took place in the education system. For that we need to look much deeper into the English social structure. There has long been a minority view which expresses dislike of government planning and a preference for *laissez-faire*. Thatcherism represented a revival of those values in a form described by Andrew Gamble as 'free economy and strong state' (Gamble, 1988). The 1979 Election was an opportunity to translate Hayekian ideas into policy — including education policy. The surprising feature of the education debate was that even those moderate Conservatives I have described above as pluralists seemed to have been converted to the language and ideas of the marketplace: they talk of the education system being dominated by 'the producers' rather than by 'consumers'. Parents must be allowed to choose because — it is alleged — they know better than the educational theorists and even better than good teachers. Not all Conservatives have succumbed to these neo-liberal doctrines: see, for example, Ian Gilmour's book *Dancing With Dogma* (1992).

In any system there will be some schools more attractive than others, but if you excite parents' interest in 'choosing' (and give them the impression they will get what they want), then the result is inevitably a number of disappointed parents. Where there are more applications than places, it is the schools that do the choosing by selecting students with fewest problems. It is surprising that politicians, hard-headed in other respects, were willing to put all their trust in such utopian dreams as the hidden hand of the market — the panacea of parental choice.

Chubb and Moe should have looked at the evidence about choice in Scotland. By chance, earlier legislation gave Scottish parents very similar rights of choice in 1982 to those English parents received after the Education Act (1988). The effects of much increased parental choice have been carefully studied by Adler, Petch and Tweedie in *Parental Choice and Educational Policy* (1989). The results cast doubt on choice as a panacea.

For example, Adler and his colleagues found that many schools attracting more students as a result of 'open enrolments' found it difficult to cope with the increased numbers. (Eton could in the 1980s have expanded to meet tremendous demand, but chose not to. Why? Well-established schools know only too well that such changes alter the character of the school and ultimately its quality.) Good schools did not improve as a result of choice, but some schools certainly deteriorated — they lost students and staff and found it difficult to keep up standards. No school had closed as a result of market forces, but those schools losing students found it impossible to respond positively to some kinds of complaint — there was little they could do, for example, about making access to the school safer. And once in decline, it was very difficult for schools to recover, however hard the teachers tried. The idea that competition makes teachers work harder and thus improve standards is not borne out by the evidence. There were, however, signs of increasing inequalities, widening of the gap between schools, and the danger of a 'two-tier' system developing. There was a growing problem of disappointed choosers, including some who were refused a place in the nearest comprehensive school. Another kind of disappointment also began to appear: having chosen a school because it had good, uncrowded facilities and plentiful resources, parents found that it was now packed to capacity and no longer so attractive. One of the fallacies of choice is that you usually have to make a choice without knowing how many others are going to make the same choice (Hirsch, 1977). The result of aggregating individual rational choices is a situation which is no longer rational: parents choose a school for certain qualities which cease to exist when many other parents choose the same school and thereby reduce the quality of its service — for example by making the school overcrowded.

Choice, although desirable in principle, and having some benefits in practice, is not a panacea. Market competition does not automatically solve problems of school organization or raise standards. But the White Paper *Choice and Diversity* (DfE, July, 1992), which became law in 1993, comes very close to putting the Chubb and Moe doctrines into operation. We now have a possible scenario of more emphasis on the market; more Grant Maintained Schools (GMS) (that is, those schools which have opted out of local education authority control); less national coordination from Her Majesty's Inspectorate (HMI); and a real danger of the development of a three-tiered or multi-tiered system of schools.

Adler (1993) in a paper for the National Commission on Education, drew on the Scottish experience in an attempt to evaluate how parental choice would work in England. As well as those of Munn (1991), the Scottish Office Education Department (1992), and Willms and Echols (1992). The evidence indicates that parents tend to choose schools in 'better' social areas with superior (unadjusted) examination results, but contrary to much right-wing propaganda, parents found it difficult to make adjustments of a value-added kind (that is, to distinguish between apparent and real quality). Schools in poorer areas tended to lose students and then face problems of viability. Social segregation tended to increase. Adler concludes that on balance parental choice had resulted in less effective use of resources. In cities, two-tier systems were beginning to emerge, and the existence of a number of 'sink' schools was a serious cause of concern. Those who had gained from choice had done so at the expense of 'losers', the community as a whole had not benefited. At the end of his paper, Adler sets out an interesting alternative plan for preserving some choice without the disadvantages of destructive competition.

In the Summer of 1993, teachers in primary and secondary schools decided to take action. In an unprecedented demonstration of unity, the six professional associations (teacher unions) representing teachers and principals, produced a joint document protesting against the tests which were proposed for 7 and 14-year-old pupils. For legal reasons, the protest concentrated on the additional workload of teachers, but underlying that complaint were objections to the kind of tests and the use of the results of assessment being published in league-table form. More than 90 per cent of schools either refused to administer the tests or to report the results. The assessment programme for 1993 collapsed, and a working party was set up to make recommendations about the national curriculum and its assessment in order to make it more workable.

The whole episode is an interesting example of the failure of politicians and bureaucrats to consult the professionals — especially the teachers themselves — about a radical programme of 'reform'. A top–down model has been rejected and the government will have to start again after many millions of pounds Sterling have been wasted, as well as many hours of teacher — and student — time has been lost. There are several lessons to be learned from the events of 1988–93.

Conclusion

Several broad observations can be drawn from this. Politicians should be careful to distinguish between areas of legitimate concern, and direct interference in areas where they lack competence. Where obvious political transgressions or incursions occur, they should be challenged to avoid long-term pain. The national curriculum innovation can be regarded as a case study of transgression beyond the competence of government, in which an opportunity for planning a good curriculum has been lost, and the desirable TGAT assessment model has been seriously distorted.

Application of market models to education is very misleading. Although there is evidence that most people want some choice in education, they would prefer good local schools to a market in education. Establishing a market in education is a poor substitute for planning. Further, the use of national curriculum and examination assessment data to provide market information is dangerously misleading, masking as it does many of the other factors in the education equation.

Chapter 4

Educational Reform and the Politics of the Curriculum in New Zealand

Michael Peters

There has been a massive restructuring of the education system in New Zealand since the late 1980s. Reforms have been advanced at all levels, from early childhood to tertiary education, and instituted at an unprecedented pace by two successive governments. The Fourth Labour Government (1984–90), beginning in 1987, undertook the reform of educational administration. The reforms, based on neo-liberal principles of individualism and strategies of deregulation, corporatism and privatization, represent a commitment to the market distribution of public goods and services. Those reforms were dressed up in the language of devolution, community empowerment and democratization yet, in effect, they served to commodify education and culture, to deprofessionalize teachers, and ultimately to disempower communities. The structural reforms instituted by the Labour Government also served as the context within which, subsequently, the National Government has focused on 'reforming' the curriculum and qualifications systems. In essence, the National Government has introduced the national curriculum of New Zealand, which is an attempt to build a national culture of enterprise and competition. This chapter reviews these developments, arguing that there is an essential continuity in ideology and approaches to reforms adopted by the Labour and National Governments.

The Fourth Labour Government and the Reform of Educational Administration

The Politics of Reform

The Fourth Labour Government's strategy was first to form committees to report on each of the areas of preschool, primary, secondary and tertiary education; second, in response to these reports, to produce a government policy document in each of these areas; and finally, to establish working parties to restructure the sectors and implement changes according to their policy decisions. As an indication of the speed of these changes, the committee on secondary education was established on 21 July 1987; it reported in April 1988 in a publication entitled *Administering for Excellence* (known as the Picot Report, 1987); the policy decisions were announced in August 1988 in *Tomorrow's Schools* (Ministry of Education, 1988); and the reforms were put in place on 1 October 1989, only to be reviewed and further reformed a mere six months later (Ministry of Education, 1990).

The rapidity with which the reforms were carried out is primarily due to two factors. First, these reforms were based on neo-liberal ideology, the organizing principles of which had been operationalized and instituted much earlier in the restructuring of the 'core' public sector. There is great political significance in the sequencing of reforms which reshaped the New Zealand State; in the fact that for reasons to do with mass threats to legitimacy the restructuring of education, health and welfare should be carried out later in the reform process. Second, the pace at which the reforms were carried out was part of a deliberate strategy embraced by the Labour Government. Roger Douglas (1989), then Minister of Finance, in a paper to the Mt Pelerin Society entitled 'The Politics of Successful Reform', listed ten principles which underlay Labour's strategy for politically successful reform, including the following three:

- Implement reform by quantum leaps. Moving step by step lets vested interests mobilize. Big packages neutralize them.
- Speed is essential. It is impossible to move too fast. Delay will drag you down before you can achieve your success.
- Once you start the momentum rolling, never let it stop. Set your own goals and deadlines. Within that framework consult in the community to improve detailed implementation.

Notice here, in particular, how the process assumes a small policy elite and, equally, negates any possibility of wide public consultation or community participation. Consultation in this process is seen purely in terms of improving detailed implementation after the major decisions have been made. My point is that the process is profoundly anti-democratic.

While the education reforms had been advanced as changes in administration which would lead to more effective delivery of education through the devolution of power and responsibility to the community, and by the promotion of excellence and equity in the areas of ethnicity, gender and class, they represented the insertion of New-Right thinking into education, almost exactly as presaged by the New Zealand Treasury's *Economic Management* (The Treasury, 1984) and *Government Management* (Vol. 2 *Education Issues*) (The Treasury, 1987). Labour's *Tomorrow's Schools* (1988) and to a lesser extent National's *Education Policy* (Ministry of Education, 1991) together established the conditions necessary for the operation of a decentralized, deregulated competitive market catering for self-interested individuals. Further, both documents used the discourse of participatory democracy and community empowerment to mask their policy interests.

The Reforms and their Intellectual Sources

The contemporary rejuvenation of classical, liberal economic theory which has informed the New Right has taken form in the work of Friedman and the Chicago school; Buchanan and Tullock and the public choice school; Hayek and the Australian school; and the British Institute of Economic Affairs. The strands of thought which together comprise New-Right thinking include: public-choice theory, agency theory, transaction-cost analysis and the 'new managerialism'.

These theories take as their central assumption the notion that all human behaviour can be explained by reference to self-interest. Individuals, in other words, are 'rational utility maximizers'. Concepts such as altruism or public interest have relevance only insofar as they mask attempts by interest groups (e.g., education unions) to maintain or enhance a privileged position. Most important, perhaps, is the notion that the self-seeking behaviour of individuals in the market-place leads to the most effective and efficient distribution of public goods and services. This argument is used by the New Right to oppose the ideology of the Welfare State which stresses the importance of redistribution of goods and services through the State. The 'new managerialism' which has recently been applied to public administration in many countries (Britain, New Zealand and Australia included) represents a strong move away from the ideology of welfarism. Boston (1991, p. 9) summarizes its central tenets:

- an emphasis on management rather than policy; in particular a new stress on management skills in preference to technical or professional skills;
- a shift from the use of input controls and bureaucratic procedures and rules to a reliance on quantifiable output measures and performance targets;
- the devolution of management control coupled with the development of new reporting, monitoring and accountability mechanisms;
- the disaggregation of large bureaucratic structures into quasi-autonomous agencies, in particular the separation of commercial from non-commercial functions, and policy advice from policy implementation;
- a preference for private ownership, contracting out, and contestability in public-service provision;
- the imitation of certain private-sector management practices such as the use of short-term labour contracts, the development of corporate plans, performance agreements and mission statements, the introduction of performance-linked remuneration systems, and a greater concern for corporate image;

- a general preference for monetary incentive, rather than non-monetary incentives, such as ethics, ethos and status; and
- a stress on cost-cutting, efficiency and cutback management.

These principles are reflected in the reviews of education and in the accountability mechanisms eventually adopted. For instance, the *Hawke Report* (1988, p. xi) reviewing post-compulsory education advocates the following framework of principles based on the Picot model:

- a simple administrative structure, in which decisions were to be made as close as possible to where they would be executed;
- a move to national objectives;
- clear responsibilities and goals;
- decision makers to have control over resources, and to be made accountable for outcomes; and
- a system which is open to scrutiny and is responsive to client demands.

There is a clear fit between the central tenets of the 'new managerialism' and the framework of principles adopted on the basis of the educational reviews. This relationship is also exemplified in the accountability mechanisms recommended by the reviews.

The crucial accountability mechanisms are identified as consisting of: first, a set of contractual relationships between (i) the government on the one hand and the chief executives of the Ministry of Education and other education agencies on the other, (ii) providers (i.e., councils and boards) and their chief executives; second, charters setting out intended outcomes and performance measures; and third, audits of performance in accordance with charters. The contract becomes the central underpinning concept, and genuine devolution based on principles of participation and partnership at the level of the local community becomes transformed into a form of *delegation* of power between individuals.

The Politics of Devolution

The original *Tomorrow's Schools* document seemed couched in the language of participatory democracy and community empowerment, where schools, managed collaboratively, would be governed through a partnership of interests of parents and teachers. The opening pages of *Tomorrow's Schools* is graced with a quotation from Thomas Jefferson in both English and Maori:

> I know of no safe depository of the ultimate power of the society but the people themselves and if we think them not enlightened enough to exercise their control with a wholesome discretion, the remedy is not to take it from them, but to inform their discretion. (T. Jefferson)

The idea of participatory democracy was underlined by the creation of a number of organizational innovations: the Parent Advocacy Council, Board of Trustees, Community Education Forums, and the National Policy Council.

Of these organizations only the boards remain. The rest have been abolished. The main thrust of public-choice theory is preserved in this policy of 'devolution'. Since boards, in conjunction with school principals, are responsible for hiring, firing and controlling staff this effectively transfers power from the 'agents' (teachers) to the 'consumers' of education (parents), thereby circumventing the prime 'danger' of interest group or 'provider capture'. Second, substantial savings are realized because of the wide range of administrative costs devolved from central agencies to the voluntary labour constituting the boards of trustees (Gordon, 1992a).

Peter Bushnell (an economic adviser in the Treasury) and Graham Scott (secretary to the Treasury) addressed the question of devolution from an economic perspective, at the time of the major educational reviews. They approached devolution in terms of agency theory, arguing that accountability is inseparable from devolution. At one point they write:

> Some of the key costs in economic transaction are those related to the formation, monitoring and enforcement of a set of contracts with agents whose interests may diverge from those of a principal. (Bushnell and Scott, 1988, pp. 22–3)

They argue that the contractual relationship needs to be structured through a system of sanctions and rewards so as to counter any tendencies to opportunism. The important point to understand is that Bushnell and Scott interpret 'devolution' as a form of delegation of power where three conditions must be met: first, 'objectives should be clearly identified and conflicts avoided'; second, 'performance must be monitored'; and third, 'incentives and sanctions should be in place to encourage managers to act to meet objectives rather than follow their own goals' (Bushnell and Scott, 1988).

Devolution has been redefined through an interpretation of agency theory to become an important element of the 'new managerialism'. It has everything to do with management but nothing to do with community empowerment and democratic participation.

The complete corruption by the New Right of the notion and promise of genuine devolution, based on access, participation and collaboration, and of any possibility of establishing 'community' social relations in education is given very clearly in the account by Stuart Sexton (1991). Sexton, a member of the Institute of Economic Affairs and one-time adviser to Margaret Thatcher, was contracted by the Business Roundtable to review education reforms in New Zealand and comment on their possible future direction. There is some evidence that the Sexton Report, which was written and available in draft form, greatly influenced the Lough Report (*Today's Schools*, 1990), particularly in its attack on the size and scope of the Education Review Office — the organization responsible for monitoring equity and Treaty of Waitangi obligations under school charters (see Marshall, Peters and Smith, 1991).

Sexton's (1991) argument is revealing because it represents a celebration of the free market in ideologically transparent terms. The State's role in education, according to Sexton, should be reduced to a bare minimum and could be fulfilled merely by requiring all children to attend school, providing parents with funds, and then letting the market take over.

The quality and quantity of schooling is then dictated by consumer demand and competition. Sexton's radically decentralized schools would be managed by a body analogous to 'a non-executive board of directors of a company'. Neither teachers nor students would be eligible for election to the board, and school principals would be non-voting members. Any notion of participative democracy or community representation is ignored. In Sexton's (1991) terms, education is a market commodity and schools are enterprises or businesses which compete for consumers in the educational market-place. In fact, Sexton completes his report by advocating the adoption of a full voucher system. Not surprisingly, much the same framework has been applied to tertiary education in another report commissioned by the Business Roundtable (Blandy, 1988).

Recent Development

When National became the Government in late 1990, it continued the implementation of Labour's reform process. Since its term of office, there has been ongoing concern about the huge proportion of work that has fallen onto boards and school principals. Concern also came from boards claiming to be underfunded, although this has, to some extent, been rectified for the 1991 year. There has been a continuing struggle in relation to the bulk funding of teachers' salaries. While the present Minister of Education (Dr Lockwood Smith) is still pushing for salary bulk funding, the available evidence shows that, by far, the majority of boards do not want it. The reasons given for this included fears of the extra workload involved and the possibility of negative effects in board–staff relations (Wylie, 1990, pp. 66–7). Most recently, the minister has decided to impose bulk funding on schools for senior management staff. This unilateral Government action, along with conflict over pay claims, has led to a series of rolling regional one-day strikes by secondary-school teachers. Further, teachers have threatened to disrupt the implementation of the Minister's national-curriculum reforms.

In relation to the issue of board–staff relations, some believe that the Government will dump its fiscal crisis onto the schools, with teachers taking the brunt of cost-cutting. Two factors indicate that the Government has this in mind. Firstly, teacher registration has been made voluntary and schools are able to employ non-registered teachers. Secondly, boards opting for bulk-salary funding can transfer money from salary to operational areas, choosing, should they wish, to employ fewer, or less qualified teachers, or even to impose pay reductions on existing staff. Without doubt, the controversial, anti-union Employment Contracts Act 1991, which provides employers with the means to undermine national awards, leaves the way open for such treatment of teaching staff.

What is more the Minister of Education has recently de-emphasized all issues pertaining to equity and empowerment (Gordon, 1992b) and has made a commitment to repeal the statutory requirement that schools include equity clauses in their charters. Claiming that the New Zealand curriculum has an 'excessive focus on social issues . . . poor preparation for the competitive world [and] inadequate skilling in technology' (*Education Policy*, Ministry of Education, 1991, p. 1) the minister has argued for an education which is responsive to business and is imbued with a new culture of enterprise and competition in our curriculum.

The answer to the 'crisis' in education of handing power, control and responsibility back to the community has appeal on the surface to the full spectrum of pressure groups, from those on the far right to those who have traditionally made the call for a community development approach. But only on the basis of a clear understanding of both the notions of community, and its place within various socio-political paradigms, are we really in a position to determine whether particular proposals for devolution are genuinely concerned to promote community or are a cost-cutting mechanism for the New Right, which is intent on reducing the role of the State on the basis of an ideological commitment (Peters and Marshall, 1988a, b).

The National Government and the Politics of Curriculum Reform

Background to the National Curriculum

Labour's reform of educational administration did nothing positive for the reform of curriculum in the schools sector. Indeed, the 1989 Education Act actually dismantled the Curriculum Division of the Department of Education which prior to 1989 had been responsible in developing and trialling new syllabuses with teachers in both the preschool and school sectors. One explanation that has been advanced for this 'black hole' in Labour's reform process suggests that 'the dismantling of pre-existing curriculum development structures and processes was a deliberate consequence of Treasury's dissatisfaction with the way in which they had operated' (Capper, 1992, p. 16). In support of this claim, Capper cites the way in which the *1987 Curriculum Review* — the result of the work of a representative group that held wide public consultations — had been attacked by the New Right. It was criticized as a liberal document not sufficiently aware of the needs of the economy. In this vacuum, the New Zealand Qualifications Authority (NZQA), one of the new educational agencies established by the reforms, seems to be in control of the school curriculum, almost by default. In lieu of any one agency which, officially at least, picked up the mantle of responsibility of the now defunct Curriculum Division, the control and development of the national curriculum has come formally under ministerial control, creating greater centralization than at any point in the past. This has clauses at a time when, as Capper (1992, p. 17) argues 'the capacity of central agencies to facilitate change at the institutional level had been reduced in the compulsory schools sector'. This degree of centralization has been augmented by two factors: first, the ministry now relies on contract research for issues concerning curriculum development; second, the minister has had a strong influence over the selection of members appointed to working parties for mathematics, science and English.

By May 1991, a little more than six months after the National Government was elected to power, the Minister of Education had published his plans for comprehensive reform of the school curriculum — reform, as Dr Smith (Ministry of Education, 1991, p. 3) said in one of his speeches, 'that will bring our schooling system into line with the needs of the 90s and the 21st century and the imperatives of the modern competitive international economy'. This was to become a favourite theme of the minister's, together with an emphasis on the subjects of science and technology, and an attack on the current standards of the educational system.

The National Government's education policy has focused on four initiatives. They are:

- Parents as first teachers: a new parent education and support policy designed to assist parents in fulfilling their role as their child's first teachers.
- The achievement initiative: a policy designed to refocus school education on the basic subjects of English, mathematics, science and technology.
- The national certificate: a new vocationally-orientated qualification for sixth and seventh-form students that could be studied in part at school, polytechnics, or in approved workplaces.
- The study right: a scheme to provide school leavers with access to tertiary education and training according to their needs (see Peters, 1992a; Peters *et al.*, 1992).

Here I shall concentrate on the proposal for the development of a national curriculum, incorporating the achievement initiative.

The National Curriculum

In May 1991 the Ministry of Education published *The National Curriculum of New Zealand: A Discussion Document* (Ministry of Education, 1991) and the

Principles

The set of fundamental principles which give clear direction to the national curriculum.

The national curriculum describes essential learning areas and skills; gives greater emphasis to core subjects; establishes clear achievement standards; challenges all students to fulfill their potential; is based on equal educational opportunities; recognizes the experiences, values, cultural traditions, histories and languages of all New Zealanders; ensures that learning progresses throughout schooling and builds on students' prior knowledge and experience.

Essential Skills	**National Curriculum Objectives**	**Essential Learning Areas**
The essential skills and qualities to be developed by all students.	The clear learning outcomes to be achieved by all students in the basic and other subjects. The objectives will: define the knowledge, understanding, skills and qualities stated in essential learning areas and skills; describe levels of achievement; facilitate assessment and monitoring; be used by teachers to chart individual progress; provide students and parents with specific information about students' achievement.	The essential areas of knowledge and understanding for all students.

Essential Skills

- Communication skills
- Numeracy skills
- Information skills
- Problem-solving and decision-making skills
- Self-management skills
- Work and study skills
- Social skills

Essential Learning Areas

- Language (English)
- Mathematics
- Science /environment
- Technology
- Social sciences
- The arts
- Physical and personal development
- Core curriculum subjects

Assessment Methods

Classroom and national-assessment procedures arising from the national curriculum.

- Diagnostic monitoring classroom-based assessment.
- National monitoring assessment to monitor national standards.
- Age-specific, transitional monitoring assessment at transition points (e.g., new entrants, Form 1, Form 3) to determine allocation of resources.

Figure 4.1:   The Framework for the National Curriculum of New Zealand

Minister launched it in a speech to the PPTA (Post Primary Teachers' Association) Curriculum Conference. As Capper (1992, p. 18) notes the Minister in his speech to the PPTA 'made frequent reference to labour-market needs, and a very narrow and functionalist core curriculum', ignoring the needs of Maori students and, indeed, all socio-cultural aspects of schooling.

The proposed national curriculum of New Zealand comprises five essential elements: the curriculum principles, essential learning areas, essential learning skills, and the national curriculum objectives, underpinned by new assessment methods. A diagrammatic representation and description of the framework of the national curriculum is given in Figure 4.1. The seven essential learning areas describe in broad terms the fields of knowledge which all students must study during compulsory schooling. Up to the fifth form, all students will be required to take the core subjects. The essential learning skills will be developed across the whole school curriculum. Subsequently, so-called 'competitive skills', 'teamwork skills' and 'responsibility skills' have been added under these group-ings since the first draft. The national curriculum objectives are meant to define more specifically in terms of outcomes the knowledge and skills identi-fied in the essential learning areas and the essential skills, as well as providing a clear continuum of learning goals and levels of achievement to be expected of students at particular stages of learning through the years of schooling.

The new assessment methods are to be developed to enable student progress to be systematically monitored against the achievement objectives of the national curriculum at key stages throughout schooling.

In conjunction with these developments, the New Zealand Qualifications Authority has released its discussion document *Designing the Framework* (1991) which is based around the national certificate. The national certificate is sup-posed to be a coordinated set of units of learning which is available to students at senior levels in secondary schools, polytechnics, colleges of education, universities, wananga, and private training establishments. The qualifications proposal is based on the Scottish model and it seems that New Zealand's and Australia's frameworks are identical in terms of numbers of levels and their descriptions. I will not dwell on the certification system suffice it to say that the idea of units of learning assessed by standard-based criteria, together with the capacity to recognize prior and experiential learning, has been received very positively by some who argue that it can only empower students (e.g., Capper, 1992). Others have criticized both the national curriculum and the NZQA system of certification in terms of their centralized control and in terms of the 'busnocratic' fragmentation of principles, skills, learning areas and assessment (Marshall, 1992).

A Curriculum of Enterprise and Competition

The notion of competition is one that the minister has dwelt on in a number of recent speeches. For instance, Dr Smith entitled his speech to the APEC (Asia Pacific Economic Co-operation) Education Ministerial Conference at Georgetown University, Washington DC, in August 1992, 'Achieving Excel-lence in a Competitive World'. In that speech he recounts policy develop-ments in New Zealand since 1984, describing them as 'an all-encompassing economic reform programme'. By returning to 1984 and tracing develop-ments in outline since that time he is tacitly approving and 'owning' reforms undertaken by the Fourth Labour Government (1984–90) based around the strategies of corporatization, privatization and deregulation. In a speech to the Auckland Division of the National Party, the Minister (1991, pp. 15–16) stated:

Over recent years the word 'competition' has disappeared from the vocabulary of educationalists. Yet, the world is a competitive place. Our standard of living as a nation now depends on our competing successfully in the international environment. We do our young people a grave disservice if we shield them from that reality and if the curriculum ignores it . . . The imperatives of the modern world require a new culture of enterprise and competition in our curriculum.

The emphasis on a new culture of enterprise and competition is part of the New Right discourse which represents a deliberate and sustained attempt at cultural reconstruction. Central to the notion of 'enterprise culture' is the importance of restructuring education so that it will deliver the necessary research, skills and attitudes required for New Zealand to compete in an increasingly competitive international economy. The message is quite clear: in the past there has been too much emphasis on social and cultural objectives and insufficient attention paid to economic goals in our education system; henceforth we must invest heavily in education as the basis for future economic growth by redesigning the system so that it meets the needs of business and industry.

Underlying the Budget 1991 and the Government's enterprise strategy is the explicit assumption that our education and welfare systems have failed us: they have allegedly created a 'culture of dependency' (p. 20, p. 26). The answer to these problems at the broadest philosophical level is to develop an enterprise culture based on a form of individualism promoting concepts of 'choice' and 'greater self-reliance'. According to the Budget document education is regarded as 'a key investment in our economic future' and the Government is committed to providing 'an environment that enables businesses and individuals to develop internationally competitive and innovative skills' (ibid., p. 20). Government spending has been redirected 'towards areas important for long-term economic growth and security, including: larger commitments to investments in *education, skills* and *research and development*' (ibid., p. 41). The Education Policy document, *Investing in People: Our Greatest Asset* (Minister of Education, 1991) reiterates these claims. The foreword by the Minister of Education begins with the assertion that the Government came to office with a clear policy 'to enhance educational achievement and skill development to meet the needs of a highly competitive, modern global economy'. It continues:

Studies like the Porter Project, questioned the relevance of our current curriculum with its excessive focus on social issues and poor preparation for the competitive world. It confirmed other recent studies that show inadequate skilling in technology compared with other qualifications.

The Porter Project is the popular title given to a study of the New Zealand economy organized around the theory and methodology of Michael Porter, a professor at Harvard's Business School who has made his reputation specializing in improving international competitiveness. Published as *Upgrading New Zealand's Competitive Advantage* (Crocrombe *et al.*, 1991), the project received funding and support from the Fourth Labour Government to the level of $1.75 million. From the beginning the project was bedevilled with internal disagreements over the Porter methodology, its applicability to New Zealand, and the selection of New Zealand industries to be incorporated in the study (see Edwards, 1991). Doubts about methodology have also been raised by Philpott (1991) who suggests, in addition, that the project relies excessively on management jargon and unproven assumptions, all at the expense of proper scientific enquiry. The Porter Project maintains that national prosperity is not inherited but created. National economic success is not simply a matter of cheap land and labour, or even, primarily the rate of capital accumulation. As the project notes: 'The industries that support a high and rising standard of living today are knowledge intensive' and 'success in international trade has become more a function of the ability to develop and deploy technology and skills, than of proximity to low-cost inputs' (Crocrombe *et al.*, 1991, p. 26). Under the Porter prescription New Zealand must become more 'innovation-driven' rather than factor-driven or investment-driven. The emphasis on innovation provides the link to sustained investment in 'human resources', the development of new skills, and the need for the reform of education.

As I have provided a critique of the Porter Project elsewhere (Peters, 1992b) I will not engage the substance of its arguments here. Suffice it to say that the Porter Project has served to legitimate aspects of past and existing policies and it has also served to provide legitimations of current and future policy initiatives. For example, the project has been used to legitimize the experiment of 'Rogernomics' (New Zealand's variant of Reaganomics, named after Roger Douglas) and the market oriented macro-economic policy framework; it has been appealed to in the need to avoid devaluation and as a vindication of privatization strategies. It has even helped to legitimize the further privatization of the remaining state sector: electricity generation, postal services, state television and radio. It has provided ammunition for those politicians who wish to roll back the Welfare State, to curtail both the type and level of government spending in areas of superannuation, health and welfare.

The project's ideological function is, perhaps clearest, in the realm of education policy where it has been referred to as a buttress for launching the Government's so-called 'achievement initiative', including the national curriculum. In particular, the Minister of Education has referred to the Porter Project to warrant claims concerning: the way 'imperatives of the modern world require a new culture of enterprise and competition in our curriculum'; the need to give greater emphasis to core areas, including a new subject called 'technology'; greater recognition of the new technologies; and emphasis on skills development at the expense of a traditional concern for knowledge and understanding; the concern for internationally competitive academic standards; and so on. In particular, the Porter Project has been a major inspiration for the notion of developing a culture of enterprise and competition in New Zealand.

The notion of enterprise culture is one that has been imported into the local context from Thatcher's Britain where, increasingly, questions of national economic survival and competition in the world economy have come to be seen under the Conservative Government as one of cultural reconstruction (Keat and Abercrombie, 1991, p. 1). The task of constructing such a culture has involved remodelling social institutions along commercial lines and encouraging the use and acquisition of so-called 'enterprising qualities'. The ideological function of the political rhetoric of enterprise, according to Keat and Abercrombie (1991), is to make sense of the kind of economic and cultural changes that have been variously described under the notions of post-industrialism, the information society, and post-Fordism. Morris (1991) traces the genesis and development of the concept of enterprise culture from its beginnings in the thinking of the Centre for Policy Studies, in the link between Christianity and the 'new conservatism', and in the work of Lord Young. He distinguishes three phases, the latest of which he christens 'partnership in cultural engineering'. The third phase, which represents a massive cultural reconstruction, has concerned policies involving 'unprecedented government intervention in education (at all levels)' (Morris, 1991, pp. 34–45).

The notion of 'enterprise culture' and the emphasis on enterprise, more generally, appeared relatively late within the New Zealand context, surfacing under the current National Government (Peters, 1992c). The present Prime Minister set up both the Enterprise Unit (within his own department) and the Enterprise Council. The Employers' Federation has organized a Schools Industry Links Development Board. The Enterprise New Zealand Trust operates the Young Persons' Enterprise Scheme. The Prime Minister recently organized the Enterprise Conference and the Education for Enterprise Conference.

The Prime Minister's 'Education for Enterprise' Conference held at the Beehive in early February this year (1992) became the basis for considering the following questions: how can we improve the responsiveness of educational institutions to the needs of enterprise? What is the Government's role in promoting better links between education and enterprise? How can secondary schools best prepare young people for future working life? And, how can we improve the quality of training by enterprises? The conference was convened 'to bring together leaders in education and industry to forge a vision of how these two sectors can work together to upgrade the New Zealand economy'. Submissions were received from a variety of sources including industry, government and education representatives. The three key themes to emerge from the submissions, as analysed by the Ministry of Education, included the need for:

- Processes to improve business sector input into the development and implementation of education policy at the national and local levels.

- Mechanisms to encourage and coordinate business–education partnership activity at the national and local levels.
- Processes to enable the business sector to identify medium and long-term skills needs for education and training purposes.

This statement of themes reflected the preponderance of industry representation and the choice of education representatives. As can be readily seen from the statement of these themes the emphasis was on a notion of enterprise synonymous with business and with business interests. This was reflected in the way business interests dominated other prominent themes at the conference: the need for business to have a greater say in curriculum formation; suggestions for changes in the processes of teacher training and recruitment to better reflect the world of commerce and business; better representation of business in tertiary decision-making; the opening up of the education system to greater competition. In all of this the appropriateness of business as a model of enterprise for education was taken for granted. There was very little discussion of the notion of enterprise at all except in terms of creating closer industry–education links or of modelling education on business. Clearly, the notion of enterprise culture had been construed in the narrowest economic sense. The national curriculum as a reflection of enterprise culture, therefore, would simply embody those skills thought necessary for creating an internationally competitive economy. Indeed, one participant at the conference suggested that the subject 'international marketing' become part of the core curriculum!

Politics of the Curriculum

In New Zealand since 1984 there has been a massive restructuring of education. The Labour Government, driven by New Right ideology, reshaped the State privatizing much of the 'core' public sector, deregulating and commercializing the 'peripheral' public sector, including the areas of state housing, health and education. Thus, when the national Government came to power in 1990 the New Right reform of educational administration was largely complete: the new structures and accountability mechanisms were already in place. Significantly, only the issue of bulk funding of teachers' salaries (part of the original proposal of the Picot task force), remained to be forced through against teacher opposition. Perhaps, the major single piece of legislation enacted by the National Government has been the Employment Contracts Act 1991, which in the name of efficiency, has dismantled an industrial relations system that, since its establishment in the late nineteenth century, has been 'oriented towards industrial stability, social equity, and economic efficiency' (Walsh, 1992). Pressure for radical deregulation of the labour market had been provided previously by the Business Roundtable and the Employers Federation. With the Employment Contracts Act, the National Government has pursued an aggressive agenda most recently, against both teachers and nurses.

The National Government could afford to turn its attention away from overt structural concerns to concentrate its energies on curriculum, qualifications and testing issues. Under both the Ministers of Education (Lockwood Smith) and of Labour (Bill Birch), the teaching labour market has been deregulated (registration of teachers was abolished in 1991), bulk funding of senior teaching staff has been imposed, and a new qualifications system has been established which, in effect, collapses the distinction between education and training. It is in this wider context that the introduction of the national curriculum, with its pragmatic and instrumental emphasis on essential, generic skills, must be viewed. The national curriculum is a socio-cultural construction which reflects the presuppositions underlying the notions of enterprise culture and competition. As Michael Apple argues:

> Education is deeply implicated in the politics of culture. The curriculum is never a neutral assemblage of knowledge, somehow appearing in the texts and classrooms of a nation. It is always part of a *selective tradition*, someone's selection, some group's vision of legitimate knowledge. It is produced out of the cultural, political, and economic conflicts, tensions, and compromises that organise and disorganise people. (Apple, 1992, p. 1)

The fact that the national curriculum of New Zealand tends to ignore questions about the nature and structure of knowledge, choosing to speak of learning theory, areas of learning, and, most importantly, 'skills', only more firmly endorses the point Apple is making. For by reducing knowledge to skills, the authors of the national curriculum have achieved a number of 'political' purposes. First, 'skills' can be more easily related to individual performance and thus more easily measured than 'knowledge' and 'understanding'. In this sense, 'skills' lend themselves to packaging and, thus, to commodification. Second, a skill is like a technique; it is a performance, an action, a doing. Like a technique, and like technology more generally, 'skills' are often seen as neutral or as value-free. 'Skills' are, therefore, considered to be generic, separable from their learning contexts, transferable or transportable from one context to another. Third, a skills-based orientation towards learning and the curriculum provides both an analogue of, and an easy transition stage to, the labour market with its emphasis on employable skills, new skills, skill needs of industry, 'upskilling', etc. In other words, a skills-based perspective contains an in-built bias towards a vocational education.

Richard Bates (1991), in an address to the New Zealand Post Primary Teachers' Association Conference, considers the question of who owns the curriculum in relation to two opposed interpretations: the market model of the curriculum and the curriculum as a form of cultural politics. The first is clearly meant to apply to New Zealand. Backed by public-choice theory, it argues that teachers have 'captured' the curriculum and constructed it in their own self-interest. It is the role of politicians, under this view, to reclaim the curriculum for those who are the 'end-users' of the 'products' of schooling. The language of public choice, argues Bates (1991, p. 4) 'appears to be about introducing a new democracy of service . . . whereby demands made of the State can be satisfied through individual choice within a market supplied by multiple, competing producers'. The role of the State on this model is, first, to ensure that service delivery in education is not captured; second, to put an end to monopolistic interests of teachers through the mechanism of deregulation; and third, to provide quality checks by controlling and monitoring national standards. Public-choice theory, Bates maintains, emerges as the dominant ideological response to the problems of diverse cultural demands currently besetting the corporate State — problems which cannot be solved within the framework of a Fordist state. While touted as a new model of the State, public-choice theory, Bates maintains, rejuvenates old Fordist principles. One indication of the continuing Fordist character of the State is the notion of the contract as the central institution of the so-called new order. The contract by defining relationships and responsibilities in terms of measurable performance, instantiates market relations in the public sector and thereby redefines public culture as consumption. Another indication of the continuing Fordist nature of the State is the increase in its centralized powers — the so-called strong but limited State. Nowhere is this more clear than in the realm of education with the development of the national curriculum which rests on a revival of the principles of 'scientific management' (Taylorism), involving the clear separation between responsibility for the specification of the curriculum (Government with input from big business) and responsibility for its execution (teachers, monitored by middle-level management).

As Bates (1991) argues, the political effects of this ideology were disastrous. First, it removed the control of the curriculum from educationalists and schools, separating the specification of the curriculum from its execution, and thereby turning teachers into technical functionaries (the deskilling hypothesis). Second, it defined and reduced culture to individualized patterns of consumption: 'the contractual nature of market relations . . . removes this cultural project from the public sphere by privatising the realm of values' (Bates, 1991, p. 8). Third, it defined the curriculum as a thing, a product, a piece of intellectual property which can be bought and sold in the market. The curriculum became commodified and individual consumers can purchase customized curriculum goods designed to suit their individual needs.

Against this view, Bates (1991) puts forward the conception of the curriculum as a form of cultural politics. This is a view shared widely by critical educational theorists. It encourages us to question what counts as knowledge and the ways in which it is organized and taught. It suggests that the curriculum is never an innocent or neutral cultural representation but rather reflects dominant values and interests, mapping the complex relationships between economic and cultural capital. The curriculum, on this view, can also be seen as a continuing debate which links knowledge, values and interests in particular ways and which provides the conversation within which particular historic settlements can be reached through negotiation and compromise (Bates, 1991, p. 16).

Such a view of the curriculum — as a form of cultural politics — is consonant with a policy of genuine devolution which would permit the necessary community participation in order to reach a democratic settlement. This grass-roots approach to curriculum development would also require structures which helped to develop a partnership of interests between teachers and parents. Such local-community curriculum planning and development could take place within a national framework which permitted flexibility and reflected the cultural and value diversity of the larger society. Against this view and under the New Right in New Zealand we have witnessed an increase in the power to decide curriculum matters centralized in the hands of the minister, who has constructed a national framework reflecting a new curriculum of enterprise and competition.

Part 2

Policy

Chapter 5

An Analysis of the Policy Contexts of Recent Curriculum Reform Efforts in Australia, Great Britain and the United States

Kerry J. Kennedy

Reform efforts relating to the school curriculum have been a prominent feature of educational policy-making in Great Britain, the United States and Australia since the 1980s. These countries share much in common in terms of cultural heritage, political ideology and general social aspirations. It is perhaps not unexpected, therefore, that they would pursue a similar path in relation to such a sensitive issue as the content and structure of what is taught in their schools. A common element that dictated policy responses was what Coombs has called 'a crisis of confidence in education itself' (1985, p. 9).

In the United States the crisis was highlighted by the Secretary for Education when he asserted that 'though our allegiance to quality education remains firm, our confidence in the ability of schools to realise that ideal has been battered by signs of decline: falling test scores, weakened curricula, classroom disorder, and student drug use' (Bennett, 1988, p. 1). In Great Britain, the government's White Paper, *Better Schools* (Department of Education and Science, 1985) was unequivocal in expressing the view that 'the standards now generally attained by our students are neither as good as they can be, nor as good as they need to be for the world of the twenty-first century. Schools should promote enterprise and adaptability and fit young people for working life in a technological age . . . high standards could be achieved by all schools rather than some' (p. 2). In Australia, the newly appointed Federal Minister for Employment, Education and Training was more oblique, perhaps in deference to his social democratic political orientation, yet equally as concerned about the health of the education system. He called for a 'regular assessment of the effectiveness and standards of our schools' involving the 'need to examine how our schools can report to parents and the community on their aims and achievements; how school systems can report on broader objectives, strategies and educational outcomes'. He wanted to move beyond state boundaries to develop 'a method of reporting to the nation on how well our schools are performing against established goals' (Dawkins, 1988, p. 5).

How did Great Britain, the United States and Australia each respond to this general level of concern expressed across international boundaries? Did their responses have anything in common? Is it possible to talk about the internationalization of curriculum reform? This chapter will address these questions in an attempt to portray the policy contexts that have shaped current approaches to the reform of the school curriculum.

Curriculum Reform — the Broader Context

Curriculum reform has been described as a type of educational reform that focuses on changes to the 'content and organisation of what is taught' (Ginsburg, Cooper, Raghu and Zegarra, 1990, p. 475). Carnoy and Levin (1976, p. 43) have pointed out that reforms of this type are limited or constrained by the social, economic and political context that gives rise to them. They have argued that unless educational-reform efforts are consistent with the values and interests of the larger society they will not be successful. This leads them to the conclusion that '. . . only when there is a demand for educational reform from the polity will education reform succeed'.

While such a view would not go unchallenged by many educators, it serves to remind us that any study of educational reform must be firmly embedded in contexts outside of the somewhat narrow realm of education. This involves acceptance of the notion that education is very much a public-policy issue — as much an instrument for local state and national policy development as for developing sensitive and caring relationships among young people.

Educational reform viewed as an instrument of public policy highlights the motives and objectives of governments rather than the intrinsic value of the particular reform effort. Ideally, in a democratic society, governments seek to mediate conflicting opinions and pressures in order to produce policies for the common good. Yet this mediation process can often result in outcomes that favour dominant groups in society or simply self-interest on the part of a particular government. Thus at times the rhetoric of educational reform may be more significant than the reality (Merritt and Coombs, 1977; Weiler, 1988; Ginsberg, Cooper, Raghu and Zegarra, 1990).

Educational reform, therefore, if it is to be properly understood, must be viewed in its broader ideological context. In particular, it needs to be recognized that educational-reform efforts may serve as symbolic political gestures so that purely educational assessments of such efforts may mask their real intention.

Finally, some consideration must be given to the way in which the international context to be discussed in this chapter influences local initiatives. Wirt and Harman (1986, p. 4) have argued that national and international influences on educational reform interact so that 'national qualities operate like a prism, refracting and adapting [global] influences, without blocking all of them'.

Ginsberg, Cooper, Raghu and Zegarra coming from a different ideological perspective, agreed that it was necessary to try and balance national and international influences on reform:

> . . . when we examine educational reform efforts in any country or region, we need to investigate how the global, structural and ideological contexts constrain and enable individuals and group actors' transactions concerning education . . . (while not ignoring) national — (regional — and local —) level cultural and political dynamics. (Ginsberg *et al.*, 1990, pp. 493–4)

Such interactions are clearly complex and not amenable to any kind of simplistic analysis. Throughout this chapter references will be made to international influences on national decision-making and these will recognize the problems of attributing cause and effect and the difficulty of unravelling direct and indirect relationships. In the end, judgments will be made about international and national influences on the curriculum of schools — judgments informed by an understanding of contexts and events that seemed to shape action on the curriculum throughout the 1980s.

The Context of Curriculum Reform: Political Corporatism in Relation to the Economy and Education

Recently a number of writers have suggested that corporatist political theory influenced the process of educational reform that occurred in the 1980s (Rust and Blakemore, 1990; McLean, 1988). At the heart of corporatist theory is a strong role for central governments. Thus if the recent history of education in Great Britain, the United States and Australia seemed to suggest that more and more autonomy would be granted to local-level decision-makers, the 1980s made it clear that central governments were not prepared to preside over the fragmentation and disintegration of national educational effort. In contrast to the 1960s and 1970s, there was an assertion of 'the idea that state education is integrated organically into the nation state' (McLean, 1988, p. 206). In this context, educational decision-making in the 1980s was not seen as the sole preserve of professional educators or educational bureaucracies but of governments that had much broader social, political and economic agendas to which education was expected to contribute.

While the government plays a central role in corporatist theories of the State, it does so in conjunction with other major players. It does not simply mediate conflicting interests as in a pluralist conception of the State and it does not merely respond to social tensions and economic problems as Marxists highlight (Rust and Blakemore, 1990). Rather, it purposively seeks to dictate policy outcomes that are seen to be in the 'best interests of the nation'. A strong version of corporatism would have governments directly intervening in private companies to ensure particular economic outcomes. A softer version would emphasize cooperation among government, employers, unions and other interest groups so that government objectives can be achieved with a minimum of disruption. This may involve a process of bargaining over specific policy outputs but the real outcome is commitment by all groups to the implementation of the agreed policy (Sullivan, 1988).

Rust and Blakemore have highlighted the structured nature of corporatism as follows:

> Corporatism emphasises the significance of interest groups rather than social classes or class conflict. But rather than competitive pluralism, a structured pluralism is portrayed in which the state acts with corporate groups in policy formation . . . government and private interests function as partners . . . In terms of education, professional groups in a corporate system not only work to gain sectional advantages but help maintain the system's authority and legitimacy as a whole. (Rust and Blakemore, 1990, pp. 502–3)

Rust and Blakemore (1990) also talk about strong and weak versions of corporatism with the main differences being the degree of centralized control, the status of professional teacher groups, the inclusion or not of the private education system and the degree of continuity that desired educational reforms will achieve. Both versions of corporatist theory have attracted criticism from political theorists (Sullivan, 1988) yet the main tenet of corporatism, viz. a powerful alliance between a range of interest groups, provides a framework in which the process of curriculum reform in the 1980s can be analysed. The framework is all the more interesting because each of the three countries under discussion has not traditionally been associated with corporatist state structures. Following Middlemas (1979), therefore, it might be more realistic to talk about 'corporate bias' in the development of curriculum policy in the 1980s rather than to infer the existence of corporate structures or corporate states.

The strength of a corporatist interpretation of curriculum reform efforts in the 1980s can best be demonstrated with reference to the needs of national economies. Control of the national economy is a central tenet of political corporatism (McLean, 1988) and during the 1980s in Great Britain, the United States and Australia there was a general concern about future economic growth and competitiveness.

Levin and Rumberger (1989, p. 209), for example, have pointed to efforts by all advanced industrial countries throughout the 1980s to maintain or regain 'economic progress and competitiveness'. The emergence of the European Economic Community as a single trading bloc, the rapid growth of newly industrialized economies (NIEs) such as Korea, Taiwan, Brazil, Singapore and Hong Kong, and the economic dominance of Japan has led not only to a major reassessment of economic policies but of education policies as well.

The argument has been that if the traditional western industrialized countries are to compete effectively in the international market-place they will need to develop a highly skilled and adaptable workforce. Such an argument has not been without its critics. Levin and Rumberger (1989) have amply demonstrated that the argument may have some validity in terms of the aggregate demand for skills. Yet they have shown that at either end of the occupational spectrum there is the possibility of both overeducation and undereducation for certain job categories. Nevertheless, the demand for a more highly skilled workforce became a significant policy prescription throughout the 1980s.

This line of argument has been advanced most assiduously by the Organisation for Economic Cooperation and Development (OECD). Impediments to the development of a competitive edge for OECD countries (including Great Britain, the USA and Australia) were identified (OECD, 1989, p. 17): 'high levels of unemployment and long-term unemployment; sluggish output and employment growth; sharp declines in manufacturing employment and expansion in service sector employment; intensified international trade competition; changing requirements within occupations; technological innovation permeating production and consumption'. These problems were not seen as temporary aberrations in national economies, but as medium-term problems in need of fundamental structural adjustment if western economies were to be competitive internationally.

As a solution to the problem of structural adjustment, the so-called 'human factor' emerged as a prime consideration:

> Whether it is the labour complement to technologically advanced, 'smart' capital equipment in the manufacturing sector or the very embodiment of productive capacity in the expanding service sector, the skills and qualifications of workers are coming to be viewed as critical determinants of effective performance of enterprises and economies. (OECD, 1989, p. 18)

Schools, traditionally criticized for failing to equip young people with adequate workplace skills, came to be seen as the location for significant reform if the economic needs of western industrialized nations were to be met. Education and training came to be regarded as micro-economic tools that could contribute towards effective control of the economy of the future. The perceived link between economic and education needs meant that education policy had to be aligned with economic policy. Such an alignment required new coalitions and new ways of thinking about education if governments were to be successful in harnessing education to the economic bandwagon. It was in this context that corporatist approaches to educational reform emerged in the 1980s and have continued into the 1990s.

It should also not go unnoticed that human-capital theory emerged once again during the 1980s in recognition of 'the growing knowledge-intensiveness of the pathways to sustained economic growth' (OECD, 1989, p. 20).

This attachment for human-capital theory was referred to by the Australian Minister for Employment, Education and Training in his address as Chairman of the OECD Intergovernmental Conference on Education and the Economy in a Changing Society:

> We accept, pragmatically, that the relationship between economic performance and human capital investment can never be measured with any precision . . . the vital question for this Conference is not whether education and training are factors in economic growth and performance, but rather what needs to be done to improve their provision, by what means and in which directions, and where responsibilities for action should lie. (OECD, 1989, p. 11)

This kind of thinking was not simply abstract and theoretical on the part of policy makers — it had quite practical implications at the national level for the curriculum of schools as governments sought to solve economic problems with supply-side economic tools.

National-level Responses to Economic Concerns

United States

The United States has traditionally been viewed as pluralist rather than corporatist in its orientation. Yet there has not been much evidence of pluralism as far as education or reform has been concerned in recent times. The federal government's education agenda became very clear following the release of *A Nation at Risk* — to restore confidence in the nation's schools by improving academic standards and raising the quality of the teacher workforce. This agenda was pursued relentlessly by successive secretaries of education. While federal funding for education initiatives may have decreased, there was no mistaking the objectives and priorities of the federal government in education. The 'bully-pulpit', rather than elaborate funding programmes, was used as an effective platform to spread the message.

Yet the federal government did not work alone in prosecuting its agenda. State governments sensed the need for action and across the nation, state initiatives in educational reform emerged throughout the 1980s (Pipho, 1987). Indeed the National Governor's Association made education a priority and saw the need for a new partnership:

> There is something else that Governors must do that takes them beyond the borders of their states. They must help renew an historic relationship with the federal government. Recent American educational history is disjointed. The federal government once moved powerfully in this arena . . . The states now make the nation's education policy.

But state leadership is not enough. We have to put rhetoric aside. We need each other . . . Governors must join those willing to link the energy of the states and localities and the federal government. (National Governors' Association, 1987, p. vi)

There were new partnerships at the local level as well — especially with the business community. It has been argued that educational reform in the United States in the 1980s was driven more by politicians and business executives than by educators (Australian Education Council, 1987). There is also evidence that the results of the reform movement would have been much less had they not been supported by the business community (ibid., 1987).

There was, then, a political consensus between federal and state governments and between state governments and business interests on the need for, and the direction of, educational reform. Governor Kean of New Jersey indicated the reason for such an alliance:

. . . the quality of education is intensely competitive. Our trading partners remind us of this. When Governors visit Japan, Korea, and Europe to see the business leaders, we can't help but see something else — the commitment other nations make to education. Their question — how to recruit and retain able teachers, how to improve the skills of the workforce, and how to enable citizens to achieve a fuller life — these are our questions, too. We take their commitment very seriously when we remember that their education systems already produce results. (National Governors' Association, 1987, p. v)

This view has been supported by US businessmen so that James Campbell, Chairman of the Board and President of the Mississippi School Supply Company has argued that the '(United States') ability to compete, perhaps even to survive, as an industrial leader among countries depends largely upon our education system' (Australian Education Council, 1987, p. 40). Bill Kolberg, president of the National Alliance of Business agreed with this view when he commented that: 'the quality of human resources is the key to competitiveness, to the United States and Australia and to every other country' (ibid., 1987, p. 38).

The direction of education policy was not lost on the American left as Giroux's comments indicated:

Much of what has passed for educational reform in the 1980s has represented a sustained effort by business interests and right-wing cultural elitists to redefine the purpose of public schooling, putting economic considerations first, and touting the alleged virtues of a 'unitary' Western culture. In the first instance schools are expected to provide the skills necessary for domestic production and expanding capital. (1988, Giroux, 1988, p. 4)

Coming from a different ideological perspective, John Jennings, counsel for the Committee on Education and Labor in the US House of Representatives, seemed to agree with Giroux's analysis when he claimed that 'economic competitiveness is the Sputnik of the 1980s' (Jennings, 1987, p. 109). It remains now to review the outcomes of this new political and economic consensus on the curriculum of schools in the United States.

A Nation at Risk had criticized the curricula of US schools as being 'homogenised, diluted, and diffused to the point that they no longer have a central purpose' (Bennett, 1988, p. 14). The report recommended a set of 'new basics': 'four years of English, three years each of mathematics, science and social studies, one half-year of computer science; and, for those students planning to attend college, two years of a foreign language' (Bennett, 1988, p. 14). The new basics were, in fact, the old academic curriculum with the addition of computer science and the reappearance of foreign languages.

The US Department of Education reported that in 1982, only 1.9 per cent of high-school graduates completed a programme in the 'new basics' but this had increased to 12.7 per cent by 1987. Timar and Kirp (1988, p. 29) have reported that by '1985 forty-three states had raised high school graduation requirements . . . ; thirty-seven had initiated statewide student assessment programs; seventeen had increased college entrance requirements; twenty-five instituted academic recognition programs; and thirty-four had created academic enrichment programs'. Core graduation requirements in most states, four years of English, three years of social studies and two each of mathematics and science (Timar and Kirp, 1988) fell a little behind the demands of the 'new basics' but nevertheless substantially ensured the survival of the academic curriculum in the American comprehensive high school in the 1980s.

How was this curriculum related to the economic needs of the nation? It could be argued that mathematics, science, computer science and foreign languages provide an important instrumental link to economic needs. Yet the point to note is that there was no radical shift to a vocationalized curriculum — the prescription for the 1980s in the United States was a general education for all students, strongly oriented to mathematics, science and technology. This did not mean, however, that vocational education was seen to be unimportant.

There has also been a strong agenda for the reform of vocational education. It was recognized that preparing students for single occupations was outmoded and that students needed to be multiskilled (Naylor, 1986). They also needed to be prepared with basic skills in numeracy and literacy, including technological literacy, as well as be able to participate in work teams and groups. To achieve these objectives a number of specific initiatives have been adopted. There has been a strong emphasis on integrating academic and vocational education in order to eliminate the narrow focus of traditional vocational education (Naylor, 1986). TECH PREP courses have been developed articulating high-school courses with two-year courses in community colleges (Kennedy, Cumming and Catts, 1993) as well as with the first years of work

(Del Valle, 1993). In some states, career academies have been established as schools within schools to promote certain vocational areas and skills (Grubb, 1992). In an important sense there has been an agenda for the renewal of vocational education that has complemented the emphasis on a more traditional academic curriculum, especially for the later years of schooling.

Great Britain

In 1976, the British Labour Prime Minister, Mr James Callaghan, launched the so-called 'Great Debate' on education. At the heart of the debate, according to Dale (1985a, p. 3) was the proposition that 'schools should emphasise the contribution of the economy to national life and prepare students to take their place in the economy as it now exists'. While this was by no means a new proposition it did serve to reassert the link between schooling and economic needs. As Dale (1985b) has pointed out, it highlighted the inadequacy of existing curriculum provision and especially its relationship with the world of work. Chitty (1989, pp. 95–6) has also pointed out, the groundwork was laid 'to construct a new educational consensus around a more direct subordination of education to what were perceived to be the needs of the economy'.

The Labour government did not last long enough to oversee such a reform and was replaced by a Conservative government in 1979. Yet, as Lawton (1989) has shown, this did not mean there was a break in educational policy directions. Rather, there was a continuity on the issue of seeking widespread curriculum reform. Indeed, under the Conservative government curriculum reform was given a high priority and its first substantial effort — the Technical and Vocational Education Initiative (TVEI) was designed to ensure that school curricula were practical and relevant with control placed in the hands not of educators but labour-market specialists. This was a tacit recognition that education was too important to be left to the educators. If education was to serve the needs of the economy, it had to be linked more directly to policy mechanisms that could guarantee an alignment between economic objectives and outcomes. Thus it was, that for the first time in the history of Great Britain, a significant curriculum reform for schools was administered by the Manpower Services Commission (MSC) — an unmistakable indication of the links that were seen between education and the economy and of radical processes that could be used to secure significant objectives.

TVEI has attracted a good deal of attention from writers concerned with the curriculum of schools (Dale, 1985b; Pring, 1986; Cattell and Norton, 1987; Chitty, 1989; Saunders and Halpin, 1990). Much of the comment has been favourable although the initiation process often comes in for criticism. There seems to have been, however, general support for the philosophy underlying TVEI, especially its active-learning pedagogy and integrated approach to learning. Yet, was it a major attempt to vocationalize the secondary-school curriculum? Chitty (1989) has argued that it was not, since it was not intended for all students but principally for the less academically inclined. That is to say, TVEI was designed to vocationalize the curriculum for some students but not all. Chitty (1989, p. 175) has called it 'a major vocationalising strategy' and the centrepiece of the Conservative government's education policy until at least 1985. Yet TVEI does not tell the whole story on curriculum reform — it seemed to be the first step in a vocational direction but it was a step that was quite limited compared with what followed it.

The challenge to TVEI came from the 1988 Education Act which, among other things, prescribed a national curriculum for all schools in Great Britain. There have been severe reservations about TVEI's role in this new frame-work (Chitty, 1989; Saunders and Halpin, 1990). The direction of the national-curriculum initiatives under the 1980 Act was to reinforce traditional acad-emic areas and to impose a centralized assessment regime. This meant that centralized monitoring of educational outcomes became a feature of national-curriculum reform. Yet outcomes of the national-curriculum initiatives are primarily measured in academic terms. In reinforcing a traditional academic curriculum, the national curriculum has looked to the past rather than the future. Keating, for example, has indicated that:

> Curriculum and qualifications in England and Wales are shaped on the bedrock of the A-levels. Frequently referred to as the 'Gold Stand-ard', the A-levels are narrow and deliberately highly selective, with only 22% of the cohort achieving a pass. (Keating, 1993, p. 2)

There is no evidence that there will be any shift from this emphasis on maintaining an academic stream that will feed directly into higher education. Yet it does appear that it will be supplemented by additional streams relating to vocational education and training. This would maintain the present govern-ment's philosophical commitment to choice in education as well as contribute to a more effective skills-development process for the training sector (Keating, 1993). Yet it also maintains the supremacy of the academic curriculum and the pathway to higher education.

The rigidity of Great Britain's commitment to academic education has recently been criticized as 'narrow and elitist', but perhaps more importantly as totally unsuitable to national needs:

> The qualitative issue is whether expanding participation on the basis of the existing curriculum, even were it to prove possible, would provide young people with the kind of skills and knowledge that are necessary in the likely circumstances of the 21st century. (Young, 1993, pp. 203–4)

The government does not appear to be overly concerned about this issue. The recent review of national-curriculum initiatives seems to have focused on amending aspects of curriculum and assessment practice that have emerged over five years of experimentation rather than seeking new solutions (Dearing, 1993). Some private-policy prescriptions seek solutions by bringing together academic and vocational education (Young, 1993) while others have identified a more flexible system over the border in Scotland (Keating, 1993). Academic commentators rate the national curriculum as a failure, not because it was national but rather because it was not designed to meet real and emerging needs (Lawton, 1994). As one editorial claimed:

> There is a case for a national curriculum for the nation's schools, but not the one written on the back of an envelope by Kenneth Baker and his civil servants in 1987. (*Forum*, 36, 1, p. 3)

Australia

The Australian Minister for Employment, Education and Training, the Hon. J.S. Dawkins, was the driving force behind shaping a new philosophical direction for the curriculum of Australian schools but he started somewhat later than his American and British counterparts. He took office towards the end of 1987 and soon issued *Skills for Australia* in which he made his position clear:

> A high quality basic education is an essential prerequisite for a vocationally skilled and adaptable labour force. More needs to be known about the levels of competence achieved by our students at school, especially in the core disciplines of language, mathematics and science . . . We also need to examine new ways to impart less measurable skills on which future prosperity depends — life-time learning, enterprise and initiative, pursuit of excellence, communication skills, teamwork and responsibility. In other words, we need to lay the foundations of a productive culture. (Dawkins, 1987, pp. 8–9)

In a subsequent publication he focused more clearly on his objectives for schools which he portrayed as central to the processes of economic and social adjustment being pursued by the third Hawke Labour government:

> Schools are the starting point of an integrated education and training structure in the economy. They provide the foundation on which a well-informed, compassionate and cohesive society is built. They also form the basis of a more highly skilled, adaptive and productive workforce. As skill upgrading and retraining of adults becomes more necessary, so will the quality and nature of schooling received by individuals need to change. It will need to be more adaptable and prepare for, lifelong education. We need to ensure that every young Australian gets a general education of quality which provides both personal and intellectual development as well as broadly based and adaptable skills. (Dawkins, 1988, p. 2)

To achieve these ends, he proposed the development of a common curriculum framework

> . . . that sets out the major areas of knowledge and the most appropriate mix of skills and experience for students in all the years of schooling . . . [it would] emphasise higher general levels of literacy, numeracy and analytical skills across the nation . . . [it would] acknowledge Australia's increasing orientation towards the Asian and Pacific region . . . [it would] provide the guide to the best curriculum design and teaching practices. . . . (Dawkins, 1988, p. 4)

In order to further these ends he met on a regular basis with his ministerial colleagues from each of the Australian states in a forum known as the Australian Education Council (AEC), and, from 1988 onwards, he used this as an instrument to elicit ministerial agreement with respect to the curriculum agenda he had outlined in *Strengthening Australia's Schools*.

There are several outcomes of this process to date which are worth reviewing. First, Mr Dawkins managed to get his colleagues to agree to a set of 'Common and Agreed National Goals for Schooling in Australia' which spelled out the knowledge skills and understandings that all students would be expected to acquire over their period of formal schooling. The substance of these was somewhat conservative: largely academic in nature with some leaning towards general problem-solving skills and a concern for the environment. What is more, there were no plans to implement the goals in any way. Their declaration was more a symbolic statement rather than suggestive of a prescription for action.

The second initiative undertaken through the Australian Education Council mechanism was agreement on a series of what were called 'curriculum mapping exercises'. These were designed to review existing curriculum requirements across a range of areas. The first to be undertaken was in the area of mathematics, followed by others concerned with literacy, science and technology, human society, environmental studies and aboriginal studies. Additional national-curriculum initiatives have been undertaken for the arts, health and physical education, technology and languages other than English. Together, these areas have been designated as the eight-key learning areas for the national curriculum. National-curriculum statements have been produced outlining sequences of content and skills accompanied by subject profiles that outline suggested outcomes to be achieved by students at different levels of development. These profiles provide a framework for reporting student progress but do not indicate how assessment is to be conducted. Nevertheless, the profiles foreshadow a more common approach to assessment than has been the case in the past.

Even though national-curriculum statements and profiles have been produced for eight key areas of the curriculum, it is not clear exactly how they will be used or what impact they will exert in classrooms. With respect to the mathematics statement, one senior officer of a State Education Department indicated that it 'could be used as a reference point for systems as they develop their own curriculum documents' (Eltis, 1989, p. 9). This comment has to be understood within the context of a federal system of government in which constitutional authority rests with the states/territories rather than the federal government. The notion behind the comment was reinforced when in December 1993 the AEC agreed that the statements and profiles would be released to the states/territories to be used at the discretion of local education authorities. This signalled a breakdown of the political process that had created a national approach to curriculum development but it left a significant resource and a culture that valued national consistency, particularly in relation to the assessment and reporting of student progress.

In addition to developing a national approach to general education, the AEC also established a number of committees in association with the Ministers for Vocational Education Employment and Training (MOVEET). The first of these recommended the development of a set of employment-related key competencies to be achieved by all 16–19 year olds (Finn, 1991). These were not seen to be specific to any particular curriculum area but rather were designed to be generic and thus applicable to a range of curriculum areas. The point was made often in the report that 'employment-related competencies' were simply a subset of a broader range of outcomes that students should achieve by the end of their formal education and training. A second committee took up the Finn recommendations concerning the development of such competencies and consulted widely with educators and trainers to see how they could be linked with existing curriculum provision (The Mayer Committee, 1992). A significant outcome of this process was the dropping of the description, 'employment related' so that what Finn originally envisaged as 'employment-related key competencies' became simply 'key competencies'. This has been the most overt attempt to incorporate a vocational component as part of the curriculum for all students but as Marginson has pointed out it represents a new approach to vocational education:

> It is not quite true to say that the Finn report is narrowly vocational. There are two processes at work here. There is both a broadening and a narrowing. Finn wants a vocational education to be broader than before, which is good. At the same time it wants vocational competencies to dominate the curriculum, pushing other roles of education to the margins. In that sense there is a narrowing. (Marginson, 1991, p. 5)

In Australia, therefore, there have been clear intentions to align the needs of education and the economy. These efforts commenced in 1988 and were formally concluded in June 1993. The emphasis on employment-related competencies suggests a vocationalization of the school curriculum in the post-compulsory years.

Conclusion

Governments in Great Britain, the United States and Australia all sought to respond to economic problems that emerged during the 1980s — problems that were international rather than national in nature. A part of the solution was seen to be forging strong links between the needs of the economy and education. In doing so, governments of different political persuasions (Conservative in Great Britain and the United States and Social Democratic in Australia) sought to use the school curriculum to achieve their purposes.

In each country, the objective was regarded as so important to national policy that traditional methods of educational reform were rejected by politicians. In Great Britain, labour-market bureaucrats were initially seen to be more trustworthy than either the Department of Education and Science or the Local Education Authorities (LEAs). Eventually, the government resorted to legislative mandate in order to achieve and implement a national curriculum. In the United States coalitions appeared between the federal and state governments and between state governments and the business community. In Australia, a purely political process through the Australian Education Council and more recently the Ministers of Vocational Education Employment and Training became the driving force for educational change. In some senses, this might seem to defy corporatist theory since major education interest groups were excluded. Yet in reality it was corporatism at the strong end of the spectrum that was being enacted. There was no room for compromise on the issue of curriculum reform so that traditional interest groups were discarded and new ones arose to take their place. A new constituency of politicians and business groups was created for recent curriculum reform efforts and it seems likely to dominate ongoing curriculum reform in the 1990s.

In this educational climate, what about the nature of the changes to the curriculum itself? The curriculum for the final decades of the twentieth century was to be uniform rather than diverse; emphasis was to be on the core rather than optional subject matters; and the assessment of outcomes was to be accorded high priority. Each of the countries reached different levels in this regard, with Great Britain achieving the most concrete outcomes embodied in its legislated national curriculum. The United States probably came next with state governors working very closely together on specific reform initiatives. Australian governments had the best of intentions and the national-curriculum statements and subject profiles bear witness to this. Despite these differences, however, the basic academic curriculum is probably still in place in each of the three countries at least in the compulsory years of schooling. If anything, reform efforts have worked to entrench this pattern of curriculum organization even further. As a complement to these efforts, however, there have also been attempts in the three countries to reinstate vocational education, or at least a vocational perspective, into the school curriculum. It has taken different forms in the three countries and it represents new thinking about vocational education. Such an emphasis provides a contrast to the solidification of the academic curriculum and perhaps the future lies in bringing together these two historically diverse approaches to the education of young people. It seems clear that new approaches will be needed if social and economic problems are to be addressed adequately.

There seems little doubt that in recent times education, and the curriculum of schools in particular, was reclaimed by governments in Great Britain, the United States and Australia and utilized as an instrument of public-policy development. A distinct corporatist bias was noted in the actions of different governments as they sought to align school curricula with the needs of their respective economies. In general, it was improved educational standards rather than fundamental curriculum change that was seen to be the policy priority. The real litmus test of the new reforms will be whether they can deliver a satisfying and rewarding life to young people personally and to society as a whole.

Chapter 6

From Policy to Classroom Practice: Beyond the Mandates

Shirley M. Hord

From other chapters in this book, it is easy to conclude that educational reform is everywhere. It is being targeted at the local, district, state, and national levels in the US — and similarly around the globe. It is simultaneously the focus of discussion and debate by educational professionals, parents, and the press. But, can it be found, however one defines 'it', in the daily teaching–learning interactions of teacher and student?

A Funny Thing Happened on the Way from the Forum

Education, in the 1960s, was the focus of exploration similar to that of the 1980s — and now, the 1990s. The launch of Sputnik catalyzed attention at that time on maths and science curricula, in particular. During that period of rapid development of innovative instructional programmes and processes, Chin and Benne (1969) articulated several theories that represented how the change process works.

Assumptions about Change

In Chin and Benne's 'empirical-rational' theory, an idea well tested by research and developed into useful programmes and practices is provided to a well-intentioned receiving group — teachers and administrators in this discussion. The theory suggests that because the new programme is 'good' and the people are 'good', the programme will be adopted and find its way into classroom use. This notion seems valid for a very small number of teachers (Bush, 1984, indicates 10 per cent) who can read about or learn modestly about a new practice and put it into place. It has not proven sufficient to cause widespread, or schoolwide, change.

A second theory, 'power-coercive', described by Chin and Benne, presents a well thought-out policy to receivers, and delivers it by an authority figure or strong power base. Policy makers and decision makers at all levels (if they have not consciously espoused this approach) have unconsciously assumed that their policies, based on the assumptions about change noted above, will be incorporated into educational practice and thereby 'do good'. These assumptions remain in vogue today, although they have not resulted in successful educational change.

Several Waves of Reform

If the process by which change and reform might successfully occur were not being given attention in the 1980s, what to change certainly was being addressed by policy makers as several waves of reform suggest.

A first wave of reform, 1982–6, called for fixing the existing educational system (Murphy, 1991). Raywid (1990) characterized this period as that of 'pseudo-reforms' calling attention to needs by mandating cosmetic approaches and seldom touching classroom practice. These 'quick fixes' articulated by policy makers had insignificant impact. (Note, various writers refer to two, or three, or four waves, thus, the period of years is not consistently divided. The exact number of years is not important. What is interesting to note is the consistent sequence of attention by writers to an ever-widening target for change.)

The second wave, 1986–9, was characterized by proposals to improve individual schools, to increase achievement through providing access to appropriate curriculum and instructional strategies and classroom-focused needs. These reforms were labelled 'incremental reform' by Raywid, and were the focus of widespread planning for school change, but few plans moved beyond the written page.

If these reform efforts bore little fruit, then it was thought that changes of greater magnitude would be given more productive attention. Many concluded that 'schools failed because of the bureaucratic structure of schooling' and that important reform would require change in the fundamental arrangements by which schools operate, thus 'restructuring' the education system was the focus (Bjork, 1993; Raywid, 1990). This third reform wave gave attention to such arrangements as shifting administrative authority to the building level and professionalizing teaching (Darling-Hammond, 1993).

Bjork reports on the emergence, during 1988, of new policy-maker targets. Restructuring the education system was beginning to be seen as inadequate, and new proposals addressed the 'need to alleviate the environmental factors that contribute to the failure of school children and called for redesigning the fundamental *structure of schooling* (my italics)' (p. 248). Such a model would develop integrated service-delivery systems across school, health, and community organizations to provide services to children and families. This structure would be much more comprehensive and fundamental and policies espousing such models would be wide-reaching in their intended impact.

Similar to the series of waves, an analysis of historical approaches to school reform was conducted by Sashkin and Egermeier (1992). In their review they cite four approaches; the first of these is 'fix the parts'. This approach involves the introduction and adoption of changes in curricular programmes and new instructional practices, proven by field test and trialling to be sound. Change is seen as the exchange of new educational products for old (curriculum), and/or new tasks to be done (instructional processes). Sashkin and Egermeier's second approach is 'fix the people'. In this case educational personnel are influenced to change through the application of training and development. This training is typically 'sent' as a policy directive from upper-level decision makers and is intended to change attitudes, behaviours, values, and beliefs.

The third approach is 'fix the school' and has been a strategy extensively applied in school-improvement efforts. The school is the unit of change, and a school-improvement committee or council leads the school in analysing needs, identifying solutions, and planning for change.

From these three approaches Sashkin and Egermeier conclude that successful change has not been wholly achieved, but that the fourth and current approach, 'fix the system', or restructuring, can be effective. These four approaches ranging in magnitude from 'parts' to 'system' resonate compatibly with the waves of reform already described. There appears to be general consensus, particularly from writers espousing restructuring, that bigger is better and if we can just cast the net wide enough, reform will be successful and education improved. The Sashkin and Egermeier review permits the identification of another factor associated with successful change, the human interface that supplies information, support, and technical assistance, to which we will return.

A Multiplicity of Reform Menus

Over the course of some years, school districts and state departments of education have been directing schools' involvement in specific educational programmes, processes, and practices. The effective schools process, strategic planning, and outcomes-based education (OBE) are some of these. Local schools and systems are also being asked to take on board practices imported from the corporate sector — such as site-based management (SBM) and total quality management (TQM).

The proliferation of these innovation possibilities has confused and overwhelmed school practitioners. They report that they are trying to stay abreast of the mandates by taking training at national and state conferences and forums. They are trying to learn about OBE, SBM, and a myriad of others. But they do not know what to select for the school or district's entrée for reform, nor do they wish to scrape the plate clean and start totally afresh when some initiatives are already underway. How to incorporate local preferences for desired changes with those mandated by higher-level decision makers into an integrated vision of change and improvement has been challenging.

	Effective Schools	SBM	Strategic Planning	OBE	TQM
Constancy of purpose	*		*	*	*
Customer-driven	*			*	*
Counting	*		*	*	*
Culture	*	*			*
Collegial leadership	*	*	*		*
Decentralized		*			*
Comprehensive					*
Continuous improvement			*	*	*

Figure 6.1: Factors Associated with Effective Schools, Site-based Management, Strategic Planning, Outcomes-based Education and or Total Quality Management
Source: Adapted from National LEADership Study Group on Restructuring (1993)

Analyses to demonstrate the similarities of these initiatives, in terms of their philosophy and operation, have produced some clarity. For example, a matrix (Figure 6.1) that allows comparison of five initiatives on eight selected factors from Deming's principles of quality can be useful in understanding the value-added properties of the various initiatives. The factors briefly defined by the National LEADership Study Group on Restructuring (1993) are:

- Constancy of purpose — organizational commitment to exceeding clients' needs in an environment where all persons work to move the school or district in an identified direction for the long term.
- Customer driven — identification of clients' needs and satisfying those needs in an ongoing process.
- Counting — utilization of tools and processes by all persons in the organization in order to solve problems and make decisions based on data rather than on opinions, feelings, or yesterday's myths.
- Culture — shared understandings and ways of working in an organization, representing the norms, attitudes, and beliefs of the organization.
- Collegial leadership — cooperation and teamwork by all people across all divisions of the organization in order to solve problems and pursue quality improvement by all employees.
- Decentralized — empowerment of those making decisions for improvement and solving quality problems.
- Continuous improvement — commitment to ongoing improvement and refinement of services and products for clients, based on review of the system at all times.

This matrix represents but one interpretation of the traditionally perceived attributes of the five educational initiatives. It does, however, provide a means by which educational practitioners might review programmes or processes being promoted by their district or state policies to identify commonalities or parallel features. It makes possible, also, identification of each initiative's contributions to change and reform.

Similarly, Lesley (1993) reviewed eight restructuring initiatives and found them 'remarkably similar' (p. 6) to each other and to the factors found in TQM. Lesley, too, identified the congruence of 'effective schools correlates' with quality factors. In addition, her analysis of Henry Levin's 'accelerated schools' model indicates this model targets curriculum, instruction, and organization change in concert with 'unity of purpose, empowerment with responsibility and building on strengths . . . taking stock to examine data on an ongoing basis and on study, research, piloting, and evaluating' (p. 6).

William Glasser's 'quality schools', Lesley reasons, are built on his belief in the importance of self-responsibility and on his concern that many children do not have their needs met any other place, therefore schools should be as satisfying as possible for children. Glasser proposes moving toward self-assessment, with the elimination of 'fear and coercion' so that self-directing students will be an outcome. Collaborative decision-making exemplifies leadership in Glasser's quality schools.

Lesley describes Carl Glickman's 'league of professional schools' as based on a faculty/staff collaboratively developed definition of beliefs about teaching and learning. This 'covenant' serves as the school's constancy of purpose. A second requirement of professional schools is a collaboratively developed charter that defines their decision-making processes. Third, they must make a commitment to critical study.

Lesley equates Deming's quality principle of continuous improvement with the 'effective schools correlate' on constant measurement and monitoring, with Levin's taking stock, with Glasser's self-assessment for increasing quality, and with Glickman's action research or self-study. This identification of similarities contributes to sense-making of these models by busy practitioners who have the challenge of selecting new practices for improving schools.

Lesley found four additional restructuring models *simpatico* with quality. The central purpose of Theodore Sizer's 'coalition of essential schools' is that students use their minds well — a quality goal. In these schools, administrators and teachers share decision-making and leadership responsibility. Participation of staff in continuous, long-term professional development is essential to the 'essential schools.'

James Comer's developmental model, designed to support and guide children's learning of social skills as well as their cognitive development, is another version of the quality school. In these schools, staff, parents, university, and mental-health professionals work together to create a unity of purpose and practice to support continuing learning.

The purpose of John Champlin's 'outcomes-driven developmental' model is realization of high expectations — an indicator of demands for quality. Involvement and collaboration of all staff is an important component. Major investments in training to empower staff by knowledge and enable them to realize high expectations are parts of this model.

The values and commitments of 'twenty-first century schools', proposed by Phil Schlecty, reflect their constancy of purpose. In these schools, leaders have a responsibility to 'conceptualise, articulate, and communicate that purpose'. Staff participation in decision-making increases the likelihood of quality results. There must be development of the staff for continuous improvement; 'ongoing support and training . . . are an absolute prerequisite'.

The continuing introduction of educational reform possibilities — all of which promise to produce higher-quality schools and make students more successful — has resulted in educational leaders jumping on the band wagon of successive programmes and models. All too frequently energies are spent running to the educational buffet to acquire the latest line of goodies, persuaded by the most recent advertising jingle to hit the journals. If leaders are befuddled by the parade of many dishes out of the educational reform kitchens, then an analysis of their components such as those above could enable the integration of new mandated programme policies with the existing or old.

Streshly and Bernd (1992) observe 'the insatiable appetite for reform which grips politicians . . . [who] feel obliged to discredit the status quo and pose quick fixes that sound superficially attractive to voters' (p. 321). When this happens, 'each month or year brings a new reform agenda — before the preceding efforts were given a chance or even tried' (Deal and Peterson, 1992, p. 13). The current practice of mandating bigger and bigger reforms, and more and more changes, appears based on flawed assumptions. One of these assumptions, Lewis (1993) maintains, is that legislative policy makers think there is 'a direct, clear line between policy making at the national level and changes in the classroom' (p. 670). It is expected, according to Lewis, that setting content standards that are challenging and tying new assessments to the standards will cause 'miracles to follow soon'. Such an assumption — provide educators with important new work to do and they will do it — is only half the story. The second half is addressed in the next section, in which an understanding and management of the change process itself is deemed to determine whether reform is ever implemented.

Meanwhile, Back at the School

For the last decade, abundant attention and pronouncements have targeted educational reform. Some wags say we've been in the wilderness for more than ten years, wandering about, trying to 'fix' schools. Others decry the large-scale systemic 'volcano' approach. We've tried changing schedules, elongating the school day and year, upgrading curriculum, demanding higher standards for student promotion and graduation. Much attention has focused on organizational governance and structure. Thus, much attention has been given to the 'what to change'.

What change is really about, rather than structures and strategies, is people. We have given much less attention to 'how to change' the practices of people in classrooms. Change is about each and every individual who will be involved in implementing new policies, programmes and processes. It is also about the individuals who will facilitate the implementors in doing so. In this section, the result of reviewing stories of schools and districts and other educational agencies successfully implementing their identified reforms are reported — to understand not what to change, but how to change.

Brief Historical Review: the 1970s

Early attention and studies in the 1970s focused on adoption of innovations, and connecting potential users with new information or programmes. Such studies were characterized as diffusion or dissemination, and 'linking agents' (whose job it was to connect the two alienated worlds of users and useful new programmes) were much examined. In the Sashkin and Egermeier paper, referenced earlier in this chapter, the authors included citations of these studies in the fix-the-parts approach. Even in the 1970s, an early finding in the studies, and what Sashkin and Egermeier's analyses and conclusions show was, *not* that the various approaches to change didn't work, but in fact they did work when there was a person present who provided information, support and ongoing assistance to the users. In the early studies there appeared to be a clear connection between the amount of help and technical assistance provided with the innovation, and the amount of implementation of the innovation by the user.

The 1980s

The 1980s was the era of the 'hero principal'. Examination of successful school-change stories almost always reported the same bottom line: an energetic and proactive, enthusiastic and committed principal. The linking agent role was being taken on by the principal who brought new ideas and information for the staff to use with students. Frequently it was noted that the principal enlisted the help of others to implement change; however, the principal seemed to retain star billing. In any case, these proactive principals were doing things on behalf of their change efforts, therefore studies began to centre on the principal (and team) and their actions or behaviours that contributed to their school's successful reform. In synthesizing the data from these studies, six categories of behaviours emerged that could describe actions necessary for change. Distilling these actions to their basic essence, the six sets of actions represent forms of pressure and support for encouraging individuals to change, although in the 1980s it was not politically correct to use the terms 'pressure and support'.

The 1990s

In the 1990s, decentralization of privilege and authority from central office to schools, and from principals to be shared with teachers, has been the order of the day. Shared decision-making and site-based management have been mandated as cornerstones of new governance structures. With this move have come school leadership teams that share leadership, collegial school-improvement councils that serve as leadership consortiums, and a host of other labels and terms announcing a new order of sharing authority and empowering teachers. On the one hand it seems as though leadership might become sufficiently diffused so that leaders would be invisible. On the other hand, there is more for leaders of change to do than ever as they prepare their staff for more involvement in decision-making, planning, and implementation. Furthermore, it appears that the same six categories of actions or strategies used in the 1980s to facilitate change are viable and necessary for reform in the 1990s. And, currently, it is *en vogue* to discuss pressure and support. Thus, that is precisely what we shall do, as these dimensions are seen as absolutely vital to bring about implementation of reform. We will see the pressure and support dimensions play out across the six strategies.

Pressure and Support

Milbrey McLaughlin set the matter straight when she noted that 'policy implementation is incredibly hard . . .' (1987, p. 172), and that 'successful implementation generally requires a combination of pressure and support' (p. 173). Pressure, alone, may be sufficient if implementation of the policy does not require resources or normative change. However, in isolation pressure cannot change attitudes, values, and practices that have become routinized. Nor can support, alone, bring about significant change because of the demands and tasks already required of people in the system that is attempting implementation of new practice. Crohn, Hagans, and Olson (1989) add that pressure can be very positive. They note that if pressure is provided without support, 'alienation results. Conversely, if support exists without pressure, the result is wasted resources' (p. 1).

In a review of one large district's experience with study groups to foster faculty learning, Murphy (1992) notes productive functioning of groups during the first year when pressure was exerted for attendance and involvement. While the groups were still working to become legitimized, pressure was removed. Murphy concludes, as have others, that even when innovations and new practices are judged to be effective, they will not automatically be embraced 'into the existing culture without on-going pressure and support' (p. 74).

And, in a roundtable discussion, called by *Education Week*, eleven school reformers provided ideas of 'how we get from where we are to where we want to be' (April 21, 1993, p. 21). The hope of the group was to develop an action plan or implementation strategy for the next phase of school reform. The participants provided various perspectives. In response to *Education Week's* assessment, 'after more than a decade of school reform efforts, there is no shortage of ideas about what needs to be done . . . But there is no clear idea of how to actually do it' (p. 22). One participant cited Fullan and the need for the right mixture of pressure and support, 'We've got the pressure, but we don't provide the support' the speaker opined (p. 22).

Huberman (1992), too, affirms the power of pressure and support, but points out that there must be 'intelligent combinations' of the two. 'Too much pressure is bullying; too much support suggests to teachers that they will need crutches for years on end' (p. 14).

It is one thing to enunciate the need for pressure and support on behalf of policy implementation in schools and classrooms. It is quite another to orchestrate intelligent combinations of the two. In this final section, how leaders do this across the six strategies they employ to facilitate change will be reviewed. The six strategies are:

- developing and communicating a shared vision;
- planning and providing resources;
- investing in continuous staff development;
- assessing progress;
- providing ongoing assistance; and
- creating an atmosphere for change.

Developing and Communicating a Shared Vision

Newton's First Law of Motion: Every body continues in its state of rest, or of uniform motion in a straight line, unless it is compelled to change that state by forces impressed upon it. (Hazen and Trefil, 1990)

Vision refers to the mental picture of what a school or other organization or its parts (practices, processes, etc.) might look like in a preferred image of the future. 'The starting point for any change is a clear vision' (Mendez-Morse, 1993, p. 1). While this statement may not seem very profound, it has profound implications for policy implementation. District and school leaders use 'vision engineering' to focus community and staff on the picture of improvement to which attention and movement will be given. Superintendents initiate a vision through the introduction of research findings, new ideas and possibilities, or by providing a beginning picture, then challenging principals and staff to generate input and share in shaping and clarifying the vision (Paulu, 1988). Introducing the new idea or policy is the pressure; inviting expansion and clarification of it through interaction is support.

When leaders are involved with staff in such an activity, all persons feel an obligation to contribute. When individuals contribute, they feel ownership and commitment develops. This subtle pressing people for involvement makes them also feel valued and supported. The leaders press and keep the vision clear to all through communicating about it regularly and frequently in multiple settings.

District-level administrators spend time in schools — and campus-level administrators spend time in classrooms — articulating a consistent message regarding the vision and priorities. Radio and TV interview/public service announcements may be used. The forum may be weekly meetings of service organizations such as Rotary. And, of course, the community's most popular coffee house is a good place to disseminate information about the district's or school's vision of a new policy for improvement.

Administrators use an increased flow of information to keep the vision priorities, and the vision's attendant goals and objectives foremost in staff's attention (Hill, Wise, and Shapiro, 1989). Staff and community feel supported and included when information is provided regularly and frequently. Including recognition of those contributing to the vision in the school or district newsletter is both a powerful pressing and supporting action. Other rewards can be used for recognition.

Policies initially developed at national, state, and district levels may be further articulated at lower levels soliciting and using the broadest input possible. Committees and task forces of community and staff may be organized to shape and clarify the original skeletal vision. A prime consideration is clarity. When the vision is clear, pressure is stronger for there is less fuzziness in which to hide. Clarity also is supporting because people understand and frustration is diminished. When there is collaborative development of the policy vision, pressure is more likely to be exercised by peers *and* by supervisors. Collaborative development is supportive since authority, responsibility, and influence are shared.

Another means to press staff's involvement in vision development is through the study of student-performance data. Policies that require schools and districts to develop a vision of change and to write improvement plans are frequently based on the review and interpretation of multiple student-data sets. In this way the policy mandates a product but also suggests a means of how to get there. In this way the state's vision is of schools developing their own vision and plans for change; the state further clarifies its vision by specifying how this should be done.

Finally, leaders share stories of success and describe pictures of success with the staff to establish the belief that the vision can be achieved. They demonstrate visible commitment to the vision, and reflect a personal belief in the goals of the vision. In these multiple ways they bring pressure and support to the development and continuing communication of a policy vision for the school or district.

Planning and Providing Resources

Effective implementation requires a strategic balance of pressure and support . . . (McLaughlin, 1987)

Leaders may develop plans single-handedly or a plan may evolve as a result of interactions with the staff. In the latter, staff feel more commitment and support from their involvement. In either case, leaders may 'steer' planning so that it accommodates implementation of policy and achieves the policy vision. A clear and well-communicated policy vision provides the basis for clear planning. Thus, these actions mutually reinforce each other and give clear signals to staff, signals that press them to implementation action. Of course, leaders can simply require plans from staff, that address policy implementation. Historically, this pressure without support for the planning process does not produce high-quality plans.

Leaders can entice staff to policy implementation through provision of resources. They reward (support) those staff who have acted in accordance with implementation and encourage (press) others by withholding resources until compliance occurs. This balancing act can be very subtle, open to staff's interpretation. Superintendents exercise this kind of indirect control with their principals, who appear to understand what is intended.

On the other hand when leaders visit schools and classrooms and observe first-hand the status of implementation, they are more informed and can more appropriately supply required resources to support staff in their policy implementation. Successful leaders are effective in putting fiscal resources where they can make a real difference (Louis and Miles, 1990); successful leaders provide materials and resources that directly focus on the policy being put into place. Time is one of the most necessary and expensive of resources, and most frequently the scarcest. When leaders provide time for staff to deal with implementation issues and concerns, they strike a strong chord of support with the staff. It is not only material resources that are important, but also time and energy for staff to plan, share, and act (Fullan, 1985).

Investing in Continuous Staff Development

Reasons given for adoption: administrators — improve classroom instruction; teachers — administrative pressure. (Crandall and Associates, 1982)

Many implementation efforts stall and fail because staff have not been trained in new skills. This leads to frustration and undercuts the implementation plan. Providing personal and professional development is viewed by many staff as highly supportive, although others may not agree. The use of formal and informal data to identify individuals' needs for training increases the supportive attributes of this strategy. Many leaders demonstrate their commitment and support of staff by participating in training with the staff. They also take an active role in planning, conducting, and evaluating staff development. Superintendents, for example, participate in staff development with principals and teachers, demonstrating that they are part of the learning community in support of policy implementation (Murphy, Hallinger, and Peterman, 1985).

Study groups (Murphy, 1992) have become increasingly used (see reference to this earlier) to promote staff reflection, discussion, and learning. In this strategy staff can provide the peer pressure that engages a faculty. However, leaders (until this practice becomes institutionalized) will need to support and push staff to be initially involved. When leaders arrange time and secure resources for the purchase of materials and other needs, this supportive action makes study more feasible. When studying together becomes common practice, then staff will take the lead and identify and manage material and initiate topics for review.

A tactic that some principals use is to arrange for faculty members to provide staff development for the school. This may encourage wider participation from the faculty. Should participation in staff development be required of people (pressure) or be voluntary (support)? A blend of the two with possible incentives and rewards (as additional pressure and support) may be an answer.

Assessing Progress

Administrative decisiveness bordering on coercion, but intelligently and supportively exercised, may be the surest path to significant school improvement. (Huberman and Miles, 1986)

Policy implementation, like all change efforts, never proceeds as planned, no matter how well the planning is done. There will be unanticipated issues and events. More importantly, people will need help in changing their practices and aligning them with new policies. Change is a process, not an event; so it is for the individuals in classrooms. Monitoring this process so that implementation can be orchestrated and coordinated at the school and classroom level is of the utmost importance.

When planning for the change moves off the planning book, initial staff development has been provided, and first implementation is being tried, it is at this point that checking on progress is vital. Effective leaders regularly and frequently check on the implementors to solicit needs and inquire 'how things are going'. This action is two-fold: implementors feel valued and cared for, and a clear signal is given that the change is of high priority and deserves attention.

Effective leaders visit classrooms often to lend this support, and to provide pressure as they are discovering what is happening in classrooms. They collect data through formal observations and instruments, but through informal methods also — walking the hallways, dropping in on classrooms, visiting departments and grade-level meetings, and having casual conversations in the cafeteria, workroom, or while crossing the parking lot.

Collecting classroom products is another way of expressing interest and monitoring classroom implementation of policies. Such products may be exhibited in public areas of the school — serving as support and a press for implementation. Student data may also be reviewed to monitor impact of new practice. Murphy and Hallinger (1986) report that superintendents make school and classroom visits to assess progress of implementation. They hold the principal accountable by using information collected in their supervision and evaluation of principals.

In monitoring implementation at the individual implementor level, leaders have data-collection techniques and tools from the 'concerns-based adoption model' (Hall and Hord, 1987; Hord, Rutherford, Huling-Austin and Hall, 1987). One technique focuses on the concerns of users or implementors of new practice, and provides a means to clearly shape support for people. Other tools assess the degree of implementation, again making it possible to provide more appropriate assistance — the next strategy.

Providing Ongoing Assistance

> To create effective change, the leader must always be patient and persistent. (Blokker, 1991)

Support and assistance are ongoing needs of implementors. Implementors' needs change as they move from introduction and early use of new practices to becoming experienced and expert. Assessing progress provides the data about needs; appropriate assistance then follows. When this occurs, implementors are supported but they are also pressed to continue implementation and refine their use. For instance, if staff do not know how to manage new practices, then leaders can provide information on this problem, demonstrate how it might be done, or arrange visits to other schools or classrooms so staff can see how others have managed successfully.

Recognizing and praising positive implementation efforts is both good psychology and an impactful tactic, that implicitly provides pressure and support. Celebrating progress is done publicly and privately, in large and small ways. Through a focus on positive use and problem-solving, leaders support staff's efforts and press forward to improved implementation.

Leaders may press for more complete implementation if individuals are not putting all parts of a policy into place. They can support this effort by helping to develop lesson plans that focus on the new policy and by demonstrating how the lessons might proceed. Leaders can arrange for staff to be assisted by peers, getting help and support from fellow implementors.

Arranging released time for teachers to meet for regular sharing of experiences in the change is seen as a profoundly supportive intervention. These meetings provide opportunities for teachers to support each other and a form of peer pressure can result. Change may be successful, or not, dependent on the time and quality and appropriateness of assistance received by implementors.

Creating an Atmosphere for Change

> Change encompasses a world of complexity, and realising and maintaining the delicate yet crucial balance between the humanitarian concerns of supportive behaviour and the pragmatic dictates of responsible authority could be fairly said to constitute the fundamental practical problem of change management. (Hord, 1987)

In a review of the literature, Boyd (1992) found particular contextual factors that support school change. The factors were of two dimensions: ecological and cultural. Ecological factors include physical facilities, structures and schedules, policies and regulations, and resources. Cultural factors are represented by attitudes and beliefs, norms, and relationships of all within the school. Cultural norms that seem especially facilitative of change are: 'a norm of continuous improvement, a widely shared sense of purpose, and a norm of involvement in making decisions' (p. 3). Leaders take actions to create these norms.

For instance leaders take actions to stimulate staff to create and introduce innovative ideas, and to initiate improvement efforts. To support such a climate, they arrange for staff to share ideas at meetings. They encourage staff's risk-taking with the proviso that when mistakes are made, learning must result from these mistakes. Superintendents push on all principals by endorsing those who initiate change; they do not applaud the status quo. Principals develop this kind of supportive and encouraging climate in their schools with their teachers, symbolizing action by their highly visible presence in classrooms.

Superintendents work to ensure that 'a harmonious environment pervades the district in order to nurture the internal creativity of the school staffs' (Hord, 1992, p. 32). They provide this supportive context (Murphy, Hallinger and Peterson, 1985) by:

- communicating openly and frequently with staff;
- building team spirit and team work and working on teams him/herself;

- expressing concern for staff and supporting staff morale; and
- solving problems rapidly.

Principals shape the school culture to be both supportive of change efforts and demanding of improvement. Deal and Peterson (1990) cite six ways principals do this. They work with the community and faculty to develop a mission and purpose of the school. Second, they select staff who share their values to build their preferred culture. They deal with disputes and conflict, and in so doing build unity. Four, through their own daily behaviours they model their values and beliefs. And they tell stories to exemplify their values. Six, they define and support the school culture by establishing traditions and rituals.

Conclusion

Nearly any of the actions classified in the six strategies leaders use to implement new policies and practices can be delivered with a tone of pressure or emphasis on support, or a combination of the two. Some actions are employed solely for pressure; others are utilized only to support. Effective leaders determine the appropriate needs of individuals and then act to work with them in policy implementation.

Abundant research has provided better understandings about the complexity of any change effort. No longer is it possible to imagine that reform of education will 'just happen' because well thought-out and developed policies are delivered to good people by an authoritative agency or power figure. Policies can contribute to reform only when effective leaders facilitate policy implementation through attention and action. Attention is used to balance support and pressure in leaders' actions representing six strategies found necessary for successful change. Policy makers and reformers would do well to be mindful of these issues.

Chapter 7

The Local Educational Change Process and Policy Implementation[1]

Gene E. Hall

One of the largest perennial gaps in understanding and area of misinterpretation is that between 'policy makers' and 'practitioners'. Unfortunately this gap in perspectives, semantics, and scope is not only true of the 'doers' in policy and practice; it also is characteristic of the researchers of policy and practice. The gap has been maintained over the last twenty to thirty years while the interrelationships between policy and practitioner players have become increasingly intertwined, as a result of the greatly increased involvement of federal and state policy makers in education.

At this time, it is even more difficult to talk about policy and practice in the same breath, due to the many paradigms that can be used. Depending upon the paradigm selected, one's assumptions, perspectives, values and language shift. When two or more actors attempt to communicate using different paradigms, there is a concomitant increase in difficulty in being understood. Some of the paradigm options include:

- policy–practice;
- development–implementation;
- behaviourist–constructivism;
- large scale–small scale;
- process–product;
- organizational development–concerns-based;
- intervention–innovation; and
- change agent–change facilitator.

Although these paradigm alternatives contribute to miscommunications, they are also representative of the rich resources now available, and signify the tremendous increase in knowledge and wide array of conceptual and technical tools now available for understanding the dynamics of social systems such as schools. An understanding of how change takes place in these systems is vital to those who are concerned about achieving success with policy initiatives.

In this time of popularity of cognitive psychology, perhaps a metaphor will be helpful to illustrate the array of semantic, conceptual and perspective opportunities (as well as sources of confusion) for analysing change. One useful metaphor is that of a tunnel. The traditional use of this metaphor is in terms of 'light at the end of the tunnel'. A related use of this metaphor is to equate looking through the tunnel to looking down a railroad track. As one looks down the railroad track, two rails appear to converge to a point. By combining the images of how things at a greater distance appear to merge with the idea of a tunnel, one way of explaining policy–practice perspective differences is possible. This metaphor is pictured in Figure 7.1. The various educational system actors are placed on a continuum from policy to practice. Each actor has the opportunity to look along the tunnel to other positions in the system.

One of the most serious problems in education today is the overly simplistic view that various role groups have of actors at other points along the policy–practice continuum. Thus, it appears that policy makers see the life and work of teachers as straightforward and relatively simple. There is a failure to recognize, or accept, the complexities of life in the classroom. At the same time, teachers, at their end of the tunnel, see their world as extremely complex and they have little empathy for what they perceive to be the relatively easy life of policy makers, who keep announcing 'simplistic' solutions. At the outset there is a problem of perspective, between policy and practice, that is affecting the ability of the educational system to make meaningful change. Further, this perspective problem is affecting success rates in curriculum development and implementation evaluation. The initiatives to improve science education are excellent examples of the clash between efforts to change and (excuse the pun) tunnel vision. The policy-led initiatives to develop curricula have not transferred automatically to widespread implementation in classrooms.

Another way to use the tunnel metaphor is to imagine the tunnel being a highway tunnel, with all sizes and types of vehicles rolling through. If each vehicle represents an educational innovation, or change, then one can envision the current situation where there is an increasingly dense stream of traffic flowing through the tunnel. Further, currently the dominant pattern is a flow from the policy end toward the practice end, with each vehicle carrying the newest solution/fix that the policy makers have derived for practitioners to implement. At this point there is little real forward movement in the tunnel. The educational highway system is in a major traffic jam (i.e., gridlock).

Well, enough about metaphors, and the different frames and perspectives that can be used to set the stage for a discussion of educational policy, and implementation. Currently, multiple frames and perspectives are being applied. There are differences in frames of reference of policy makers and practitioners. Note that these differences in perspective, and status, also apply to those who are doing research on policy and research on implementation. The absence of shared paradigms, in combination with the intense needs for change have led to intense pressure from policy makers for schools to change, and educators in schools feel that they are drinking out of a fire hose. This situation

Figure 7.1: *Different Points of View along the Policy-to-Practice Continuum*

has accumulated to the current condition of system gridlock. The continuing bombardment of practitioners in combination with their sense of low status has resulted in pragmatic and self-protecting resistance to change. The reaction of school-based practitioners has been initial willingness to attempt change, followed by frustration at the failure of others to support their efforts, and increasing cynicism, 'What will it be this year?' As practitioners have increasingly felt overwhelmed, undersupported and resistant, policy makers have become impatient and pushed harder, by creating more piercing initiatives. In all of this discussion, the central theme is *change*.

During the last two decades, while education policy makers and school practitioners have become more active, researchers have made a number of important breakthroughs in understanding how change takes place. One of the major directions for research on change during this time has been to examine closely how implementation works in schools and classrooms. The purpose of this chapter is to briefly summarize the major research studies of implementation during the 1970s and 1980s, and then to use selected findings from those studies to propose a number of issues and suggestions about how the educational change process should be approached in the 1990s.

The term 'change process' has been deliberately selected here. One of the basic discoveries in the 1970s was that change is a *process*, not an event. This key assumption was first stated in 1973, by Hall, Wallace and Dossett, in the original concept chapter for the Concerns Based Adoption Model (CBAM). However, as with many statements from theory and findings from research, this basic premise is often ignored. Much of the educational system still behaves as if change is an event; that change simply can be mandated, with a set date for accomplishment (which is well before the next election). Grudgingly, policy makers provide occasional support for development, but little for dissemination, and nearly none to support implementation in individual schools and classrooms.

This is another important point to highlight during the introductory part of this chapter, implementation as a phenomenon has been a relatively recent discovery. What is still recognized by only a few is that implementation *costs* just as much (if not more) as development. The traditional view, as defined in policy and practice, has been to place most of the available resources (i.e., time, dollars and personnel) into the development of an innovation, e.g., multi-year projects with special staff to create new curricula. Since the major announcement by researchers and theorists on change in the 1970s that there was an aspect of the change process called implementation, there has been limited acceptance by policy makers of the need to support the implementation phase at the practitioner level.

There are other aspects of the imbalance between development and implementation that could be pointed out, such as the major differences in the role of leadership for change during the development and implementation phases. However, the main point here is that implementation is an equally costly phase of the change process. Effective implementation requires parallel

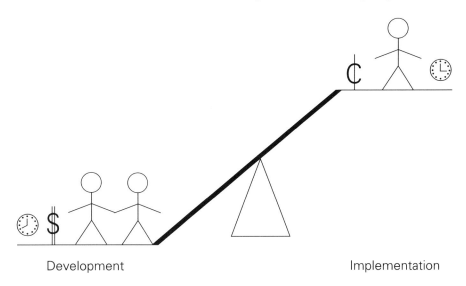

Development   Implementation

Past and Present

Reality is

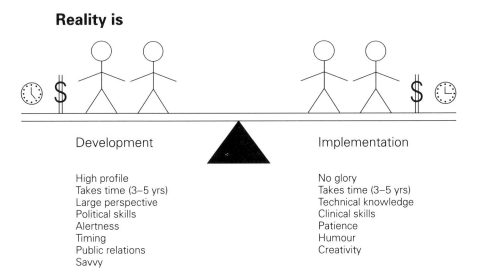

Development   Implementation

High profile   No glory
Takes time (3–5 yrs)   Takes time (3–5 yrs)
Large perspective   Technical knowledge
Political skills   Clinical skills
Alertness   Patience
Timing   Humour
Public relations   Creativity
Savvy

Figure 7.2:   Balancing the Costs of Development and Implementation

policies and procedures, to those that are addressed routinely for development, and implementation takes time.

As this chapter unfolds, the next section provides a brief summary and
commentary about the major implementation studies that occurred during the
last twenty years. Following this is an extensive discussion of issues and

implications of the studies for policy, curriculum development and practice, including suggestions for how to have successful change efforts in the 1990s. The chapter concludes with some related speculations and suggestions for how policy, practice and research need to shift from a vertical top–down paradigm, to a horizontal and more systemic approach for transforming the educational system. This approach will require trust and understanding of the roles and responsibilities of all participants in the system.

Prior to the 1970s, change was rarely if ever viewed as a process. Approaches to change in the earlier decades of this century, as well as the research on change, treated the phenomena as an event. In the classic studies conducted by rural sociologists, of farmers adopting such innovations as hybrid corn seed and in the studies of technology transfer to third-world countries, the event perspective was an implicit assumption. This event orientation is reflected in the terminology through the use of concepts such as 'adoption'. Given the relative simplicity of the innovations being studied and that the, adoption decision was most frequently done by an individual (e.g., farmer), it was easy for early research, to preserve this change-as-an-event assumption. Farmers either did or did not use hybrid corn seed. Physicians either did or did not shift from sulphur-based medicines to antibiotics. Third-world farmers either did or did not use steel tipped ploughs.

Analyses of this classic research in such sources as *Communication of Innovations* (Rogers and Shoemaker, 1971), illustrate that the event mentality was preserved throughout this rich research tradition. Ironically, even the early studies of change in schools, by Mort (1953) and others, tended to focus on 'adoption' of educational innovations such as kindergartens and driver education. The intent here is not in any way to diminish the merit of these earlier studies, instead the objective is to point out how difficult and slow the 'change' has been in thinking of the researchers in this field. For many reasons it has been easier to view the utilization of an innovation as an event, rather than as a phenomenon that has a timeline and process. In addition, there has been slowness in understanding that teachers are not equivalent to farmers in making an adoption decision. The milieu of the educational system is significantly more complex.

One of the contributors to the gradual shift in thinking about change in schools was the national-curriculum development movement of the 1960s. With major support from the US National Science Foundation, a number of revolutionary curricula were developed in mathematics, science and other subjects. These were an attempt to update the content as well as the process of teaching subjects in the nations' classrooms.

There are two interesting aspects of the national-curriculum development movement of the 1960s that continue to be a part of our thinking today, especially from the policy end. One theme was federal involvement in curriculum development. The second theme was multi-year funding of development projects, and in terms of today's levels of funding, large budgets were involved (many of these were multi-million dollar projects). An important premise in these efforts was the focus upon developing 'teacher-proof' curricula. The intent of this objective was to develop curricula that would be so well refined and defined that teachers would not adapt or mutate the prescribed practices. In a somewhat ironic twist, these materials ended up being teacher-proof in another way. There failed to be widespread 'adoption' of these curricula, and the majority of the nation's science classes were affected very little (Stake and Easley, 1978). The experiences of these national-curriculum development projects forced the discovery of implementation. These projects represented extensive investment on the development side and a near complete denial of there being any need to address implementation at local sites. It was explicitly assumed that after extensive and thorough curriculum-development processes were completed, widespread adoption and use would follow automatically.

Thus the stage was set for the discovery and study of implementation in the 1970s. The decade began with the Rand Change Agent Study (1974–8), which was established and funded as a policy study. However, due to the sensitivities of the researchers and the design of the study, they more or less got sucked in to an examination of implementation phenomena. The Rand Change Agent Study was of four federally funded programmes that offered four different ways of temporarily funding local sites to create new local practices. A key concept out of the Rand Change Agent Study was the concept of 'mutual adaptation'. This concept suggested that in the 'effective projects', a reason for success was that there was an adaptation of the innovation to fit the local setting *and* adaptations by the local users to fit the innovation.

As with most major studies, there are criticisms that can be raised (e.g., Datta, 1980), and in hindsight, a number of nuances that one could argue the investigators should have anticipated and understood. For example, the generalizations from this major study, as with a number of the other major studies, tend to go beyond the types of change projects that were being studied. In this case, the federal projects studied were designed to provide seed monies to the local level to create local process and product changes. However, the findings of the studies were extrapolated to all types of changes, including those without extra seed money and those situations where innovations developed outside were being introduced at the local level. In general, extrapolations of this type are dangerous and that has proven to be the case with the Rand study. As McLaughlin (1990) pointed out in revisiting the Rand Change Agent Study, most of the basic findings hold. Yet there are areas where we now understand more and some of the extrapolations, as well as a few of the interpretations, need to be adjusted, given our greater current understanding of implementation.

Another national study that dealt with implementation was launched in the late 1970s, the Dissemination Efforts Supporting School Improvement (DESSI) study. This study had an implementation emphasis and looked at the National Diffusion Network (NDN), as well as two other types of federal policy supporting change efforts. The trends and findings in this study are mainly the reaffirming of earlier studies and intuitively make sense. There has been little commentary and systematic criticism of this study, although it too tends to have findings that are extrapolations beyond the study design and the types of data that were collected. For example, in this study, the majority of the innovations selected for study would be implemented by individual teachers, not schools as a whole. However, in their reports, the DESSI investigators offer a number of conclusions about the role of principals and draw implications for school-wide change efforts.

An important note about the Rand Change Agent Study, the Emrick, Peterson and Agarwala-Rogers study, and the DESSI study is that all three were supported by federal funds to study federal-policy initiatives for the purpose of evaluating the effectiveness of those policies. In each case, the study design forced a look at the local level. In each case teachers and classroom practices were assessed to some extent. However, the amount of direct measurement of classroom practice was minimal, and the focus on individual schools as units was limited. The need to sample for national 'representativeness' worked against detailing individual schools and classrooms, as did the designs of the projects studied. The use of case studies did enrich interpretations. However, the purpose for doing each study was to evaluate the success of policy initiatives and to inform persons at the policy end of the continuum. These were not commissioned as studies to develop understandings of the practice end in order to inform practice.

The other major set of studies of implementation was based on the practice end with heavy focus on schools, individual teachers, and classroom practices. This project was the multi-disciplinary effort centred around development, initial verification and widespread application of the Concerns Based Adoption Model (CBAM) (Hall, Wallace and Dossett, 1973; Van den Berg and Vandenberghe, 1981; Hall and Hord, 1987). This cross-national team effort now is celebrating twenty years of concentrated study of the dynamics of the change process as it is experienced by individual teachers and schools as units. Three diagnostic dimensions, 'stages of concern', 'levels of use', and 'innovation configurations' have offered ways to describe and document the change process from the perspective of the individual classroom and school staff as a whole. More recent research in this area has focused upon how the principal's 'change facilitator style' affects teachers' success in implementation (Hall, Rutherford, Hord and Huling-Austin, 1984). Where other researchers have ebbed and flowed in their involvement in studies of implementation, those involved with the CBAM work, both in the US and in other nations, have continued to conduct studies that have been systematically focused on the change process in schools. Thus at this time, they have an extensive database, verified concepts and measures, and an array of research reports to undergird this approach to documenting and facilitating all phases of the change process, from initial conception of the innovation, to development, through dissemination, implementation, and on to institutionalization.

One of the key perspectives in the CBAM approach is that there must be an understanding of how the individuals within a school become confident and competent in using educational innovations. It is argued from the concerns-based perspective that a school has not changed until the individuals within it change, and that is done on an individual basis. For each individual, (i.e., teacher) change is a developmental phenomenon, thus during the introduction, implementation and institutionalization phases, change facilitators must provide leadership (i.e., interventions) differently in order to best address the developing concerns and use of teachers within the school. All of these in-school implementation-support activities require resources, time and personnel.

Also, almost every developer of an innovation sooner or later, (unfortunately it is usually later rather than sooner) discovers that implementation has to be addressed. Rarely a month goes by, that one of my CBAM colleagues or I, do not receive an urgent phone call from another innovation developer who is chagrined to discover that not everyone automatically is willing to use his or her innovation. As a rural sociologist pointed out some forty years ago, the 2.5 per cent of the population that work and behave as 'innovators' do not heavily influence the other 97 per cent of prospective adopters. Specialized dissemination and implementation-support strategies are essential, if most teachers and schools are to successfully implement a new practice.

This tour of the key implementation studies is meant to be short and only to highlight key themes in the work. One of the themes is the general reluctance to accept implementation as being a reality. One conclusion is that neither the development of a policy, nor the creation of exciting new curricula, lead to successful change processes in schools and school classrooms without the phenomena of implementation being addressed. A second theme is that in the 1970s and 1980s there was a thorough recognition and documentation by researchers and theorists of a special phase called implementation. The conclusion is that the implementation phase can be assessed, planned for, and facilitated. One set of tools that can be applied in the implementation process is the three diagnostic dimensions of the CBAM. In addition, these dimensions provide ways to monitor and suggestions for facilitating the full change process, of which implementation is one phase.

One way of thinking about these different concepts and components is presented in Figure 7.3. To understand implementation a distinction must be made between the innovation (the change that is being sought) and interventions (the actions of policy makers and change facilitators to assist teachers in using the innovation). All of this is taking place in the context of the user system, which includes the classroom, the school, the school district and perhaps the State. In order for a change process to be successful, change facilitators (e.g., science consultants and principals) must make interventions in ways that address the developing stages of concern and levels of use of each teacher and the configuration of the innovation that is being implemented.

Change Process =

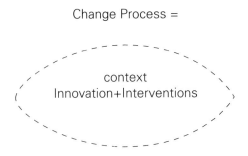

Figure 7.3:   The Change Process in Context

Implementation Issues and Implications for the 1990s

There is much that we have learned from the accumulation of policies, the wide array of curriculum-development efforts, the intense experiences of implementation, and the research that has been done during the last two decades. The items presented here are in no particular order, but each has direct implications for how we should go about the change process during the 1990s.

1   There is tremendous need to have clearer and deeper understanding of the concept of an innovation.

When we began our research around the Concerns Based Adoption Model (CBAM), some twenty years ago, we were amazed to discover that little attention had been given to carefully defining concepts in the earlier research on change. For example, in one classic book on change, the term 'adoption' was regularly used with multiple implicit definitions (i.e., as a decision point and as a phase). The concept of interventions was not mentioned! This lack of definition of concepts has added to the confusion and helped preserve many misunderstandings about the change process. The concept of innovation has been no exception.

   In the CBAM model, the concept of innovation has been defined operationally (Hall and Loucks, 1977; Heck, Stieglebauer, Hall and Loucks, 1981). In this approach the innovation is defined in terms of key operational components and distinctions are made between the different working variations that can occur for each component. For example, one component of an innovation could be the grouping of students. This component could vary from the teaching of the whole group, to three small groups, to individual work. Configuration component maps are developed for each innovation and used to document behaviourally how an innovation has been implemented in each classroom. The documenter circles the variation of each component that is in use. Each pattern of circled component variations represents a different configuration. A simple example checklist is presented here as Figure 7.4. This

Component 1: Units Taught

(1) All units and most activities are taught	(2) Most units and activities are taught	(3) Some units are taught	(4) A few selected activities are taught	(5) No units or activities are taught

Component 2: Use of materials

(1) Students are constantly manipulating science materials	(2) Selected students only and the teacher handle the materials most of the time	(3) Typically, the teacher does demonstrations and the students watch		(4) Memorization of facts and reading about science are emphasized

Component 3: Student grouping

(1) Students work individually and in small groups	(2) Students are kept in 3–5 permanent groups	(3) The whole class is taught as a group		(4)

Component 4: Process/content emphasis

(1) Science content and science processes are emphasized equally	(2) Science content is given major emphasis	(3) The processes of science are given major emphasis		(4) Memorization of facts and reading about science are emphasized

Component 5: Assessment

(1) All TSP assessment activities are used	(2) Some TSP assessment activities are used	(3) Teacher-made tests are used all of the time		(4)

Figure 7.4: Simple Innovation Configuration Component Map

technique offers a concept and a tool to systematically address the phenomena Gallagher (1967) had observed earlier. In a classic study of four BSCS class-rooms, Gallagher systematically documented that although the name and curriculum materials were the same, classroom practice varied dramatically from teacher to teacher. This finding makes common sense once it is pointed out; however, to this day major research and evaluation studies fail to docu-ment the innovation configuration in use in each classroom. This failure to document configurations leads to major sources of uncertainty in explaining observed (and unexpected) outcomes. If teachers don't do the new then it will be highly unlikely that the desired outcomes in students will be found.

There are a number of other ways do define the concept of an innovation. A regularly occurring problem today is that in most change efforts there is no clear agreement about the underlying definition and elements that comprise the innovation. Thus, without a taxonomy or categorization system, many different types of 'changes' are being implemented simultaneously and the inherently different experiences and effects that these different types and cate-gories of innovations accrue are not being distinguished. For example, one current innovation in the US is 'restructuring', another is 'Site-Based Decision Making', (Hall and Galluzzo, 1991). In both cases, what is being done in dif-ferent schools and school districts under these labels is amazingly different. The lack of clear definition is a contributor to the uncertainty and confusion that so often is observed around these efforts. This ambiguity clearly explains the regularly observed 'no significant differences' between the new and the old. When there is no clear agreement about what the innovation looks like *in use*, then there can be no certainty about determining implementation success, attaining outcomes, or measuring the right things.

Two other levels of distinction about an innovation that have been pro-posed in the literature need further thought in the 1990s. One was proposed in relation to the CBAM work, that is, the concept of an 'innovation bundle'. Instead of a particular change being one innovation, a number of distinct innovations are packaged as one. A name is given to the set, such as mastery teaching, choice, or middle school, and the implementation effort addresses the innovation bundle as a whole, rather than attending to each innovation in the set. Currently, innovation bundles are the nominal approach to change in North American schools. Rarely is a single innovation implemented, instead a bundle of loosely defined innovations is being implemented.

By way of contrast, the concept of 'large-scale innovations' has been proposed by van den Berg and Vandenberghe (1983). In Belgium and The Netherlands a different approach to change in schools has been the norm. Rather than many single innovations and relatively small innovation bundles being disseminated in a short period of time, in these European countries, national policy efforts are directed towards the creation of large-scale change in schools. Characteristics of a large-scale innovation include: the innovations tend to be 'big' and require all to make changes from what they are currently doing. Further, there is a five-to ten-year commitment on the part of the policy level to support the implementation of these innovations. Along with the expectations of large-scale change comes a structuring of the entire educational system to support the change effort. Special roles are created and supported for external facilitators, and there is an expectation of ongoing support to facilitate sites as they implement the changes. Researchers are contracted to study, evaluate and advise the process as it unfolds. This is in sharp contrast to the one- to two-year event-oriented perspective of change efforts in the US.

In summary, the key issue here is that definition of the innovation is important in terms of theory, as well as in terms of operation. For most change efforts, this lack of definition contributes significantly to confusion during implementation and mixed interpretations of change-process success. If you don't know what it is that is being implemented, then it is relatively easy to make quick judgments about success or failure, and it is nearly impossible to offer empirical confirmation. Shymansky, Kyle and Alport (1983) experienced this problem in their meta-analysis of effects of new science curricula. They observed:

> Assuming discernible, qualitative differences between new and traditional programs actually exist, the degree to which these programs were translated into reliably distinct treatment conditions in the original research studies is a critical issue which defies resolution a posteriori. For example, could the traditional classes in some studies have been taught by highly creative, innovative teachers and actually have been more a 'new' curriculum than the new curriculum to which it was being compared? Similarly, could not the treatment described as new programs have been equally distorted and very traditional? (Shymansky, Kyle and Alport, 1983, p. 402)

A related problem with large-scale innovations and innovation bundles is that each of the innovations has to be implemented before one can talk about or review effects of the complete set.

2   Conditions that are supportive of implementation.

We have learned a great deal about the roles, responsibilities, and actions of those in positions to support teachers and schools as they are involved in implementation. As the innovation or change that is being considered becomes larger and more complex, there is greater need for *ongoing active* support by the principal, from those in the school district, and facilitators beyond the school's district such as university faculty.

As one moves from implementing the type of innovations studied in the DESSI study and by Emrick, Peterson and Agarwala-Rogers (1977), to innovations requiring whole-school use, there is greater need for ongoing support. In other words, as one moves away from the type of innovations that tend to be adopted by individual teachers toward large-scale innovations, the more critical it is to involve other decision makers and more elaborate change-process support systems. For example, the four following conditions are basic to the success of most change efforts:

- Larger conceptions (i.e., systemic)

In order for change to be successful, the leadership needs to have an understanding of the systemic nature of the change process. Change is not done solely by individuals, and it is certainly not done by each in isolation of others and the larger system. Even site-based decision-making cannot work in isolation of the rest of the system. Leader involvement in facilitating the change process must keep in mind the various subsystems and how their interconnectedness will affect the change process as it unfolds.

In recent research on principals as change facilitators (Hall and George, 1988; Vandenberghe, 1988) the concept of 'strategic sense' has been proposed to address this dimension of leadership. Some principals are able to envisage the larger picture and to consciously place their day-to-day actions into the whole. In their schools all actions and events add up, they accumulate in moving the school in mass toward the desired goal. Other principals have only a day-to-day perspective. Implementation is much less successful in their schools (Hall, Rutherford, Hord and Huling-Austin, 1984; Schiller, 1988; van den Berg and Vandenberghe, 1983).

- Removal of rules and regulations

In the site-based decision-making movement we have observed in district after district where the 'top' makes a decision to have site-based decision-making, but removes none of the existent rules, regulations and policies that were inherent to top–down control of the site. It seems ironic that so many districts are advocating site-based decision-making from the superintendent's office, while the same controls for budgeting, hiring, scheduling the class day, and determining the curriculum are in place as were prior to the site-based decision-making initiative.

A partial exception to this effort would be in Dade County where the assistant superintendent, who was placed in charge of the effort, has as his basic job description the role of removing district and state rules and regulations that interfere with the schools moves towards site-based decision-making. Most change efforts would benefit from having the capability to remove old rules and regulations.

- Site need for time

In order to implement an innovation bundle or a large-scale change, a minimum of five to eight years is necessary. For obvious reasons, policy makers are unwilling to launch and support change-process initiatives over this extended time period. However, the reality is that it takes this magnitude of time to bring about meaningful change. This fact of life needs to be a cornerstone of all change efforts.

• Change facilitator teams

We know the change facilitator style of the principal is important ($r = .76$). In The Netherlands, Wijlick (1987) has documented the importance of external facilitators. Hall and Hord (1987) have pointed out the importance of the second change facilitator or 'consigliere'. All of the studies are documenting the importance of leadership by *many*. In the 1990s, implementation plans and supports need to be designed with an understanding of the critical role of the change facilitator team. No one actor does it alone, instead the site-based and external facilitators must work as a team. Planning staff development, and ongoing support for the change facilitator team is as important as training programmes for teachers (Hall, 1992).

3   Who, what and how?

We are at a time when it is important that the simplistic approaches to system-wide change be dropped. In the last twenty years we have tried 'top–down', 'bottom–up', 'mutual adaptation', and various forms of organized and disorganized anarchy. In all cases, researchers can provide testimony that there are instances where there has been successful change and instances where there hasn't. At this point, we need to begin to accept and recognize the importance of each of the work groups playing out their essential part, and that the system will only change when each person does his or her job.

The 'top' has to encourage or mandate 'do something'. However, the top should not be over prescriptive in controlling how it is to be done. The 'bottom' has to assume responsibility for implementation and have the opportunity to participate in defining the configurations that will be implemented. Then *all* need to understand and accept the goals of the change effort and do their own job, instead of micro-managing others. It is unacceptable to think that one part of the organization can succeed without the participation, ownership, understanding, and full involvement of other parts.

4   Middle-level guiding parameters.

Another key to change-process success has become clear in two current studies of school districts involved in implementing large-scale innovations. In each case, the top has set 'middle-level guiding parameters'. The people at the so-called 'top' strove to monitor themselves to not be overly prescriptive. When tasks are defined too tightly, teachers and principals do not have the flexibility to customize the innovation and change it to fit their specific situations (shades of mutual adaptation). On the other hand, when the top is overly vague and general, teachers and principals are unable to receive sufficient guidance and structure to understand what the change effort is really about (increased ambiguity means higher self and task concerns).

Some still cling to the belief that 'top–down' is wrong; however, most of us have experienced first-hand, at one time or another in our careers, attempts to bring about and sustain change from the 'bottom–up'. After two to three years the change effort fades, and everyone leaves discouraged and disillusioned about the possibilities for successful change. These feelings of futility come about when the top does not provide the ongoing support, encouragement, *and* day-to-day sanctioning that is so essential for change to be successful. There is a critical, necessary and ongoing role for all who are involved in implementation.

Back to the importance of setting middle-level guiding parameters. Currently, in one school district there is a major initiative to create a new type of teacher leadership role. This district, Douglas County, Colorado, has merged the previously established school consultant roles of mentor teacher, TOSA'S, curriculum specialist, and gifted and talented coordinators into a new single-person role. The old functions are to be accomplished in a new way by having a full-time specialist teacher called a Building Resource Teacher (BRT) in each school (Hayes, Grippe, and Hall, in press). In setting up this effort, the district set the educational and experience qualifications for persons who wished to be BRTs. The district established a pool of persons who met these qualifications. The district then said to each school that the school site needed to identify its needs and its philosophical position before interviewing candidates. The schools then selected from the district pool the person that the school believed would be right for them.

This has turned out to be a very powerful initiative and one of the keys to its success has been the insight of the district leadership. Setting middle-level guiding parameters, rather than being overly prescriptive or overly vague, empowered the school sites. The district didn't say to schools 'do whatever you want', nor did it say to schools 'here is the person we have selected for you'. Instead a middle position was taken, where the district set expectations and guiding limits, while leaving it to schools to select the person that would best fit their perceived needs. It is difficult to develop and maintain this middle-level perspective; however, it appears to be essential to having success in system-wide change efforts.

5   The innovation is in the mind of the beholder.

Cognitive psychology and the constructiveness–interpretivist paradigm has a very interesting set of implications for change research, policy, development and implementation practice. One of these ideas is related to defining the innovation from a constructivist perspective. In this approach, it does not matter what the innovation is or how the innovation is defined operationally, or necessarily what the goals are. Rather, an innovation is defined in terms of the meaning ascribed to it by the participants in the change process. Based on their past experiences, perceptions of the interventions (e.g., memos, announcements and workshops) that are made, and perceived needs, each teacher, principal, and policy maker (and developer, and researcher) will construct his or her own definition of the innovation *and* its implications. This construction of definition will occur individually and collectively (i.e., social construction). With the constructivism paradigm, the meaning of change success through implementation will be constructed by individuals and groups as they experience the change process. Thinking about development and implementation this way raises many new and interesting research opportunities.

For example, this is an area where the 'stages of concern' (Hall and Hord, 1987) work can be helpful. That participants in the change process go through different stages of concern about an innovation has been clearly documented (see Figure 7.4) (Fuller, 1969; Hall and Rutherford, 1976; James and Hall, 1981; Hall and Hord, 1987). Another way of saying this is, depending on their stage of concern, teachers will construct meaning of the innovation and interpret the innovation differently at different times in the change process. At the beginning they are likely to interpret the innovation in terms of their *self* concerns. The meaning assigned to the innovation is moderated in terms of perceptions of what it means for them personally. As implementation begins, *task* concerns become more intense. Here the interpretation of the innovation is done more in terms of perceptions of the amount of time, logistics and scheduling challenges that are associated with use. Ultimately, if the principal and others do an effective job of change facilitation, the concerns of teachers and others may shift to having more *impact* perspectives, where there is an analysis and interpretation of the innovation in terms of its consequences and effects upon students. Depending on the persons' stage of concern, they will construct different understandings of what the innovation is.

The point here is that there is variation in the assignment of meaning and what understanding of the innovation is depending upon where the person is in the change process. During the change process there are developmental shifts in perspective, that have been well documented in the last twenty years of implementation research. It would seem sensible and practical to take these different constructions of meaning into account at the policy level, as well as in future research, development and implementation activities. To continue to naively assume that everyone will see the innovation the same way, and at the same time, will continue to be wasteful and debilitating.

6 Use of an innovation is not dichotomous.

A basic assumption in traditional experimental studies and summative evaluations is that one set of people receive the treatment (i.e., use the innovation) and the people in the other group receive no treatment (i.e., no use). In other

- **VI Renewal**: State in which the user re-evaluates the quality of use of the innovation, seeks major modifications of, or alternatives to, present innovation to achieve increased impact on clients, examines new developments in the field, and explores new goals for self and the system.

- **V Integration**: State in which the user is combining own efforts to use the innovation with related activities of colleagues to achieve a collective impact on clients within their common sphere of influence.

- **IVB Refinement**: State in which the user varies the use of the innovation to increase the impact on clients within immediate sphere of influence. Variations are based on knowledge of both short- and long-term consequences for clients.

- **IVA Routine**: Use of the innovation is stabilized. Few if any changes are being made in ongoing use. Little preparation or thought is being given to improving innovation use or its consequences.

- **III Mechanical use**: State in which the user focuses most effort on the short-term, day-to-day use of the innovation with little time for reflection. Changes in use are made more to meet user needs than client needs. The user is primarily engaged in a stepwise attempt to master the tasks required to use the innovation, often resulting in disjointed and superficial use.

- **II Preparation**: State in which the user is preparing for first use of the innovation.

- **I Orientation**: State in which the user has recently acquired or is acquiring information about the innovation and/or has recently explored or is exploring its value orientation and its demands upon user and user system.

- **O Non use**: State in which the user has little or no knowledge of the innovation, no involvement with the innovation, and is doing nothing toward becoming involved.

Figure 7.5: Levels of Use of the Innovation

words, use of an innovation in this paradigm is dichotomous — some use it and some do not.

In the concerns-based adoption model a different paradigm is presented: levels of use (LoU) of an innovation (Hall, Loucks, Rutherford, Newlove, 1975; Hall and Loucks, 1977; Hall and Hord, 1987). This dimension, as the name states, proposes a range of different behavioural patterns of 'users' and 'non-users'. Three different non-user patterns and five user patterns have been operationally defined (see Figure 7.5). There are a number of implications of the 'levels of use' studies that should be considered by policy and curriculum developers, and evaluators, for example:

- Facilitating interventions need to be different in form and content for persons at different levels of use. For example, persons at levels of use I, 'orientation', are looking for descriptive information about the innovation that can help them shape an 'adoption decision'. Persons at levels of use III, 'mechanical use', are looking for how-to-do-it tips, not presentations about theory and philosophy.
- During the strategic planning for dissemination of an innovation (e.g., efforts to create nationwide awareness of a new science curriculum),

interventions can be identified and designed to address potential adopters differently depending on their non-use levels of use. For example, interventions targeted toward persons at levels of use 0, 'non-use', should be inexpensive (e.g., custom-designed brochures), while the more expensive personal contact type of interventions will be more effective with persons at levels of use I, 'orientation'.

- Most persons when they first use an innovation will be at level of use III, 'mechanical use'. Specialized coaching and on-site technical assistance will be important here.

- Summative evaluations should not be done with 'users' who are at level III, 'mechanical use'. When use is disjointed, there is a near term focus and inefficiencies, that is not the time to conduct the standard treatment-group control-group assessment of outcomes. That most evaluation studies report 'no significant differences' is not surprising, when the so-called users tend to be first-time users and are still trying to figure out how the innovation works (i.e., LoU III). It is unlikely that they will be optimizing effects of use on students.

- For summative evaluations, the users should be at level of use IVA, 'routine'. They are stable in their use, they anticipate problems and have alternate steps in mind when problems occur.

- For all comparison studies, use and non-use must be assessed at the individual level. Testimonials about use from principals/superintendents and others are not reliable. For example, in one early 'levels of use' study (Loucks, 1975; Hall and Loucks, 1977), a school district was engaged in summative evaluation of an innovation bundle that had been implemented in eleven schools. The district evaluators matched the treatment schools with eleven comparison schools. The treatment schools had received three years of extra resources and support to implement the innovation bundle. Then the school board wanted to know if their investment was worthwhile. The district evaluators compared student outcomes in the two sets of schools, found 'no significant differences', and the board discontinued extra support. With cooperation from the district evaluators, a research team assessed the levels of use of each teacher in the eleven treatment *and* in the eleven comparison schools. One major finding was that only 80 per cent of the teachers in the treatment schools were 'users' (levels of use III–VI)! Further, 49 per cent of the teachers in the so-called comparison schools were 'users'! No wonder there were no significant differences in effects.

To return to the point, implementation has to be assessed at the individual level in all treatment and comparison settings. Curriculum developers, researchers and evaluators should not rely upon the testimony of untrained observers, or administrators, or the facts that the materials were delivered to the classroom and teachers received training. Use of an innovation is an individual practice and use has an array of levels, rather than simply being there or not there.

7 There needs to be an acceptance of the fact that add-ons are resulting in system overload.

Several years ago in developing a layman's taxonomy of intervention strategies I suggested that one be called the Multiple Adoption Design, or MAD strategy. This strategy is increasingly used around the world. More and more curriculum innovations, rules, regulations, policies, and prescriptions are being laid upon teachers, principals, and schools. At the same time, the demographic changes in the student population have increased complexity geometrically. Multiple innovations are being 'adopted' at once.

There has been a complete failure of the top, middle, and bottom to accept the fact that new things when added to an already full vessel have little lasting effect. Until we start understanding that there is a finite amount of activity that can be accomplished at any one time, we are going to continue to have system overload. System overload brings with it a whole new round of symptoms in addition to implementation failure. Symptoms of the MAD strategy include teacher burnout, the horrifying statistic that over 50 per cent of beginning teachers quit within five years, and the failure to be able to identify many strong persons in applicant pools to become the next generation of principals. These are just a few of the symptoms that are resulting from our continual attempts to pour more into a finite amount of time and space, where very good people are already overworked and overloaded. We need a new type of principal that sets a quota on how much change is attempted in one site at one time. Further, when something new is added something old needs to be removed.

8 Time by itself does not guarantee implementation success.

Simply extending the time for implementation is not enough. Two to four years of implementation effort, without the necessary support, will lead to implementation failure, just as now occurs in shorter time intervals. Attention needs to be given to another phase of the change process during the 1990s. That phase is *institutionalization*. Basically institutionalization is a phase where use of the innovation has become a part of the regular routine in terms of practice, organizational rules and procedures, and system support. Institutionalization does not automatically occur just because there is more time with an innovation. Institutionalization though is another one of the change-process phenomena that needs to be planned for.

9 Researchers need to become users of the findings of their colleagues research.

In preparing this chapter, I reviewed various chapters of others and reflected on the last twenty years of research on policy and implementation. An inescapable conclusion is that we have not been the best at dissemination of our own research findings, or learning from the works of others. We, as researchers, have an adoption and implementation problem of our own. As we develop new understandings we should link these to the understandings of others' research findings. The converse is that we need to become more knowledgeable of the works of others. However, it appears that we suffer from the same problem as researchers in other fields. Once we have reported our study findings, we have less interest in working to share our understandings with others (i.e., policy makers and practitioners). This is a natural tendency, since the effort to share amongst ourselves is arduous and there is a tendency to avoid taking additional time to share with the thousands of practitioners and policy makers. Unfortunately the effect is that we are not knowledgeable about the work of others and we are not building the cumulative learnings that we could (i.e., shared construction).

Finally, we are all part of the same system and it is time that we all became players on the same level with the same footing. The last twenty years of implementation research clearly document that when any one of us tries to do it alone little is accomplished. In those instances where there have been cooperative and collegial efforts, with each one doing his or her job, exciting and amazing things have happened.

Note

1   An earlier version of this chapter was presented at the annual meeting of the American Educational Research Association, Chicago, April, 1991. A modified version of this chapter was published in the *Journal of Research in Science Teaching* (1992), **29**, 8, pp. 877–904.

Part 3

Perspectives

Chapter 8

Educational Reform and Curriculum Implementation in England: An Historical Perspective

Richard Aldrich

The chapter provides an historical perspective on the educational reform and curriculum implementation which has taken place in England since the advent of the first government of Margaret Thatcher in 1979. The word 'historical' is here taken to mean the study of human events with particular reference to the dimension of time. Such study, though principally located in the past and the present, also has implications for the future. England, together with Scotland, Wales and Northern Ireland, constitute the United Kingdom. Although the United Kingdom is one state, governed from Westminster, there are significant cultural differences between its several parts, differences which are reflected in both the formal and informal dimensions of education. The term 'England' in the title, therefore, should be taken as a recognition of these differences, rather than as any attempt to generalize from one part of the country to the whole.

Recent educational reform in England has, to a great extent, been consistent with the widespread changes in 'westernized' societies which lie at the heart of this book. Indeed in education, as in other policy fields, the radical reforms of Margaret Thatcher have provided a model for governments, both of the right and of the left, of other countries.

Since 1979, and particularly since the Education Reform Act of 1988, there has been a massive reform of the state educational system in England, certainly the most substantial since World War II, and possibly the most substantial in English history. A national curriculum of ten subjects has been established, a curriculum which is centrally prescribed and controlled. All children are to be tested at the ages of 7, 11, 14, and 16. Schools now have considerable control over their own budgets: some, indeed, have chosen to opt out of local-authority control altogether. Accordingly the powers of Local Education Authorities (LEAs) have been severely reduced. Not only has their relationship to schools been severely weakened, polytechnics (now redesignated as universities) and other colleges of higher education have been removed from their aegis. The largest and most expensive local authority, the Inner London Education Authority (ILEA), has been simply abolished.

These reforms have been justified in terms of the need to improve individual and national economic performance. The basic interpretation of the process by those who have carried it out is that in the interests of promoting national efficiency it has been necessary to wrest the control of education from the producers — teachers and LEAs — and to place it in the hands of the consumers — parents and employers. The application of market forces — for example, open enrolment which allows a school to recruit students up to the limit of its physical capacity, and the publication of league tables of examination results — will, it is argued, confirm the quality of, and provide further incentive for, good schools. Those which are identified as underachieving will be forced by parental pressure either to improve or to wither away.

It is not difficult, however, to point out certain inconsistencies and flaws which underlie these arguments. The market principle has not been applied to the curriculum or to testing. All students in state schools will follow a national curriculum which, ultimately, has been prescribed by a politician, the Secretary of State for Education. The very use of the word 'national' may also be questioned. Independent schools do not have to follow the national curriculum, nor are their students subject to national testing.

Thus the market may operate in respect of curricula in independent schools, but not in state schools. As to the operation of a market in choice of schools, although there are some 'assisted places' at independent schools for the children of poorer parents, essentially access to such schools is restricted to those who can pay the fees. The operation of a market between state schools means that where a popular school is oversubscribed, ultimately the choice will rest with the school (the producer) rather than with the parent (the consumer).

The analysis of educational reform and curriculum implementation in this chapter is grouped around three themes: culture, control and curriculum. The approach is a broad one. Other contributions by two of my colleagues at the University of London Institute of Education, Caroline Gipps and Denis Lawton, focus upon the politics of change since the 1988 Education Reform Act and the politics of assessment regarding the implementation of the national curriculum.

Culture

English culture is deeply rooted in a complex and contradictory history. The traditional rural hierarchies of the medieval period — monarchy, aristocracy and Church — and their attendant values, have been overlaid, but not yet overwhelmed, by the industrial, urban and professional revolutions of more modern times. In the nineteenth century Britain became the greatest and most confident imperial and financial power the world had ever seen. In the twentieth century, that confidence was to be shattered by the loss of empire and by relative economic decline. Though on the winning side in World War II, in peacetime, Britain was defeated on the economic battlefield by (amongst others) two of her former adversaries — Germany and Japan. British governments and business increasingly attributed such defeats not to their own shortcomings, but to the failure of the educational system.

There have been two broad interpretations of the nature of that perceived failure. One interpretation would be to point to the survival of medieval hierarchies and values. It could well be argued that the educational system reflects the strength of English conservatism. The universities of Oxford and Cambridge, the only universities in England for several hundred years, still enjoy a unique social and intellectual position — with some 50 per cent of their undergraduate students recruited from independent schools.

The most prestigious secondary schools are also medieval foundations, for example those of Winchester and Eton. Access to such schools continues to be monopolized by the sons of the wealthy. These boys' independent schools, the so-called 'public schools', have provided a model for secondary education across the centuries. The grammar-school tradition which they exemplify, with its elite connotations and classical, rural and religious values, continued to provide the model of secondary education in England until very recent times.

In 1965, for example, 8 per cent of secondary-age students were in independent schools, 26 per cent in grammar schools, a mere 5 per cent in technical and selective central schools, and 49 per cent in modern schools. (Prais and Wagner, 1983 figures for England and Wales.)

Such criticism would not deny the achievements of students in independent and grammar schools. Attainment levels at age 18 of students who have concentrated for two years on three General Certificate of Education (GCE) Advanced Level subjects are comparable or superior to those of students anywhere in the world. But at what cost have such achievements been bought? Concentration upon the success of the few at the expense of the many has made schooling in England essentially unpopular. Since the introduction of compulsory schooling in 1880 the majority of students in English schools have chosen to leave as soon as possible — currently at age 16. Secondary schools have not provided a purposeful education for all, according to abilities and needs, but rather have acted as a selection mechanism for those who would proceed to higher education or to the professions.

In consequence, in spite of the fact that some 90 per cent of state secondary-school students now attend comprehensive schools, such schools have considerable difficulty in producing an ethos appropriate to the world of the 1990s. The continued existence of the independent schools, the survival of grammar schools in some areas, coupled with the recent introduction of opted-out schools, and the absence of any strong technical or vocational tradition at secondary level, combine to create considerable problems.

Such an analysis was confirmed by the substantial research into the comparative standards of schooling in England and Germany, and their bearing upon economic performance, undertaken by Prais and Wagner. They showed that some 60 per cent of the German labour force obtained vocational qualifications (compared with 30 per cent in Britain) with a particular super-iority in the area of mathematics. They concluded that the strength of the German economy depended in part upon the amount of pre-vocational instruc-tion provided in German schools and that this had 'definite commercial and industrial (and not merely 'craft') emphasis' (Prais and Wagner, 1985, p. 68).

A more detailed analysis of curriculum will be provided in a later section in this chapter. At this point it is important to note that not only with respect to the curriculum, but also more generally, English schooling has been weak in its provision for the students of average and below-average ability, as opposed to those who are academically gifted. Too often such students have been presented with a watered-down version of the grammar-school curriculum, or diverted into studies which have had little validity and less status. Prais and Wagner concluded that 'The contrast between the growth of an intermediate stream of schooling in Germany — with its explicit educational objectives and syllabus — and its submergence in England, provides an overriding clue to many educational and social differences between these countries' (Prais and Wagner, 1985, p. 70).

A second interpretation of the weaknesses of English education focused not upon the faults of traditional educational institutions such as Oxford and Cambridge and the independent schools, but rather upon the failure of new foundations to reproduce their many virtues. The writers of The Black Pa-pers, the first of which appeared in 1969, condemned the perceived progres-sivism of the Plowden Report and of the primary school, the laxity and low standards of the secondary comprehensive school, and the permissiveness of the new universities and polytechnics. According to this analysis the English educational system, rather than acting as an agent of investment in individual and national well-being and wealth, had become a destructive force, charac-terized by consumption. It provided a haven for neo-Marxists and others of the left to encourage amongst children and students a culture of envy and enervation, of indulgence and inaction.

In October 1976, in the wake of further economic difficulties consequent upon the oil crisis, the Labour Prime Minister, James Callaghan, signalled his disquiet in a speech delivered at Ruskin College, Oxford. Though careful to distance himself from the Black Paper writers, the tone of his speech indicated that the heady days of hippy culture, of the Beatles and flower power, were over. Instead he called for greater accountability in three areas: the first was a halt to ever-increasing educational expenditure; the second a need to raise educational standards and to equip students to 'do a job of work'. The third was to pay greater attention to the needs of employers and to the wishes of parents.

Such an analysis was music to the ears of Margaret Thatcher, Secretary of State for Education and Science, 1970–4, and Prime Minister, 1979–90. Her aim was nothing less than to purge English culture of what she saw as its many weaknesses, weaknesses which had proliferated with the growth of state monopolies and state socialism. In seeking to match the competitive cultures and economies of such states as Japan and Singapore, she looked back to the nineteenth century, and drew upon the so-called 'Victorian values' of enterprise, thrift and personal responsibility. The public services would be privatized, at both national and local levels; the power of those latter-day, over-mighty subjects, the trade-union leaders, like Arthur Scargill, who had brought down the Heath government in 1974, would be broken. Members of the old professions — lawyers, doctors and university teachers — would be deprived of their privileges and brought to account. Those ministers within her governments who blanched at this attempt to reverse the course of recent history, 'the wets', many of them from the traditional ruling families, were simply removed from office. The grocer's daughter from Grantham was equally adept at disposing of trade-union barons or Conservative grandees.

Although until 1986 educational reform was of a piecemeal nature, the advent of a new Secretary of State, Kenneth Baker, with his decisive style and comprehensive approach, led to the Education Reform Act of 1988. The government believed that the brave new world which it envisaged, the world of small business, of enterprise, of competition, of individuality, was being hindered by members of the educational establishment. The thrust of the legislation, therefore, was to weaken the power of the providers, and to increase that of the consumers. Such an approach was consistent with the general tenor of Thatcherite reform. Thus the abolition of the Greater London Council was followed by the abolition of the Inner London Education Authority; the sale of council houses by the opting out of schools. Institutions of higher education were required to bid for students; the tenure of university teachers was abolished. In education, as in other areas of social policy, there was a move towards controlled competitiveness.

It is not clear whether educational policies were significant factors in the four successive Conservative election victories of 1979, 1983, 1987 and 1992. These victories, however, suggest that within England at least, the broad thrust of Margaret Thatcher's policies and those of her successor, John Major, have commanded more support than those of their opponents. One obvious feature of the Conservative period has been the decline in power of the trade-union movement, a decline which has contributed to the defeats of the Labour party with which it has always been inextricably intertwined. Such decline has meant that, in contrast to countries like Australia, the trade unions have had little or no influence on recent educational reform. What then is the future of English culture, and how will such future affect the educational reforms implemented so far?

In 1993, at the time of writing, neither the traditional institutions and values, nor the enterprise culture appears to be very successful. Some of the ancient institutions are in disarray. The concept of the royal family has been severely tarnished by marital problems which have been so prominently featured in the media. The Anglican Church, of which the monarch is the Supreme Governor, has also been weakened by these developments, and further divided by the decision to admit women priests.

Grave doubts have also arisen about the efficacy of the Thatcherite revolution. After a decade of enterprise culture, the United Kingdom, in common with many other 'westernized' societies, is in deep recession. Though inflation has declined, so too has productivity. Unemployment stalks the land, so that an ever-increasing percentage of public spending must be diverted into social-security payments. During 1993 there were indications of both a modest upturn in output and of a decline in unemployment, but the recovery is fragile and may be reversed by increases in taxation to be implemented in 1994 and 1995.

Such difficulties have called into question, once more, the nature of the United Kingdom. Northern Ireland remains a permanent problem. Nationalism and separatism have found a stronger voice in both Scotland and Wales, which have given their support to their own nationalist parties or to the Labour Party of Neil Kinnock and John Smith. On the international scene the country appears to be a half-hearted member of both the European Community (EC) and of the Commonwealth, while still trying to sustain a 'special relationship' with the United States of America.

Strong elements of competition have certainly been introduced into the educational system. Universities now compete against each other for funds for teaching and research. Schools compete against each other for students. Whether such competition will raise the overall educational standards and promote a classless society (John Major's declared aim), or simply allow those who are already successful, powerful and wealthy — the universities of Oxford and Cambridge, the independent schools, state schools in affluent areas — to become even more successful, powerful and wealthy, remains to be seen.

Margaret Thatcher exemplified the non-conformist enterprise culture of mid-nineteenth century England. The rhetoric of Conservative educational reform was consistent with the promotion of such a culture. But the non-conformist enterprise culture did not triumph in the nineteenth century in England, nor indeed in the twentieth. The open aristocracy of England, with its traditional rural and classical values, out-manœuvred the entrepreneurs. In the boys' public schools, the sons of manufacturers learned to despise their origins and to acquire the speech, manners and prejudices of the traditional land-owning and professional classes. The educational reforms of the 1980s and 1990s were largely devised and implemented by ministers who had themselves attended independent, and not state schools. Although Margaret Thatcher, herself, had attended a state school, the architects of educational reform — ministers like Keith Joseph and Kenneth Baker — were the products of independent schools. These schools remained the ideal, the jewel in the crown, and in a direct sense were untouched by the reform process. LEAs might be deprived of their schools and colleges, and teachers of their pay-negotiating rights; state primary schools would be pilloried for their progressiveness, state comprehensive secondary schools would be castigated for their confusions, but the independent schools would remain independent. And Margaret Hilda Roberts, the product of Kesteven and Grantham Girls'

Grammar School, who studied chemistry at Oxford and worked as a research chemist before turning to the law, ended up in the House of Lords as Lady Thatcher.

Control

One of the great paradoxes of the recent educational reforms in England is that, although they have been justified in terms of market forces and of freedom, their most obvious product has been a massive increase in central control. The 1988 Act, for example, has given the Secretary of State some 415 new powers (Lawton, 1989, p. 43). Other groups which might claim an increase in powers are school governing bodies, head teachers and parents. The losers have been the LEAs and teachers. The situation of students in respect of control remains unclear.

How Should this Change in Control be Interpreted?

The first point to note is that this assumption of authority by government was as much the cause, as the result of legislation. It signalled that in educational terms, as in other areas of life, the politics of partnership had been replaced by the politics of confrontation, the agenda of consensus by that of radical reform. Substantial changes in any area of human existence may either be produced by negotiation and consensus, or by imposition. The Education Act of 1944 was preceded by a lengthy round of consultations with interested parties, including the several Christian denominations. There was no such process prior to the Act of 1988. A minimal period of eight weeks was originally allowed, which nevertheless drew more than 20,000 responses, half of them on the proposed national curriculum (Haviland, 1988).

This lack of consultation stemmed not only from a change in style but also from the nature of the proposed legislation. Education acts which are designed principally to increase the amount of education may be approved by a wide range of interests. On the other hand the stated intention of the 1988 Act was not so much to improve the quantity of education but, as Callaghan had argued some twelve years earlier, to improve its quality without increasing its resources. Since the government believed that such improvements depended essentially upon weakening the power of the existing educational establishment, the actual process of legislation, as well as its outcome, necessarily involved an increase in central control. LEAs were not likely to welcome their loss of control over a range of institutions from schools to polytechnics, especially when the largest and most prestigious, the Inner London Education Authority, was scheduled for abolition. Teachers, who in 1987 were deprived of their pay-negotiating machinery which had existed for well over sixty years, were not likely to welcome further loss of control, over such matters as the curriculum. Academics were hardly likely to approve of the removal of tenure.

Nevertheless, it would be wrong to believe that central government was assuming quite unprecedented powers in respect of education. Rather it was returning some of the control mechanisms which existed at the time of British economic supremacy in the mid-nineteenth century.

Two points may be noted here. The first is that the establishment of a central authority in English education (1839), preceded the introduction of the first local-education authorities, the school boards (1870), by some thirty years. During that period of time schools were owned and controlled, as they had been for centuries, by voluntary bodies, corporations and private individuals. The role of central government was to supply financial assistance to those schools which required it, provided that such schools submitted to inspection and, from 1862, to a national curriculum and national assessment. Under the system known as 'payment by results', central-government grants to schools depended largely upon the performance of students in annual examinations in the three Rs — reading, writing and arithmetic. These examinations were not carried out by teachers, not even by former teachers, but by an august body of graduates, principally from Oxford and Cambridge, many of them clerics, who had no other connection with the elementary school world, or with its inhabitants — Her Majesty's Inspectors (HMI). At this time working-class parents paid the full or partial cost of their children's schooling. Not until 1891 was elementary education made generally free.

Conservative governments have always been wary of local-government control over education. In 1868 Disraeli's government, indeed proposed to establish a much stronger central authority headed by a Secretary of State. Two years later a Liberal government under Gladstone established the first local-education authorities, the single-purpose school boards, but even these were intended to provide a third-rate product. At that time there was no expectation, either among Conservatives or Liberals, that the mass of schooling would pass under local-government control. Nor was there any thought that such bodies would take responsibility for secondary, adult or higher education. A natural hierarchy was assumed. Parents who exercised proper responsibility for their children would send them to independent schools, and would pay the full cost of their education. Those who could not, or would not, do so, might send their offspring to the state-aided, voluntary schools, of which there were 8,000 in England and Wales in 1970. The great majority of these, some 6,000, were supplied and controlled by the National Society for Promoting the Education of the Poor in the Principles of the Established Church, a body established in 1811 under the presidency of the Archbishop of Canterbury. The role of the school boards was to 'fill up the gaps' in respect of elementary schools, principally in localities which were too poor to make proper provision on their own account.

By 1900, however, many of the schools provided by the boards, which could rely on local rates a well as finance from central government, were decidedly of first-rate quality. Conservative governments believed that the natural order of things was being turned upside down. With some justification the prelates of the Church of England argued that the schools of secular local boards were being favoured over those of the established Church. Accordingly in 1902 the Conservative government, led by Balfour, abolished the *ad hoc* school boards and handed their powers over to multi-purpose authorities. In 1902, as in 1988, the London School Board was the centre of the controversy: on the grounds of its perceived radicalism, excessive expenditure and preoccupation with matters outside its proper sphere.

Compulsory schooling was established in England in 1880. It was part of a broad movement for, as Pavla Miller has commented, 'in the last third of the nineteenth century, systems of mass compulsory schooling were established in most countries of the Western World' (Miller, 1989, p. 123). One hundred years later, in England, as in other 'western' countries, central government believed that the educational system, its administrators and teachers, had outgrown their role, and had created a state within a state, with its own priorities and values. Margaret Thatcher was Secretary of State for Education from 1970 to 1974. During that time, in spite of her own doubts and those of many of her party, comprehensive secondary-school reorganization proceeded apace — the system seemed to have a mind and a momentum of its own. Her subsequent attempts to alter this state of affairs aroused considerable hostility and led her own *Alma Mater*, the University of Oxford, to refuse to grant her the customary prime ministerial accolade of an honorary degree. The 1988 Act was designed to ensure that the education establishment — LEAs, teachers' unions and academics — would never again dictate educational policy to central government.

Thus the apparent contradiction between a substantial increase in central-government power in education and the ideal of a consumer-driven enterprise culture becomes less contradictory when viewed from an historical perspective. It could be argued that, in the twentieth century, and certainly since 1944, the distinctive feature of English education, in comparison with many other countries of a similar size and nature, has been the absence of central-government control in terms of ideology, ownership and personnel. According to this analysis central government has re-assumed, rather than assumed, several powers under the recent legislation, and the removal of schools and institutions of further and higher education from local-government control may, indeed, provide such schools and institutions (notwithstanding current financial restraint with a greater freedom both to manage their own affairs and to respond to the wishes of consumers).

One feature of this re-assumption control has been to show how ill-equipped, in terms of personnel, the government has been to implement its reforms. The Department of Education and Science (since 1992 the Department for Education) has not had teams of curriculum experts in its employ. The several quangos and working parties established to put flesh on to the bare bones of legislation have necessarily included large numbers of professional educators, educators who have produced schemes for curriculum and assessment which the government has often seen as a deliberate attempt to pervert the course of its reforms, and to win back control of the system. There is now a widespread belief that many key appointments to such bodies are being made, and will continue to be made, from amongst the ranks of 'party *apparatchiks*' (Graham and Tytler, 1993, p. 134).

The historic controllers of the school educational system, the traditional eyes and ears of the department, Her Majesty's Inspectors, have always enjoyed a certain independence from central government. For example the HMI model of a national curriculum, both before and after the 1988 Act, differed considerably from that held by other Department of Education and Science employees, and by ministers (Chitty, 1988). As Duncan Graham, chair and chief executive of the National Curriculum Council from 1988 to 1991, has recently revealed:

> Council meetings and major committees were usually attended by a deputy secretary and Eric Bolton, the then Senior Chief HMI, who did not see himself as part of the Civil Service and was fighting his own battle to regain control for HMI. (Graham, 1993, p. 17)

Such independence came to an end in 1992, the numbers of HMI were drastically reduced and the post of chief inspector became a part-time appointment. In future inspections of schools would be carried out by private teams which would include a strong representation of the 'consumer' interest.

Curriculum

The curriculum of schools and other educational institutions may be viewed in several ways: for example, as a selection of knowledge and values from the culture; as a battleground for contending pressure groups. How should the national curriculum in England be interpreted?

George Tomkins suggested that there are three broad positions in respect of curriculum: child-centred education which stresses individual development; vocational education which focuses upon the demands of the workplace; subject-based education which favours cultural heritage and traditional hierarchies of knowledge (Tomkins, 1979). Since 1976 the child-centred curriculum has found little favour with governments which have believed that the education system as a whole was too self-centred, and insufficiently aware of the real world outside the playground walls or campus gates.

Keith Joseph's concern for the neglected 40 per cent of secondary-school students who were not preparing for public examinations led him to take a keen interest in vocational education, but the major thrust in this direction came not from the Secretary of State and the Department of Education and Science, but from David Young and the Manpower Services Commission.

The Manpower Services Commission (from 1988 the Training Commission) was established in 1973 as an offshoot of the Department of Employment. The principle of a separate agency for vocational training was nothing new in English history. For example in 1853, following the success of the Great Exhibition, a Science and Art Department was established at Kensington, and pursued distinct policies from those of Whitehall until its demise in 1899.

Two major developments sponsored by the Manpower Services Commission were the school-based Technical and Vocational Educational Initiative for 14 to 16-year-olds, which was 'directed towards new technology, business studies and teaching about particular, local industries', (Ainley, 1988, p. 122) and the Youth Training Scheme, also begun in 1983, which provided a year's training for all unemployed 16 and 17-year-old school leavers. Under this latter scheme it was proposed that three-quarters of the time would be spent in work experience, the other quarter in off-the-job training or further education. Although David Young had strong backing from Margaret Thatcher — 'the only man who brings me solutions and not problems' (Ainley, 1988, p. 123) — there were widespread doubts about the somewhat haphazard way in which funds for the Technical and Vocational Initiative were being applied. As to the Youth Training Schemes, which had replaced a previous Youth Opportunities Programmes, although, in the short-term, such strategies substantially reduced the numbers of young unemployed, the long-term effects of these schemes were broadly questioned, both by employers' and trade-union organizations, and the trainees themselves. In 1989 the Confederation of British Industry adopted a radical report on vocational education and training which posed serious questions as to government policy in this area and declared unequivocally that 'the practice of employing 16–18-year-olds without training leading to nationally recognised qualifications must stop' (Maclure, 1991, p. 4).

In spite of these, and other vocational initiatives it seems clear that the curriculum reform promoted by Conservative governments since 1979 and embodied in the national curriculum as set out under the Education Reform Act may be categorized, in terms of Tompkins' analysis, as one which favours cultural heritage and traditional hierarchies of knowledge.

The curriculum is defined in terms of subjects: three core and seven foundation. Its traditional nature is indicated by the uncanny resemblance to the list set down under the Secondary School Regulations of 1904 — the curriculum of the publicly funded grammar schools established under the Education Act of 1902.

1904	**1988**
English	English
mathematics	mathematics
science	science
foreign language	foreign language
history	history
geography	geography
physical exercise	physical education
drawing	art
manual work/housewifery	technology
	music

Music, though not in the original curriculum of 1904, was added subsequently. In 1904 Latin would have been one of the foreign languages taught. In the 1988 curriculum modern languages were to be introduced from age 11. This list of subjects was not meant to comprise the whole curriculum. In response to a wide range of criticisms the government acknowledged that time should also be found for religious instruction and for other interests and activities.

Why was this curriculum chosen? Several answers may be adduced. Such a curriculum would preserve the traditional hierarchies of schools and knowledge, a grammar-school curriculum for all — at both primary and secondary levels. All children would have a sound training in the basics of mathematics, English and science: all children would be equipped for the technological age and yet would also have access to a broad range of cultural subjects. Early specialization would be avoided. Children would not be able to give up study of those subjects which they found difficult or boring.

Such a curriculum would also be easy to prescribe, to control, to test and to resource. For a government seeking to produce nationwide test results by which parents might measure the quality of schools, without itself incurring any great increase in educational expenditure, a traditional, subject-based curriculum had many advantages. National programmes of study and schemes of assessment, to be followed by all children in state schools, could be swiftly established. Most of the teachers were already in place, although in addition to the traditional shortage in the subjects of mathematics and science, more teachers of modern languages and technology would be required in secondary schools. At primary level, teachers would need more training in science and technology. The first programmes of study were introduced in 1989 and the first assessment of 7-year-old children in the core subjects of mathematics, English and science took place in 1991.

Though the general principle of a national curriculum commanded widespread support both among professional educators and the public, there was considerable opposition to the actual curriculum as laid down under the 1988 Act. Some of this criticism proceeded from those who would have opposed anything which stemmed from a Conservative government, but many of the government's own supporters were also highly doubtful of the wisdom of the proposed scheme.

Thus those 'long-serving exponents of the application of market forces to educational decision-making' (Maclure, 1988, p. 163), the economists and political scientists of the Institute of Economic Affairs, argued that:

> The most effective national curriculum is that set by the market, by the consumers of the education service. This will be far more responsive to children's needs and society's demands than any centrally imposed curriculum, no matter how well meant. (Haviland, 1988, p. 28)

The Confederation of British Industry, the employers' association, gave approval to the principle of a broad-based curriculum for all which would avoid the problems associated with premature specialization, but reaffirmed:

> The concerns expressed by industry and commerce regarding the important need to inform these traditional subjects with cross-curricular themes that relate to life after school and the world of work in particular. The CBI is concerned that the document does not contain any specific reference relating to economic awareness and understanding, or careers education. (Haviland, 1988, p. 29)

Other critics were even nearer at home. In 1985 Keith Joseph, widely regarded as Margaret Thatcher's ideological adviser, and himself Secretary of State for Education from 1981 to 1986, issued a document entitled *Better Schools*, which declared that:

> . . . it would not in the view of the Government be right for the Secretaries of State's policy for the range and pattern of the five to sixteen curriculum to amount to the determination of national syllabuses for that period . . . The Government does not propose to introduce legislation affecting the powers of the Secretaries of State in relation to the curriculum. (Department of Education and Science, 1985, pp. 11–12)

During the debates on the 1988 Bill, Joseph, now in the House of Lords, opposed the national curriculum as being:

> . . . still too prescriptive . . . I have to add that if all the foundation subjects were tested, we would impose too large a testing industry upon our schools and squeeze out some relatively widespread non academic vocationally geared subjects. (Hansard, 495, pp. 1263–4)

In spite of some modifications both to the national curriculum and to national testing, many of the questions raised in 1988 by the government's own supporters have still not been solved.

There is a widespread belief that too much has been prescribed and too much has to be tested. In 1862, under the Revised Code, the government began with the testing of three subjects and then proceeded to allow schools to add 'specific' or 'class' subjects for grant-earning purposes. In the 1990s the (widely predicted) difficulties of giving due weight to all ten national curriculum subjects are now generally apparent. Retreats have already been made, both in respect of curriculum and testing. For example some foundation (but not core) subjects have been diluted for older students so that the national curriculum for all now applies to the 5–14 age range rather than the 5–16 as originally announced. One solution, currently being canvassed, is to increase the length of the school day, but given that teachers already work well in excess of fifty hours per week, with the bulk of that time spent in non-teaching tasks, such a solution poses considerable problems of its own.

Conclusion

Political and economic rivalry are as old as history itself. For centuries 'western' nations have dominated the world in a political and economic sense, and have enjoyed a disproportionate share of the planet's goods and resources. Such domination is bound to be tested in several ways, and the lessening of the ideological and military challenge posed by the Soviet bloc in eastern Europe has only brought into sharper relief the economic rivalry between the 'western' nations themselves, and the substantial challenge currently spearheaded by the countries of Asia.

The educational reforms introduced by the Conservative governments led by Margaret Thatcher and John Major have been justified principally, though not exclusively, in terms of enabling the country to reverse its relative economic decline. It is difficult, as yet, to measure the effectiveness of these reforms, particularly in the midst of a global recession, but an historical perspective can be of value here, and is worthy of further investigation. As Martin Wiener wrote in 1981, 'The leading problem of modern British history is the explanation of economic decline' (Wiener, 1981, p. 3).

Three further concluding points can be made in respect of culture, control and curriculum.

First, in respect of English culture, the formal education system cannot be divorced from its social, economic and political contexts. Notwithstanding the undoubted capacity of teachers in state schools to transform the lives of individuals, and of groups, it is also undeniable that 'education reflects and transmits the values which are dominant in society and the values which have dominated English life for more than a century have not been those of the enterprise culture' (Maclure, 1991, pp. 9–10). Radical reform of one part of the education system will have little effect if the old social, economic, political and educational hierarchies continue in an unreformed state.

Second, the assumption of so much control by central government in education raises two issues. The first is that there is no guarantee that educational wisdom and responsibility rests predominantly with central government. Indeed central government has frequently failed to do its educational duty in the past, not least in respect of the enterprise culture. For example, the 1918 Act established part-time day continuation schools to age 16, the 1944 Act, county colleges to age 18. The failure of Conservative and Labour governments in the post-war periods to implement these reforms is the principal cause of the current deficiencies with regard to vocational education and industrial training in England. The second issue is that now that so much power in education has been concentrated at the centre, there may be violent reversals of policy, should a different government come to power. The Conservative government has sought to weaken (or abolish) LEAs, HMI and university departments of education. A government of a different political persuasion might instead target the power, influence and independence of the independent schools. Education must be a partnership, not a battleground. Now that central government has so much control, it must seek to rebuild a partnership that includes not only parents and employers, but also teachers and other educational professionals and, for the foreseeable future at least, LEAs.

As for the national curriculum, certain benefits are now becoming apparent: in terms of specifying objectives, of ensuring progression within and between schools, of improving knowledge and standards in hitherto frequently neglected areas, for example science and technology in primary schools. But three problems remain. The first is that of continuing interference by government ministers in curricular details, interference which places enormous strains upon teachers, examiners, textbook publishers, and the children themselves. The second, which is closely related to the themes of culture and control, refers to the meaning of the word 'national'. If a national curriculum and national testing are essential for the economic well-being of the nation, should they not also be applied to independent schools? Finally, the fundamental contradiction in the educational reform process must be highlighted once again. Is a traditional, subject-based, centrally controlled national curriculum consistent with a consumer-led approach to education?

Chapter 9

National Curriculum Assessment in England and Wales[1]

Caroline Gipps

The national-curriculum assessment programme is the largest assessment development to be undertaken in recent years in the United Kingdom (UK), requiring as it does detailed assessment across the core subjects of the national curriculum at ages 7, 11, 14 and 16. The purpose of the assessment programme is to measure performance of students against the national curriculum; provide accountability data for schools and local education authorities (school districts); to raise standards of performance; and to support the teaching–learning process. The original proposals for national assessment involved the use of teachers' own assessments (usually known as school-based assessment in Australia) and external tests on a performance-based model. There has, however, been a considerable retreat from this model over the four years of test development. In this chapter I will give a detailed account of developments and discuss the reasons for the shift in type of assessment.

First it is necessary to give an outline of the curriculum structure, although a detailed discussion of the national curriculum is given by Lawton in Chapter 3. In 1988 the Conservative government, under Margaret Thatcher, brought in the Education Reform Act (ERA) which legislated wide-ranging changes in education including the introduction of a national curriculum in England and Wales and a related national assessment programme.

At the heart of these developments was a concern about educational standards in terms of the range of curriculum experiences offered to students in different schools, the rigour of teaching in the basic skills, and low expectations for student performance. Both the first and last of these three had been a regularly voiced criticism by the then independent Her Majesty's Inspectorate (HMI) in England and Wales. In reality there was less curricular variation at secondary level than at primary level since the upper-secondary school curriculum is to a great extent controlled by the public or school-leaving exams at 16 and 18. The concerns at secondary level were more that students were dropping subjects, in order to specialize, as young as 13 or 14 and that the range of curricular provision for the bottom 40 per cent of the ability range was inadequate. In addition, since there were no formal assessments in the system before the public examination at 16, there being no examination on leaving primary school at 11, there was no 'hard' information on the performance of primary schools.

A significant factor in the call for an improvement in educational standards was a report published in 1983 comparing performance in mathematics standards in schools in England and West Germany. The authors reworked data from the 1964 International Evaluation of Achievement Study and claimed that German students in the bottom half of the ability range obtained levels of performance comparable with the average for the whole ability range in England (Prais and Wagner, 1983).

A number of other international comparisons also showed that English schools were not top of the league tables. The previous national-assessment programme, the Assessment of Performance Unit, which had carried out anonymous testing of 'light' samples of students, had been unable to comment satisfactorily (because of measurement problems) on whether national standards were rising or falling. These other studies shifted the argument away from comparisons over time to comparisons of English schools with those of other countries: politically a more powerful argument within the context of the discussions about economic decline.

The national curriculum was therefore to ensure that all students of compulsory school age (5–16) would follow the same course with English, mathematics, science and technology forming the core, and history, geography, a modern foreign language, art, music and physical education forming an extended core. These ten subjects together should make up 70 per cent of curriculum time.

For each subject the curriculum is enshrined in law: statutory orders describe the matters, skills and processes to be taught as 'programmes of study' and the knowledge, skills and understanding as 'attainment targets' within each subject which students are expected to have reached at certain stages of schooling. The stages are defined as Key Stage (KS) 1 (age 5–7), 2 (7–11), 3 (11–14) and 4 (14–16). The attainment targets are described in a series of ten hierarchical levels; the series of levels is designed to enable progression: most students of 7+ would be at level 2 in the system while most students of 11+ would be at level 4 and so on. The attainment targets are articulated at each of the ten levels by a series of criteria or statements of attainment which form the basic structure of a criterion-referenced assessment system.

The national-assessment programme is a crucial accompaniment to the national curriculum for it is through the assessment programme that performance is to be measured and standards are to be raised. The first stage of the development of the national curriculum and assessment programme was the setting up of the Task Group on Assessment and Testing (TGAT) with a remit to design the assessment programme. The report of this group (Department of Education and Science, 1988) put forward a blueprint for the structure of the curriculum to which all subjects had to adhere.

The National Assessment Programme in England and Wales

The national-assessment programme, as outlined in the TGAT Report and the statutory orders, required that students be assessed against all the attainment targets (ATs) by their teachers and on some ATs by external tests (called standard-assessment tasks) at the ages of 7, 11, and 14. At these ages the results of teacher assessment (TA) and the external tests (SATs) were to be combined and must be reported towards the end of that school year.[2] At age 16 the external test is to be the General Certificate of Secondary Education (GCSE) the public examination which is currently taken by approximately 85 per cent of the age group, and the grading system of the GCSE was to be merged with the ten-level national curriculum scale.

At the individual level, results must be reported to parents to allow implementation of the Parents' Charter which requires all schools to report annually on all children in relation to every NC subject, including comments on general progress and a record of attendance (Circular 14/92). At the end of Key Stages the student's performance is to be reported in terms of levels (including at aged 7 years separate arithmetic, spelling and reading levels) and comparative information is to be given about all the other students of the same age/stage. This comparative information of course makes the production of local league tables easy, even at age 7.

Indeed reporting on school performance (Circular 7/92) is now structured specifically to allow comparative tables of school performance in public examination results at 16 and 18 (which are to be distributed by primary and middle schools to parents of children about to transfer to secondary school and published by the DfE in local newspapers). Full public-examination results at school level should be available at least two weeks before choice of secondary school has to be made. Averaged figures for the whole of England will be supplied to governors to go in school prospectuses. The same procedures will eventually apply for national assessment results at the end of all Key Stages.

The only additional feature of the national-assessment proposals for Wales are that Welsh is assessed as a first language *and* as a second language. SATs are therefore available in both English and Welsh. In Welsh medium schools, students are assessed using SATs on maths, science and Welsh at age 7, and these subjects together with English at the ages of 11 and 14 years.

The first run of assessment for 7-year-olds in English, maths and science took place in 1991, the first statutory run for 14-year-olds will be in 1993, for 11-year-olds in 1994 and in that year also GCSE will be reported in line with attainment targets and national-curriculum levels. Subjects beyond the core will come on stream and be assessed in later years, with technology being the first (1992 for 7-year-olds using a non-statutory SAT, 1993 for 14-year-olds, 1994 for 11 and 1995 for 16-year-olds). All subjects should be included in the assessment programme at all ages by 1997, though teacher assessment is likely to dominate beyond the core subjects, using non-statutory SATs.

While the overall plan for national assessment is the same for all four ages, there are differences in articulation: national assessment at aged 16 is dominated by the demands of GCSE; the assessments for 11-year-olds are as yet at the piloting stage; the 14-year-old assessments were trialled in 1991, piloted in 1992 and changed dramatically for 1993. The assessment of 7-year-olds is furthest along the path of development. First therefore I shall give a detailed account of the national-assessment programme for 7-year-olds then I shall give a (necessarily) briefer account of the 14-year-old testing. The issues which are raised are, however, relevant to any criterion-referenced performance-based assessment programme used for accountability purposes.

Assessment at Age 7

During the spring and early summer term of the year in which students reach the age of 7 (Year 2) teachers make an assessment of each student's level of attainment of levels 1–4 of the scale 1–10 in relation to the attainment targets of the core subjects. Teachers may make these assessments in any way they wish, but observation, regular informal assessment and keeping examples of work, are all encouraged. In the first half of the summer term and the second half of the spring term the students are given by their teacher, a series of standard assessment tasks (SATs) covering a sample of the core attainment targets.

Because of the reliance on teacher assessment, the TGAT report suggested a complex process of group moderation through which teachers' assessments could be brought into line around a common standard and any variation between TA and SAT could be settled professionally. The combination of TA and SAT results has been a contentious area; the ruling now is that where an attainment target is assessed by both TA and SAT and the results differ the SAT result is to be 'preferred'.

Since the proposals for the SATs in the TGAT Report were innovatory and were a conscious attempt to move away from traditional standardized procedures they will be described in some detail. The TGAT report suggested that a mixture of instruments including tests, practical tasks and observations be used in order to minimize curriculum distortion and that a broad range of assessment instruments sampling a broad range of attainment targets would discourage the narrowing tendency to teach to the test. Thus the TGAT model was one which emphasized a wide range of assessment tasks involving a wide range of response modes in order to minimize the negative effects normally associated with formal assessment and a range of assessments in different contexts to ensure content and task validity. These SATs are, therefore, in the mould of performance-based assessments which are currently receiving considerable attention in the USA.

Early on in the development of the SATs for Key Stage 1 the requirement was that they should cover as many attainment targets (AT) as possible.

This proved unwieldy since there are thirty-two ATs in the original curriculum structure for the core and the mode of assessment was to be active rather than paper and pencil tests of the traditional standardized type.

In the event, the SATs used with 7-year-olds in 1991 were a watered-down version of the TGAT proposals. The style of assessment was, however, active and similar to good infant-school practice: for example, the reading task at level 2 involved reading aloud a short passage from a children's book chosen from a list of popular titles, using dice to play maths 'games', using objects to sort, etc.

Despite the reduction in the number of ATs tested from thirty-two to nine, the SAT administration in 1991 took a minimum of forty hours for a class of twenty-five to thirty students and was rarely managed without support for the class teacher, since most of the SATs were done with groups of four students. The SATs can thus be seen as matching good teaching practice, providing teachers with detailed information about individual children, but being time-consuming and as we shall see, offering limited standardization for comparability purposes.

In response to the widespread publicity about the amount of time the 7-year-old SATs were taking the Prime Minister announced in the summer of 1991 that for 1992 there would be shorter standardized paper and pencil tests. (This announcement was made *before* formal evaluations of the SATs were available). The 1992 SATs contained a reduced number of active tasks, and offered for a number of SATs a 'whole-class' administrative procedure, which in fact few teachers used. The reading SAT stayed as a reading aloud task with the teachers making a running record and in addition an accuracy score. There were also two standardized tests: a traditional group-reading comprehension test with written response, and a group-spelling test. The reading test was optional at level 2 and above and the spelling test was compulsory for level 3 and above. These two scores had to be reported separately alongside the maths 'number' score, as well as the overall levels for English, maths and science.

In 1993 there were further changes with spelling and reading comprehension tests compulsory for all except level 1 as well as the reading and writing SATs. Different ATs in maths and science are covered each year in addition to 'number' so that in 1993 7-year-olds were assessed on algebra and physics. The testing package took around thirty hours of classroom time as it did in 1992. Thus at KS1 we have a system which is a mix of SATs (performance-type assessment), more traditional standardized tests and teacher assessment.

At KS2, age 11, there are group tests (*not* tasks) in English (two hours) maths (1–1¼) hours and science (1–1¼) hours. These tests are standardized and differentiated i.e., the tests will be at three levels of difficulty covering levels 1–2, 3–5, and 6 and students must be entered at the appropriate level. As with KS1 in 1992 and 1993 the 'process' attainment targets in each subject are not covered by the SAT, but assessed by TA. Whilst this is probably a more satisfactory way of assessing these skills it does mean that we run the danger of this part of the curriculum becoming downgraded since it is not included in the 'high stakes' testing.

Assessment at Age 14

The trialling of SATs for 14-year-olds which took place in 1991 involved extended tasks taking many hours of classroom time and covering a range of activities and response modes. The Secretary of State for Education deemed this inappropriate and the pilot 'SATs' in 1992 were short written tests done by whole classes at the same time under examination conditions. Practical tests were only to be set where there was no alternative.

As with KS1 the development agencies were first asked to assess each attainment target through SATs. Not only did this make the test development task enormous, the preferral of SAT result to TA result where both were available meant that SAT results at the individual student level had to be highly reliable; more so than the TGAT report had envisaged (Brown, 1992). Furthermore, the SATs at age 14 have to cover all ten levels of the national curriculum.

For the 1991 trial the Secretary of State for Education required an element of written testing taken under controlled conditions. Again, as with KS1, before the evaluations were complete the Secretary of State — who referred to the SATs as 'elaborate nonsense' — announced changes to the SATs. Contracts with the development agencies were terminated and new contracts were put out to tender. The specifications for 1992 required three tests per subject of 1–1½ hours covering all attainment targets, except the process ones which were assessed by teachers. Papers are set at four levels each covering a range of four NC levels; teachers select the level at which to enter a student, although they will not see the examination papers beforehand. All the tests are taken on the same dates in June in formal examination conditions.

One of the reasons put forward for changing the style of the assessments was the amount of time the original SATs took, the same manageability issue that dogged the KS1 assessments. However, the evaluations showed that the KS3 teachers did not find the task burdensome and felt that the active SATs were a valid way of assessing performance (Brown, 1992; Stobart and Burgess, 1992; Jennings, 1992). It seems clear that the decision to alter the assessments from active, extended performance-based SATs to timed written examinations was essentially a political one: at KS3 the SATs did not present a manageability problem, were widely felt to be valid and were demonstrated to be sufficiently reliable.

There have been particular problems with the English tests at KS3. The Government summarily withdrew the contract from the new test developer in 1992, changed the specifications, put it out to tender and awarded it to a *third* agency for developing the 1993 materials. There was considerable debate in early 1993 therefore about the merits of these assessments, since it seemed that they could not have been piloted. SEAC and government ministers, however, insisted that the tests for 1993 *were* piloted (on a sample of 15-year-olds) in 1992 despite the change in development team and that the 1993 assessment would be a full, reported run. Interestingly, the chairman of SEAC insisted that the pilot papers were modified in the light of comments from the teaching profession, but a leak from SEAC indicated that papers with questions identical to the pilot ones were to be used in summer 1993 ('Muddling through in English', *The Guardian* 21.1.93, Melanie Phillips). Anxiety is such that many independent schools, which are not obliged to follow the national curriculum, decided not to do the KS3 tests in 1993. Eventually in February 1993 the Secretary of State agreed that the results of the English assessment would not be reported, except to parents.

Changes Made in 1993 and 1994

As well as the retreat from the very open-ended SATs at KS1 from 1991 to 1992, there were 'minor' curriculum changes and finally, a full review of the *National Curriculum and its Assessment*, by Sir Ron Dearing, which is out for consultation over summer 1994.

The emphasis given to TA was reduced in 1992/3 with test results 'preferred' over TA results where both were available; subsequently TA was restricted largely to the few attainment targets that were not being tested (teachers still had to report TA in all the ATs at KS1, but not until after the testing was done). The national curriculum itself was changed in 1992 when the number of attainment targets in maths and science were reduced. The curriculum is being changed again in 1994, with the Dearing review focusing on slimming-down the curriculum, in order to make it manageable and realistic and to allow 20 per cent of teaching time to be used at schools' discretion in KS1, 2 and 3, with 40 per cent at KS4.

The reason for the whole-scale review by an outsider (Sir Ron Dearing had been Chairman of the Post Office) was the teacher-union boycott of the tests in 1993. KS3 English teachers initiated the boycott, but were joined by their colleagues in other subjects and from KS1. The English curriculum had been changed a number of times and was highly contentious. The 'last straw' for English teachers was the formal tests to be given to 14-year-olds in June 1993, which they considered to be banal. The boycott argument was based on the extra workload caused by the tests and marking; this claim (put forward by one major, but not militant, union) was upheld in the courts and all the unions then mobilized a boycott at both Key Stages. Although a number of schools did do the tests, and indeed much of the KS1 assessment had been completed by April 1993, most did not send in their results. The Education Secretary could not therefore publish the school and LEA league tables he had planned in 1993. Sir Ron Dearing was appointed to carry out the review in March one week (approximately) before the NASUWT voted to boycott the tests; in early April it was deemed to be a legitimate trade dispute; (approximately) one week later Sir Ron was given his terms of reference. At the end of April the Appeal Court unanimously ruled the boycott as legal (Lawton, 1994). The Education Secretary never quite believed the boycott would stick: he suggested that refusal to test might result in cuts in resources; he reminded school governors that it was their statutory duty to ensure that national-curriculum assessment was implemented; he said he would be holding heads and governors to their legal duties; and he was under pressure to introduce legislation to compel teachers to administer the test. In the end only 5 per cent of KS3 schools sent in their results (Nuttall and Stobart, 1994).

The constant change in the curriculum and assessment has been very difficult for teachers who understandably feel that no sooner do they get the hang of the material than it is changed again. The Dearing review recommends no further change at all for the next five years.

Teacher assessment is also back on the agenda, with the requirement that TA and ST results be reported side-by-side, so that 'teacher assessment and test results will have equal status' (School Examinations and Assessment Council, 1993). This is a welcome move but it is not yet clear how this will look when it is reported, what weight TA will carry for high-stakes purposes e.g., secondary transfer, and what parents will make of different results for TA and tests. Apparently, the Prime Minister himself insisted to the Dearing review that TA should not replace tests, as some had been suggesting. The term moderation has disappeared unfortunately, with 'audit' appearing instead, denoting a verification or quality-control mechanism rather than professional development.

Teachers at primary level are being urged to move away from 'tick-lists' which record every Standard of Achievement (SoA) attained for each child in favour of a more holistic approach (ref. Letter to Heads 4/11/93 from Ofsted, OHMCI (Wales) and SCAA *Recording Students' Achievement*). Teachers should look across the statements at a level and decide whether, on the whole, the students' performance is closer to level 2 or level 3 (Circular 11/93). The multifarious SoAs (228 at KS1 in the three core subjects) are going to be replaced, as part of the simplification process, by level descriptions (broader descriptions of performance like the Western Australian student outcome statements and the GCSE grade descriptors).

Testing at KS1 was reduced in 1994 (and KS2 tests piloted) with no tests in science; in maths only number is tested, and in English only reading and writing tests (although spelling and handwriting will be assessed in these). The testing time should be reduced by half. TA will be required for all the ATs. The tests in 1994 for KS2 and 3 were restricted to the core (English, maths and science) and were less demanding in terms of student time (6–7 hours) and marking (quicker and simpler). Results in terms of NC levels only have to be reported to parents for English, maths and science now at ages 7, 11 and 14 (previously all the subjects of the national curriculum were to have reported in levels). In the intervening years schools can continue to report achievement in any way they choose.

In 1994 at least one union is continuing with the boycott on the grounds that testing should be suspended pending the curriculum changes. Many primary schools are, however, doing the KS1 assessment although they may not report the results and enough have volunteered to do the 11-year-old tests to make up the 2 per cent pilot planned for 1994. When I visited one of our research-project primary schools in the middle of May — they were doing the KS2 tests with their top class (11-year-olds) — both teachers and children felt it to be quite unproblematic. The school was also doing the KS1 assessment which the head described as 'routine now'.

Along with the slimming down of the NC and more recognition given to TA, the government announced in December 1993 that league tables would not be published at 7 and 14, only at 11 and 16 (these latter two being at the end of primary school and the end of compulsory school respectively).

Assessment at Age 16

The General Certificate of Secondary Education (GCSE) is the public examination currently taken by students at 16+. This is, itself, a relatively new examination with the first papers taken in 1988. The changes which were brought in with GCSE were: it involved use of coursework assessment rather than 100 per cent examination, thus oral, practical and extended project work play an important part in the assessment; it was aimed at the whole ability range; differentiated exam papers (pitched at different levels) were therefore required for some subjects; it was intended to be criterion-referenced so that candidates could be graded in relation to their own performance rather than in relation to how others performed.

The GCSE has, it is generally acknowledged, brought about changes in teaching style and content resulting in a broadening of students' curricular and pedagogic experience. A higher proportion of the age group takes it than was the case with the previous 16+ exams (over 85 per cent of the age group enters at least one subject). Coursework assessment has had a powerful effect in many schools; 100 per cent coursework-assessed syllabuses are popular in English and are available in a number of other subjects. The move towards criterion-referencing has been problematic and students are graded on the basis of rather loose grade descriptions, while the proportions achieving each grade were held roughly constant in the first two years in line with the previous public examination. Since the announcement of the national assessment proposals the search for better criterion referencing for GCSE has been halted.

Ironically, one of the justifications for making GCSE criterion-referenced was that it would help to raise standards: since there would be no limit on the number of students able to gain top grades this would encourage teachers and students to aim, and achieve, higher. The percentage of the age group gaining the top three grades has in fact risen, with the result that there are claims now being made that the exam is too easy. When aligned with national-curriculum levels, level 10 is to be harder than the previous grade A. Coursework assessment is also seen by the administration as being not sufficiently rigorous and too dependent on teachers; as a result for most subjects a maximum of 20 per cent of the marks will be awarded for coursework in future.

Since the introduction of the national curriculum into schools two changes have been announced to it which have resulted directly from the difficulties of aligning the GCSE with the national curriculum and assessment programme. The government's intention is to retain GCSE as the standards flagship and it is not prepared for a weakening or watering-down of its requirements. Since each GCSE course requires 10 per cent of curriculum time (for the two years from 14–16) it is clear that not all students could follow a GCSE course in all ten national curriculum subjects (plus religious education) since this would in theory leave no time for other non-statutory aspects of the curriculum (for example, classics, a second foreign language, personal, social and health education, etc.). At the beginning of 1991 the Secretary of State for Education thus announced that the full national curriculum would only be followed up to the age of 14. From 14–16 all students must follow a full GCSE course in the core subjects (English, mathematics and science); all students must study technology and a modern foreign language but not necessarily to GCSE level; all students must follow a course of either history or geography or half of each; only a full course will be examined by GCSE. Art and music will be optional at this stage as will physical education, although schools are expected to encourage all students to continue with some form of the latter. Subjects which are not assessed via the GCSE (all except the core) may be assessed via examinations developed by the vocational examining bodies. The expectation is that more able students will take GCSEs while less able students will go for the vocational qualifications. Thus the notion of a full entitlement curriculum for all, offering a broad general education to 16, has been watered down: the 'option' system at 14 will be similar to that already operating in many schools, and an academic/vocational divide is built in. (That said, all students must continue with a full course of science and some technology to 16.)

The second major change to come about is a restructuring of the maths and science curricula. The original national-curriculum structure gave maths fourteen attainment targets and science seventeen. The examining bodies which are responsible for producing, selling, marking and analysing the GCSE announced that they could not report performance on the ten-level scale in relation to this attainment-target structure. As a result both curricula have been streamlined to five (broader) attainment targets with approximately half the number of statements of attainment, while the programmes of study remain largely unchanged. This new structure should therefore not affect teaching plans but will make the assessment simpler for both teachers and examining bodies.

In December 1993 the government decided to leave the GCSE as it is, still reporting in grades A to G — the GCSE boards having found it difficult to switch from awarding grades to awarding levels — (with a new starred A grade in order to 'raise standards') and it will not be incorporated into the NC ten-level scale. This has compromised the existence of the ten-level scale, which the Dearing review opted to retain, since it now effectively finishes at 14. The national curriculum itself, following the Dearing review, alters at 14, leaving time for vocational options at 14–16. We then have three national curricula at 16+: academic and general (assessed through A-level) vocational (assessed through GNVQs) and occupational (assessed through NVQs).

It is a clear indication of the perceived importance of the GCSE that its requirements were allowed to modify the national curriculum and assessment programme in this way rather than vice versa. Furthermore, the return towards the domination of the formal written examination mirrors developments in relation to the SATs. This will be discussed further in the next section.

Assessment Issues

Developments in assessment in the UK over the last 5–8 years have attempted to embrace a range of new approaches: criterion referencing, teacher-based assessment, active process-based assessment tasks, and coursework assessment. This shift in assessment paradigm from a broadly psychometric, norm-referenced, examination-based model towards an educational assessment model is well illustrated by the philosophy outlined by the TGAT Report. Teacher assessment, it said, should be a fundamental element of the system and the information should serve several purposes: formative, diagnostic, summative (to record the overall achievement of a student in a systematic way) and evaluative (so that aspects of the work of a school could be assessed). The report was acknowledged as being far-sighted, professionally supportive and likely to encourage good practice in assessment and teaching. There were, however, criticisms from some educationists of the 10-level system, concerns over the extent of external testing, the playing down of teacher assessment in relation to SATs and the publication of unadjusted national assessment results as a basis for school accountability.

The move towards criterion referencing, continuous assessment based on teacher judgment, and active or extended assessment tasks are common to GCSE and national assessment. The latter two elements are time-consuming for teachers but are seen as contributing to their professional role. Where the teacher-based assessments are linked with external assessment and/or reported as part of a certification procedure, external moderation is involved, which is also time and resource-consuming, but can again act to promote professional development.

Other developments in assessment practice in the UK include graded assessment and Records of Achievement (RoA). Graded assessment developed from attempts to modularize the curriculum and to offer students shorter term goals and individual rates of progression through the curriculum. The assessments themselves can be either classroom-based or examination-based, although the latter is difficult to reconcile with the notion of readiness — this is, taking the assessment *only* when ready to pass — which is a crucial element in the argument for the motivating properties of graded assessment. Graded assessment has been a popular development at secondary-school level, in maths and modern languages in particular, and teachers have reported increased student motivation, notably among the less able. There are, however, organizational problems relating to management and flexibility, and technical problems relating to the hierarchical ordering of material and the grade descriptions on the certificates awarded. Problems of developing statements which express unambiguous hierarchies of attainment, the level of specificity of criteria and the generalizability of performance beyond the context of the assessment are the same as those raised by other forms of criterion-referenced assessment. A number of graded assessment schemes have been made equivalent to GCSE, but since the edict about the amount of terminal examination assessment required for GCSE, their future is in doubt. Graded assessment, then, is built on a model of learning which requires learners to have clear information on learning objectives and regular feedback; thus it is more interactive than the traditional secondary-school examination and course.

The model underlying profiles and Records of Achievement (RoA) is rather more interactive and dynamic. It also involves stating objectives, but these should be discussed and negotiated with the student. Dialogue with the students should include reflections on their attainment, and through dialogue, students should come to accept more responsibility for their own learning. The content of the RoA is also wider than the narrowly academic: it is an attempt to provide more comprehensive, constructive and meaningful records of students' achievement in school, emanating from an era in which public examinations were aimed only at the top 60 per cent of the ability range. 'Profiling' is the procedure in which students and teachers jointly construct an assessment record over a wide range of academic and personal objectives. The RoA is the summative document which results from the profiling process and which students have when they leave school or college. This is sometimes known as descriptive reporting or assessment, and the limitation on it as far as accountability or evaluative procedures are concerned, is that the descriptions are not amenable to numerical or grade-based summarizing. Indeed the proponents of RoA would be against such a move since modifying the summative document to produce quantitative descriptors would jeopardize the nature of the profiling process and the centrality of the formative, teacher–student interaction.

RoAs have been essentially a grass-roots development, mostly at secondary level. In 1984 the government said that it was committed to RoAs for all school leavers by the end of that decade. In 1990 the DES regulations on reporting student achievements were called Records of Achievement, but the requirement was simply for a document of record, not for the profiling process which leads up to it. This process is not forbidden: indeed the regulations state that what is being legislated for is the minimum and that good practice will suggest more. This good practice is, however, time-consuming and given the range of legally required activities it is not clear to what extent the full RoA process will survive. From 1993 all school leavers are required to be given a national Record of Achievement which will include information on qualifications, evidence of skills, attendance rate, success in non-academic spheres and a personal statement by the student.

One problem raised by the introduction of SATs into the national-assessment programme at age 7 was that of comparability. The administration of SATs is quite different from that of standardized tests: in the SATs the most important consideration is that students should understand what is expected of them. Thus there was no restriction on what was said, or on the use of the skills of another adult who was normally present in the classroom. There was no restriction on non-linguistic methods of presentation, there was no limit on students working in whatever language or combination of languages they normally use in mathematics or science. However, students were not allowed to explain tasks to each other nor could children whose mother tongue is not English have the English tasks explained to them in their mother tongue.

Standardization of these assessments was therefore enormously problematic and this raises problems of interpretation. Instructions to teachers were not specific beyond making certain that the child understood the task. Whilst this is, of course, entirely appropriate for assessing very young children the lack of standardized introduction for the assessment tasks meant that there was great variation across teachers and also between administrations by the same teacher. In addition, the statements of attainment are not sufficiently clear to allow teachers to make unambiguous judgments about performance; the criteria in this criterion-referenced assessment system were in many cases not specific enough for assessment purposes. This lack of reliability, in assessment terms, means that any use of results for comparability or accountability purposes is highly suspect.

A further issue was that of manageability, and this derives from the enhanced validity of the tasks. The 1991 SATs for 7-year-olds were by the large performance assessments. For example, multiplication, subtraction and addition were assessed through children throwing dice as in a game and having to add or multiply the numbers thrown on the dice; floating and sinking in science was assessed through a practical task in which the children were provided with a range of objects and a large tank of water. The children had to predict which objects would float or sink and try and develop a hypothesis (since it could take a week or more to assess a whole class of children on this particular task at one point in the summer term every infant school classroom could be seen to be full of water, waterlogged objects and rotting pieces of fruit: all the children were reported to have enjoyed it!); at level 2 reading was assessed by children reading aloud from a book chosen from a range of good children's story books (the list of twenty story books to be used at this level was published first in a national newspaper; within a week all the books were out of stock from bookshops); they were assessed by their teachers for fluency as they read and then asked questions when they had finished reading in order to test their comprehension. In addition there were some paper and pencil tasks to be done in maths on an illustrated worksheet and a story to be written in order to assess writing. In the majority of tasks, however, the children did not have to write their answers. Teachers were allowed to help the children produce the written answer e.g., in science, and were allowed to make their own judgments about whether the child understood or was able to do the task in hand. Bilingual children were allowed to have an interpreter for the maths and the science tasks. The tasks were therefore time-consuming but matched the real tasks and activities that we wish children to be able to do better than standardized tests or written exams can.

There is clear evidence that the 1991 KS1 SATs were not particularly reliable (Gipps, 1993); in psychometric terms they sacrificed reliability for content, even construct, validity. In assessment this is no bad thing unless one wishes to use the results for comparability or accountability purposes. This is exactly what the government's requirements for national assessment are: the publication of results and the formation of league tables (a rank order of schools) in order to implement a market model of school choice. For this purpose tests which are highly reliable are needed so that comparisons can be made with confidence. This is essentially the direction in which national assessment (and GCSE) are moving.

Policy Issues

The GCSE with its certificating role is a classic example of a 'high stakes' assessment, and it is clear that it has had an effect on curriculum and pedagogy. The national assessment SATs for England and Wales are also 'high stakes' (since students, schools and possibly teachers will be evaluated on the basis of results) and there is preliminary evidence that the style and content of the early SATs for 7-year-olds have influenced infant teachers' practice (National Foundation for Educational Research, 1992). In both these cases many of the moves are towards what educationists would regard in the main as better practice: a move away from restrictive teaching and learning styles and, at 7, towards more work with small groups of children (Gipps *et al.*, 1992). In both cases also, the central role of the teacher in the assessment process has contributed to their professional development and engagement.

Assessment trends, however, are in the process of reversal: the government is not in favour of coursework assessment, time-consuming performance-based SATs, or teacher assessment dominating at certificating or reporting stages. The move is therefore back towards the domination of traditional examination procedures and paper and pencil exercises with all that this will mean for classroom practice. That said, the traditional examination procedures are not of the multiple-choice type but allow for assessment of extended essay writing and higher-order thinking skills: thus they already involve some performance, or authentic, assessments which the USA is seeking.

The feasibility, and effect, of working to a defined progression of teaching and learning, with its underlying concept of linear progression which is at odds with constructivist models of learning, has yet to be judged. The effect of having high status external assessment in only the core can be predicted, yet the fact that the rest of the curriculum is legislated may soften the effect. It is, however, a significant reversal of the move towards an educational model of assessment, and it is important to ask why this has happened.

Assessment is being used by this administration, as by many others, to gear up the education system, to raise standards and to force accountability on schools. In this climate teachers are not to be trusted as their own evaluators. Neither are 'elaborate, time-consuming' assessment tasks considered appropriate. The formal, unseen examination has served the system well in the past, so the argument goes, and will do so again. It is seen as more objective, reliable and cheaper. It is also felt by many traditionalists that the more open relationship between teacher and student, which is a strength of the RoA movement, for example, is inappropriate.

There are two fundamental issues which, in the case of national assessment, have contributed to this reversal of fortune. The first lies in the TGAT model itself. In the TGAT report there was little mention of standards and how these could be raised by testing, and limited emphasis on accountability procedures. The tone of the report was thus at odds with the political climate within which national curriculum and assessment was introduced. Small wonder then that, as teachers complained of the workload involved in SATs and the low level of standardization became clear, the Prime Minister said the 'SATs' for 1992 would be largely paper and pencil tests, standardized, and capable of being taken by the whole class at once. In addition, the model of assessment is essentially one that is not suited to surveying the performance of *every* student of a particular age group at a certain point in time, particularly given the complex structure of the national curriculum to which it is linked. The national-assessment blueprint thus did not support the administration's requirements. Add to that the apparent lowering of standards in GCSE and the administration clearly felt that it was time to call a halt to these particular educational developments.

The second issue is that the model as it was being articulated simply did not work. Given a complex and detailed criterion-referenced assessment system, it may be possible to require teachers to assess every child on every criterion and to report this four times during their school career, but it is not possible to link this with external, project-type assessment of *every* student on a high proportion of the criteria, at a particular point in the school year. It is simply too time-consuming, and if both the TA and the SATs have to be moderated externally in order to provide for comparability the task becomes even more daunting.

The problem is that the SAT as originally conceived is simply not appropriate for assessing literally hundreds of assessment points: in any case it becomes too time consuming for testing whole age groups of students, particularly at a certain point in time. It is on the other hand ideal to support individual, formative and diagnostic assessment by teachers for their own purposes. Continuous assessment by teachers can be summed up at the end of key stages to give summative information. In the UK, however, we tend to take the view that summative assessment, particularly if it is also to be used for evaluative purposes or for certification and selection, must be taken out of the hands of teachers. Thus teacher assessment is not to be used at the end of key stages because teacher assessment is liable to be unreliable and/or biased. So goes the argument. It is of course true that teachers do need some form of referencing if their standards are to be comparable across the country, which fairness and equity demand. At GCSE and A level, external markers and moderation processes have been developed to deal with this issue and it is widely accepted (though not necessarily on a particularly good basis) that this produces reliable judgments. However, an assessment system which relied on widespread moderation and extended marking when applied to four age groups simultaneously would clearly be unmanageable. And in any case as Linn *et al.* (1991) put it '. . . if great weight is attached to the traditional criteria of efficiency, reliability and comparability of assessments from year to year, the more complex and time-consuming performance-based measures will compare unfavourably with traditional standardised tests' (Linn *et al.*, 1991).

The authors of the TGAT report maintain that their plan has been misinterpreted, hence the problems; but there are, nevertheless, major technical problems inherent in the blueprint (Gipps, 1992). And to suggest that summative assessment could wait until 16 when reporting was required at all four ages was naive, to say the least. What is almost more surprising is why the TGAT report was accepted in the first place, given the political agenda.

Another problem with the original TGAT model was that it suggested that the same system of assessment could serve all required purposes: formative, diagnostic, summative and evaluative. The notion that one programme of assessment could fulfil four functions was always questionable and has been shown to be false: different purposes require different models of assessment and different relationships between teacher and student. Assessment for formative purposes is essentially carried out by the teacher in an informal way, often with no clear conclusions, but the repeated assessment at an informal level allows the teacher to form valid assessments of the student's performance particularly because he or she is able to assess the student in a number of settings and contexts. External assessment for summative and evaluative purposes tends to be one-off and external to the teacher–student relationship. Assessment information collected formatively by teachers, when summarized can be unreliable and if used for the purposes of accountability or quality control is unsuitable; its use for this latter purpose in turn severely impairs its formative role. We knew this already, we have simply had it confirmed by the recent assessment events. It *may* be possible to design one assessment system which measures performance at school level for accountability purposes and at individual student level for selection purposes whilst at the same time supporting the teaching–learning process but we have not yet done it.

The key must be teachers' own assessments across the full range of the curriculum giving due weight to listening, speaking and higher-order process skills. Teachers must be supported in this by the provision of proper training in assessment techniques and materials — rather like our original SATs — which they can take off the shelf and use at their own discretion to support their judgment (see Harlen *et al.*, 1992). Any national or district programme, if the results are to be published or used for comparability purposes, needs to be standardized so that it can offer some reliability. It is likely to have limited validity and will not offer the same scope for supporting teaching, and thus needs to be kept to a minimum and if possible of low significance.

It is vital to resist the imposition of external assessment programmes for accountability purposes which purport to offer high-quality information when they do not, and resist any move to high-stakes testing, particularly if it involves an emphasis on narrow forms of testing, because of its effect on teaching.

Conclusion

There are three lessons to be learnt from recent developments in the UK: good quality assessment is time-consuming and requires commitment; the two general functions of assessment are difficult to reconcile; assessment frameworks which do not support the aims of a powerful administration are unlikely to survive.

The Scottish experience is particularly pertinent here: until 1992 the government did not have a strong base in Scotland; teachers are better organized professionally than in England, and parents have stronger educational rights. The result of teachers' and parents' anxieties over national assessment is that the role of external tests has changed from overriding teachers' assessments to supporting them, since they can be given when teachers decide students are ready. Furthermore, the absence of any requirement to publish school results to enable comparison shows that the Scottish model is weaker on the accountability side and stronger on the professional side. This is in direct contrast to the direction of developments in the rest of the UK.

The difference between the educational body and the political body is not just one of ideology, but also of power. It is, however, the case that enforced change does not always wipe out previous practice. There have been sufficient developments in the UK involving good practice in assessment, with teachers who have been involved in them convinced of their educational value, that it may be possible for these techniques, approaches and attitudes to survive the return to narrow testing practice, with all that this will mean for teaching and learning.

Notes

1 This chapter is based on a review produced for the OECD entitled *Pupil Assessment in the United Kingdom* (Gipps, 1993).
2 In late 1992 the SATs were renamed standard tasks or tests (STs) to distinguish them from the American Scholastic Aptitude Test. In this chapter they are referred to as SATs since that is what they were during the period described.

Chapter 10

Re-forming the Curriculum in New Zealand

Ivan Snook

New Zealand was colonized from Britain and the settlers brought with them the view of schooling current back 'home'. On their arrival, however, they found the Maori, the *tangata whenua* ('people of the land'), firmly in possession of the country (*Aotearoa*). For hundreds of years there had flourished a lively society with a material culture, a subsistence economy, a social system, an artistic tradition and, of course, education in the sense of conscious and successful attempts to hand on various aspects of the culture to the young (Davidson, 1984). Conflicts between the Pakeha (non-Maori) and Maori approaches to education seemed inevitable. Initially, however, the invader triumphed and a school system based on the imported culture was established for both Maori and settler.

In recent years, however, the dominance of the Pakeha in education has been challenged and elements of Maori culture and language have been given a more prominent place in the curriculum. In addition to the Taha Maori (Maori aspects) taught in all schools there are bilingual schools, 'cultural immersion' schools, Kohanga Reo and Kura Kaupapa Maori. These latter are kindergartens and schools organized and maintained by Maori, in which Maori language is the medium of instruction and Maori culture a major focus of study.

The other long-standing conflict relating to the curriculum was that of religion in schools. In 1877, the Colony opted for a system of primary education which was 'free, secular and compulsory'. The Roman Catholic Church found this unacceptable and set up its own system of education which by the middle of the twentieth century was so complete that almost every Catholic child could gain a full primary and secondary education at Catholic schools, staffed almost entirely by members of religious orders. Following the 1975 Conditional Integration Act, all Catholic schools became 'integrated' within the state system while the Church authorities retained control over the curriculum in relation to the schools' 'special character'.

Some Protestant schools were also set up after 1877 but the Protestant churches attacked the 'secular clause' directly and campaigned consistently to have religion included in the school curriculum. In this they were opposed by the Catholic Church (just as the Catholic claim for 'state aid' was vigorously opposed by Protestant denominations). They were unsuccessful in securing a place for religion in the official curriculum of the state school but, by the use of legal 'loopholes' and minor legislative changes, a short period of religion teaching each week is possible in state schools.

Apart from these two issues — Maori language and culture and religious education — the curriculum of New Zealand schools has not been seriously contested. In the latter part of the nineteenth century there was debate about the proper education for girls and in the early years of this century attempts were made to introduce technical subjects into the classical and scientific curriculum of the secondary schools. In fact, the aims and curriculum of the secondary schools remained basically unchanged and not until the 1940s was there really substantial change in the clientele and the curriculum: for over seventy years the secondary school remained as a 'preparatory' school through which students would gain entry to the university.

Even the advent of the technical high schools did not have the desired effect. They were founded in 1905 to provide a more relevant education for students not preparing for university careers. Yet from the outset, their aim was not as vocational as the name suggests: 'In other countries a technical school is typically a trade school serving the needs of a single industry or group of industries. New Zealand conditions have always been hostile to the development of this sort of institution' (Cumming and Cumming, 1978, p. 123). Unlike the traditional secondary schools they were, however, co-educational and from their foundation until the 1930s they offered pre-vocational training (in agricultural, industrial, commercial, and domestic skills). In addition, these schools provided an academic course for those heading for university and so became more and more similar to the ordinary secondary schools. The technical schools soon vanished in substance and, eventually, in name but the secondary system as a whole was soon to undergo a massive reorganization of aims and curriculum.

In 1936 the newly elected Labour Government abolished the proficiency examination at the end of primary school and a few years later raised the school-leaving age to 15. This ensured that, as McIlraith put it at the time, 'the doors of every secondary school . . . are open' (Cumming and Cumming, 1978, p. 257). The influx of students required a substantial re-examination of the curriculum, and the Thomas Committee (1942) achieved a major reorganization involving a 'common core': physical education, English, social studies, general science, mathematics, music, art and craft. Students who completed a three-year course in these and certain optional studies could present themselves for the School Certificate examination which became and remains today (though not without much criticism) the main national examination faced by secondary students.

The primary-school curriculum had been quite broad all along. When C.E. Beeby became Director General under the first Labour Government, he instituted a review of the primary-school curriculum, subject by subject. The review took ten years and involved widespread consultation with teachers at all levels (Beeby, 1992, pp. 138–9). This became a prominent and important part of syllabus development in New Zealand so that while the education system was very centralized and the curriculum laid down, the profession in the main identified with the content of the syllabus.

From time to time, however, the school curriculum became the symbolic focus of wider political discontent. This manifested itself in the talk of 'declining standards', 'basics and frills' and 'social engineering'. During the period of the third Labour Government (1972–5) a number of official reports advocated more stress on 'social education', 'personal education', 'values education', 'health education' and 'sex education'. These caused a great furore among the public and the reports were strongly criticized by some church groups and the business community.

Under the Muldoon government, the Minister of Education (Mr Merv Wellington) conducted a strong personal campaign to use the school curriculum to facilitate high 'standards' in the 'basics' and promote 'traditional values'. By 1984, he was ready to act and a new curriculum was produced for implementation in 1985. The key elements of the new curriculum were:

- A rigid time allocation to all the 'basic' subjects at all levels from new entrants to Form 5.
- A renewed stress on the socializing aspects of schooling ('social responsibility', 'national pride', 'work habits', and so on) and a downplaying of the themes of personal development, and individual autonomy.
- A cautious attitude concerning Maori culture, multi-cultural education, social studies, economic studies, computer education and career education.

Unfortunately for Mr Wellington's curriculum the government was defeated at the 1984 election and Mr Russell Marshall became Minister of Education in the fourth Labour Government. His educational philosophy was a liberal-progressive one and he made significant changes to the examinations and qualification system of the secondary school. He then turned his attention to the school curriculum more directly and set up his own curriculum review which, predictably, produced the sort of vaguely progressivist document typical of Labour administrations. As a result of this, the Department produced a draft National Curriculum Statement for New Zealand schools (1988). This covered the whole system from new entrants (5-year-olds) to senior-secondary classes. It was meant to be a 'draft curriculum framework' within which schools could plan their programmes. Like recent documents in other countries, it divided the curriculum into eight areas: culture and heritage; language; creative and aesthetic development; mathematics; practical abilities; living in society; science, technology and environment; health and well-being. But the real 'reforms' of education were to come from quite a different direction.

The first three years of Labour's time in office (1984–7) had been devoted to major restructuring of the economy along monetarist lines. In this context, Russell Marshall's educational programme seemed like a nostalgic rerun of earlier Labour reforms of education. His *Curriculum Review* was strongly criticized by Treasury, now exerting great power over the Minister of Finance and the Government. In the opinion of Treasury the review:

- holds unstated and narrow assumptions as to the nature and purpose of education;
- overlooks issues as to: community and education values and benefits, the relationship between education and the economy and the nature of government assistance;
- does not tackle issues of management and consumer choice. (quoted in Codd, 1990, pp. 194–5)

It was clear that Russell Marshall, Minister of Education and the liberal educators whom he represented were on a collision course with the powerful Treasury and the business interests it spoke for. On the re-election of Labour in 1987, the Prime Minister, David Lange, relieved Marshall of the educational portfolio and took it himself. Even before assuming the position, Lange had been influential in encouraging the setting up of a Taskforce on Educational Administration chaired by Brian Picot, a businessman. On 10 May 1988, its report (The Picot Report) was released with proposals for a radical restructuring of the education system. The report, virtually unchanged, became government policy with the release of *Tomorrow's Schools* on 7 August 1988. In broad terms, the Picot Report proposed that:

1 Each school would become a basic learning unit.
2 Each would be managed by an elected board of trustees to enable a 'partnership between teachers and community'.
3 Each unit would have a 'charter' to define the responsibilities of both school and government. [This was subsequently modified so that the charters became 'undertakings' of the school to the government.]
4 The regional education boards would be abolished.
5 The Department of Education with its wide-ranging responsibilities would be replaced with a ministry charged with giving policy advice through an eight-person policy council (four ministry officials; four lay people). [The policy council did not survive into *Tomorrow's Schools.*]
6 There would be a Parents' Advocacy Council (PAC) and compulsory education forums in all local areas. [Both of these were abolished in the National Government's first year of office.]
7 There would be a single authority to validate qualifications. (The New Zealand Qualifications Authority)

8 Resource groups would be private and free-standing [they were subsequently given the assets of the education board].

9 A Review and Audit Agency separate from the ministry would replace the inspectorate and report to the minister (in principle this could have been a different minister but has in fact been the Minister of Education).

Harvey McQueen, who worked closely with Lange at that time, has interpreted Lange's motivation for us. After the minister had received the Picot Report:

Lange received contradictory advice . . . Some aides and officials recommended caution, it was too big a leap. Others were enthusiastic; unless the change was big and swift it would enable a continuation of the status quo . . . The PM listened to the arguments and for a while kept his cards close to his chest. Then one day he said, 'We need more democracy not less. Picot's for democracy, so am I. Let's go.' (McQueen, 1991, p. 57)

In retrospect, Lange's position was very naive. Writing while Lange was still the minister, Gary McCullough set out several reasons why the Picot proposals were unlikely to achieve Lange's liberal aims. Among other points, McCullough argued:

If past experience in Britain and the United States, and the recent growth of a New Right in New Zealand, are any guide, the radical right will eventually seek to pursue its own interpretation of Picot into the classroom, the curriculum, the teaching force, the NZCER [NZ Council for Educational Research], the Ministry . . . Picot has, thus, the potential for being exploited for more radical and divisive ends. (McCullough, 1990, p. 66)

And so it has turned out to be. The Picot Report and *Tomorrow's Schools* can be read in two ways (and from the outset have been so read). From one point of view, they devolve decision-making to the local community, encourage partnership between parents and teachers, favour democratic decision-making, and promote equity. From another view point, they devolve responsibility while retaining control, encourage divisiveness, make decision-making less democratic and, by promoting choice, reduce equity. While many educators favour the first interpretation, Treasury and the State Services Commission constantly work to the second.

Lange and his Labour successor, Phil Goff, tried to implement *Tomorrow's Schools* in a manner most in line with the liberal interpretation:

• school charters had obligatory sections on equity;
• the (newly named) Education Review Office adopted a cooperative professional stance; and

- a committee on assessment was set up with a broad brief and its report was a judicious blend of proposals to encourage monitoring of performance without encouraging 'league tables' of school-by-school results.

Additionally, it must be noted, the Labour government backed away from extreme monetarist philosophy and, in particular, refused to deregister the labour market. This left teachers less concerned than they might have been about their working conditions and the professional future. In November 1990, however, the Labour government was defeated and the National Party came to office with vague social and economic policies and the slogan 'A Decent Society'.

Ruth Richardson became Minister of Finance. In 1987 she had been the party's spokesperson on education and had demanded that schools join the market economy: she had advocated local control, teacher accountability, decentralized financing ('bulk funding'), national standards of attainment, and parental choice. Her preferred mechanism was the voucher system. Now Minister of Finance, Richardson had the full support of the business world and was completely captive to the Treasury. Dr Lockwood Smith was appointed Minister of Education. His views on education were less well known but he soon showed that he was more than sympathetic to the New-Right agenda. Indeed the three social portfolios (Health, Education, Social Welfare) went to 'true believers' in free-market policies.

Recognizing their advantage, groups such as the Treasury, State Services Commission and Business Round Table intensified their demands for a totally deregulated economy and for a 'user pay' system of education. The Business Round Table set up an educational 'ginger group' called the Education Forum to advocate its policies in education and this it has done most faithfully.

Under National, the workforce has been deregulated by the Employments Contract Act and, in effect, most workers have lost the protection they once had. This is affecting teachers as well as other workers. At the time of writing the primary teachers have been granted a collective contract but all other education-sector negotiators are deadlocked as the State Services Commission refuses to allow collective agreements. For similar reasons, junior doctors in one board area have been on a one-month strike. The proposal of the government to bulk fund teachers' salaries has caused ructions amongst teachers and boards of trustees. Interestingly, the first meeting of the Education Forum was given a Round Table report supportive of bulk funding which was forwarded to the minister. This report saw bulk funding as part of a platform including:

- more monitoring of school performance;
- more competition between public and private schools; and
- de-zoning and voucher-based funding. (Gordon, 1992b, p. 48)

> Salaries bulk funding . . . would provide the final mechanism for the
> production of a genuinely competitive schooling system. Schools
> would compete with each other, both for students and for perform-
> ance in terms of easily specifiable outcomes. (Gordon, 1992b, p. 49)

The present government has put out a new curriculum statement. It is
important and will be discussed below. The point to be made, however, is
that although the 1989 'reforms' were not about the curriculum the forces
behind them do have their eyes on the curriculum and they are likely to have
more effect through initiatives which seem tangential than through the official
curriculum itself.

The National Curriculum

In announcing the document *The National Curriculum of New Zealand* at the
Post Primary Teachers' Association (PPTA) conference in May 1991, the
minister's rhetoric suggested a narrow 'basic curriculum' and his audience
reacted hostilely. The curriculum itself, however, is quite broad — and not all
that different from that produced by Russell Marshall. Phillip Capper, advi-
sory officer of the PPTA, makes the very interesting comment that:

> Lockwood Smith's curriculum is shaping up to have a 'conservative'
> rhetoric and a 'liberal' structure; and indication perhaps that the labels
> generate more heat in public debate than actual differences in curric-
> ulum content. (Capper, 1992, p. 26)

This seems to me to be correct but in terms of my analysis, it to some
extent misses the point. The curriculum — as a document of general policy
— is one thing. How it is interpreted, the environment in which it is implemented and assessed is another. Capper himself indicated that the minister
placed greater weight on the 'achievement initiative' than on the curriculum
on its own. Achievement-based syllabuses in mathematics, science, English
have been produced and, of course, the pedagogical and assessment aspects
rather than the content seem most significant. This view is supported by other
development which will be outlined in relation to the curriculum.

Education and 'Enterprise'

For many years the business world wanted to get its hands more firmly on the
school curriculum. As far back as 1976, the Employers Federation criticized
the Johnson Report for neglecting 'the real world of work'. The enormous
rise in unemployment in recent years has enabled business spokespersons and
politicians to criticize workers for their lack of 'skills' and schools for their

lack of adaptation to the economy. Most of this talk is based on myths and is self-serving (see Gordon and Snook, 1992) but its influence is pervasive. It is fair to say that 'school–industry links' is now a major platform of the government. Early this year, the Prime Minister himself convened a large gathering of educators and industry people, at an 'Education for Enterprise' Conference. An international conference on school–business links was held in Auckland in March 1993, with the principal aim of having conference participants leave with an understanding of the different types of school–business partnerships which they could consider in their own areas. The minister seldom misses an opportunity to exhort schools to get closer to industry.

Educational Review Office

Picot advocated, and *Tomorrow's Schools* authorized, the setting up of an independent department called The Review and Audit Agency. Its function was to 'review institutions through multi-disciplinary teams with expertise in curriculum, financial and management support, equal employment opportunities and equal educational opportunity . . . The regular reviews will be a co-operative endeavour, aimed at helping boards to meet their objectives and review their own performance'. (Picot Report, 1987, p. 21) Professional interests feared an outsider's audit and the Labour government placated them by renaming the agency the Education Review Office (ERO) with personnel from the former inspectorate and other professional agencies. Since 1990, it has conducted reviews of schools which are based on a professional model. Not surprisingly, it has been in the sights of New Right guns.

After leaving ERO untouched for a year after being elected, the National government appointed a new chief executive, Dr Judith Aitken, widely regarded as a supporter of the New Right programme. This appointment was highly significant, and clearly signalled a change of philosophy. ERO's annual report to 30 June, 1992 states:

> The Office . . . expects to see reflected in school-based curricular and educational programmes clear awareness of New Zealand's increasing exposure to global market influences and broad changes in our international relationships. (ERO, 1992, p. 7)

It also laments that 'The level of school knowledge about the achievement of students is generally disappointing'. (ibid., p. 9)

From 1 July 1992, the ERO has two distinct functions which will involve two separate reviews. (These may be carried out separately or in conjunction with each other.) The first is the 'assurance audit'. 'Assurance audits report on the extent to which a school or centre is meeting the terms of the contract it has with the Crown to provide education . . . Areas of performance include the institution's management and curriculum practices'. The second is the 'effectiveness review'. 'The effectiveness review focuses on the students (as opposed to the contract) and their achievement — both standards and progress. The review evaluates the range of factors in a school which contribute to, or hinder students' educational achievements, including school management and curriculum factors. It is therefore assessing the effectiveness of a school in terms of the achievement of its students' (Mission Statement of ERO, August 1992).

Clearly, more rigorous assessment of students is on the agenda — as the New Right has always demanded. Indeed, there is legislation before Parliament to ensure this. The Public Finance No. 3 Bill requires the Minister of Education to provide annually a report on the performance of the schools' sector in the preceding financial year. This report must contain information on:

(a)   The performance of the school's sector in the supply of outputs:

(b)   The management performance in the schools' sector . . .

(c)   *The effectiveness of the schools' sector in terms of educational achievement'.* [My emphasis]

This is all very curious. After his initial enthusiasm for national assessment, the Minister seems in his public statements to have accepted the view that national standards can be ensured and individual achievement monitored without the check points and between school comparisons favoured by the New Right. Yet, the Bill seems to cut across his position. That this clause appears in a Public Finance Bill under the control of the Minister of Finance and administered by Treasury makes the mystery deeper. Sinister interpretations suggest themselves. Will the Minister of Education and Ministry of Education be sidelined while the Minister of Finance (she of voucher fame) and the Treasury assume responsibility for the assessment of students?

New Zealand Qualifications Authority

The 1990 Education Amendment Act instituted a new statutory body which is charged with developing a framework for national qualification in secondary schools and post-school 'education and training'. It can authorize degrees outside of the universities (and in less than two years has validated some twenty-eight new degrees) and it can grant the title of 'university' to an institution not so designated. (It has done so in the case of a small business school. This is the subject of a court case brought by the Vice Chancellors' Committee which retains statutory rights over university degrees. In its turn The New Zealand Qualifications Authority may seek a revision of the Act to give it more control over universities.)

In March 1991, NZQA produced a discussion document entitled *Designing the Framework*. It proposed a system whereby

- qualifications would be developed around 'units of learning'; and
- learners would be assessed against national standards.

The framework sets out eight levels of learning, devised from those proposed by the National Training Board in Australia. (Unlike similar schemes in UK or Europe the NZ scheme includes both vocational and academic education.) Typically levels 1–4 will be completed at secondary school; levels 5–8 post-school (but the levels are intended to be flexible).

It is anticipated that:

- levels will be defined in all subjects in standards-based terms;
- units will be provided in modular form and will be 'interchangeable' within and between institutions;
- some existing qualifications will be phased out.

(The School Certificate will — illogically — remain because its retention as an examination-based credential is government policy.)

While the NZQA is not directly involved below the senior secondary school it is obvious that it will have an influence on the curriculum of the senior school. As has been obvious in the past this will tend to feed down the school, influencing curriculum at earlier stages. There will be strong pressure for 'skills' to be stressed rather than abstract understanding and, once again, business links will be pervasive since, of course, the major point of qualifications is to certify people as suitable for jobs. An express aim of the NZQA is to blur or even deny distinction between education and training. This in turn must affect curricula.

Conclusion

New Zealand has not had a tradition of curriculum theorizing. A sturdy pragmatism, liberal sentiment, and political slogans have served in its place. It is, then, an irony that when some degree of theorizing began in the 1980s, it was quickly submerged by a 'market' approach to education which may have rendered it nugatory.

In retrospect, Mr Wellington's 'conservative' curriculum, liberally interpreted, would have served the system satisfactorily. Similarly, Mr Marshall's 'liberal' curriculum, given a bit of pedagogical backbone would have worked quite well. And Dr Smith's curriculum might be 'all things to all people' — conservative rhetoric and liberal structure. But these abstract statements are not where the action is any more — if it ever was. Colin McGeorge, one of New Zealand's leading scholars of Church–State relations in education in New Zealand, once remarked that there is more religious education in NZ schools, where it is forbidden, than in British schools where it is compulsory! A profound educational truth may be buried here.

Without overgeneralizing, however, it is plausible to suggest that the school curriculum in New Zealand is shortly to face contestation as dramatic as that which faced school administration in the late 1980s — and for the same reason. There are those who wish schools to be places where the young learn to develop themselves as persons and prepare to fulfil themselves as citizens. There are others who see schools as serving the needs of the economy and preparing workers for industry. For the past few years this battle has been fought over the administration of schools; over the next few it may be fought over the curriculum.

In her 1991 Budget speech, the Minister of Finance stated:

> Tonight's announcements are not just about how much money the government will spend this year and how much it will take in tax. They are about the sort of society we will become a generation into the future. (Richardson, 1991, p. 1)

With this agenda, it is not surprising that the New Zealand government and the business interests it serves have targeted education as a way of achieving their goals. No doubt — as in the past — other interest groups will in due course set up alternative visions of the nation's future. Inevitably schools will play some part in creating that future. It would be pleasing, however, to believe that above all else they will develop a generation of people who can think critically and creatively about themselves and their world and be able to sensitively transform both. This, after all, is what the curriculum should be about.

Epilogue

Epilogue: Implementing Change in the 1990s: Paradigms, Practices and Possibilities

Gene E. Hall and David S.G. Carter

In spite of the huge, and continuing, expenditure of resources in time, money and human endeavour, recorded in an enormous body of literature on educational change, it has not been noteworthy to date in bringing about changes of the order and scale required to have a systemic and durable impact on school systems and classroom practice. Generally, the history of educational reform is one in which, with a few notable exceptions, we have persisted with the use of change models and strategies even when they have been shown at best to be ineffective (Cuban, 1990. This in spite of a steady accumulation of knowledge about the change process over the course of the last forty years. Cuban also notes the inherently intractable nature of schools and schooling, and is at pains to point out how little of the extensive reforms have made it past the classroom door (Cuban, 1988). In the current wave of educational reform in the USA, Sarason (1990) argues that once again the reform efforts are unlikely to succeed since they are reminiscent in form and substance of their many predecessors.

There is an inherent danger in the current round of educational reform that, if it becomes driven by the urge for scientific management, and from an 'over the shoulder' perspective, organizational and system structures may drive curriculum and instructional design when in fact the organization in which a curriculum is to be implemented *is part of the design itself* (Carter, 1993a). At this juncture it appears that a paradigm shift in thinking is needed.

In the following pages we return to the policy-to-practice continuum (see Chapter 7) and make some normative statements regarding what is needed in order to fully operationalize this paradigm. At source it is underpinned by a systems perspective in which education is regarded as an open system, linked to other systems through feedback loops, enjoys different ways of functioning and is amenable to analysis at different scales of resolution — all of which are interrelated. The ideal is to shorten the length of the continuum which occurs when all actors in the system enjoy a more holistic view of its dynamics and participate in its operation in an integrative fashion.

Putting this into effect will, in large measure, allow for a more inclusive framework for managing the change process than we have been able to apply coherently to date. The linearity suggested by policy-into-practice, while it takes us some distance, is overshadowed by a further shift. This is likely to occur when a new generation of information technology interacts with informed minds cooperating within an ecological paradigm to realize the ideal of the learning community. The creation of information-rich environments allowing all stakeholders in the change process to have equal access to information which is both an empowering and power-equalizing phenomenon can help us break the lock of inertia and tradition when implementing change.

Implicit to this view is a vision based on a web or network of interacting relationships that exists between policy developers, designers and implementors, irrespective of their separate roles and functions in districts, schools and classrooms linked by instant access to information and information flows ordinarily lost or treated as 'noise' in the system. Thus, later in this chapter, the implications of information management for the transformation of classrooms, schools and systems are spelled out and we then conclude with some suggestions for redirecting the research effort and speculate on the need for innovative practice that will foster the development of schools as learning communities.

From Policy to Practice — Once More into . . .

In Chapter 7 a number of implications for policy, development, and implementation in the 1990s are presented by Gene Hall and these are revisited in the following section. The basic theme to be developed here is that 'we all have to work together'. All need to develop a holistic view of the system and work with an approach that makes us interactive partners in the educational change process. Policy makers, researchers, developers, teachers, and administrators all need to work on the same plane.

The 'Status' of Policy Needs to be Balanced with the 'Core' of Implementation

Darling-Hammond (1990) pointed out in a recent article, we have to start reaching across the abyss. In her retrospective, Milbrey McLaughlin (1990) offered an olive branch too. We need to share a holistic perspective. We need to view all of us as being partners in the same user system. The playing surface needs to shift from images of verticalness, top–bottom, up–down, and the innuendo of there being something elite about working with policy, and something lowly about working with practitioners. The entire playing surface needs to become a horizontal plane with all of us at the same level engaged in ongoing collegial exchange. Note that this is a challenge for researchers too. Rather than limiting the focus of studies to the policy end, or the implementation end, studies need to be of the complete policy–practice continuum such as that discussed by Lowham in the companion volume.

Another Way of Saying this is: There Needs to be Trust

Policy persons have to start *understanding* the teacher's role, then they can trust more, and perhaps then they will talk to each other and their contract researchers a little *less* and to practitioners *more*. Teachers at the same time have to develop a larger world view than their classroom. They need to begin to understand and see their school and community as being part of the continuum, then they can begin to understand what the expressed concerns of policy makers and others are about. Developers have to broaden their perspectives by spending more time in schools and listening more to teachers and principals. At some point we all have to develop understandings of the perspectives of the others. In this way the policy–practice continuum will become shorter and the degree of understanding of participants at all points along the continuum will become greater.

There Needs to be a More Systemic View of How the Change Process Works

Change happens in individual classrooms, schools change, so do school districts and states. One of the failures of understanding about implementation twenty years ago was that we did not accept the reality that a school does not change until each individual teacher within the school successfully implements the innovation. The only way that classroom effects can accumulate to be school effects is if there is use of the innovation in each classroom. To look at the school as a whole, first one needs to look at the use of the innovation by each teacher. Each teacher individually can have an effect. The accumulation of the activities of teachers and their effects aggregate and compound to become school effects. Then, of course, as one looks at a district or a state the multiple school and districts effects can accumulate. This is shown diagrammatically in Figure 11.1. The key building block for all of this, however, is what happens in each classroom. As far away as the individual classroom can be from the policy maker and curriculum developer, it is essential for policy makers and curriculum developers to do a much better job of understanding how important the other ends of the continuum are and, especially, how the world is constructed from the point of view of individual teachers. For example, the current trend of policy makers to commission the development of more and 'better' tests of effects, without doing anything to address directly classroom practice will continue to yield poor results. Unless classroom and school practices change, the most sensitive tests possible will measure no positive changes in outcomes.

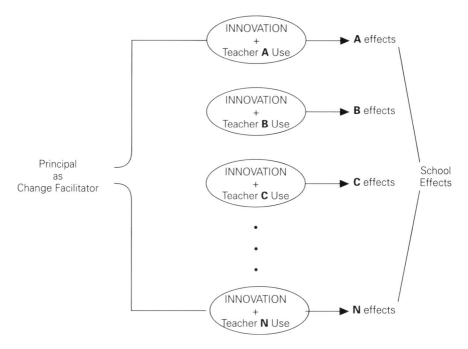

Figure 11.1: Accumulating User System Effects

So How Do We Do This in the 1990s?

At this point an array of ideas have been touched on, some of which are more segmented than may be useful. It might be worthwhile, therefore, to list some guiding principles and parameters set for those of us who are involved in trying to bring about change processes in the 1990s. Hopefully, these are reflective of the horizontal plane perspective, the holistic systemic perspective, and with the construction of meaning that is addressed in this chapter.

Deregulate

There must be fewer regulations, rules and policy mandates. If we go back to the metaphor of the tunnel and think of each vehicle travelling through that tunnel as representing an innovation (see Chapter 7, p. 102), currently, the vehicles are bumper to bumper. At this point the large number of cars, motorcycles, bicycles, hitchhikers, eighteen wheelers (i.e., lorries) and other types of vehicles, including a number of M-1 tanks, are clogging the tunnel. Most of these initiatives are travelling from the policy end of the tunnel towards the practitioner end. The system effect at this time is gridlock. There is such a jam-up of policy initiatives, mandates, rules and regulations, that teachers in classrooms have become immune to, and isolated from, the outside realities. This traffic jam of innovations must be broken. Breaking the jam can only be accomplished by reducing the number of policies, rules and regulations, and adjusting others to be more responsive to school-based realities.

Shift the Form of Policy

Currently, too many policies are written from the point of view of prescribing a particular practice or mechanism. Some of us have talked about this as setting engineering design versus function specifications. Policy needs to shift from setting some sort of implementation requirements, such as how many minutes a subject will be taught, to stating goals or performance outcomes, such as our students need to learn to be cooperative problem solvers. The mechanism to achieve a desired policy goal is best determined by developers and the professionals in schools, rather than through prescribing a specific approach in law. Another alarming part of this issue, as well as a contributor to our traffic jam, is that we are legislating more and more policies that quickly become outdated. As experience and research lead to new understandings, the 'old' policies remain in place! They are still around two and three decades later, although they may no longer be appropriate for practice. The players are so constrained that it is impossible to move.

Develop Multivariate Approaches

Currently policy initiatives deal with a single variable in isolation of the rest of the system. We live in a multivariate world; when one thing is changed, that has *systemic* effects on a number of other things. For example, the lengthening of the class day affects co-curricular activities, the scheduling of buses, the salary of teachers, the schedule for cleaning the classrooms, etc. As we move further into the 1990s, we need to think more systemically and in multivariate ways about our approaches to change. The plucking out of single-variable solutions in a multivariate world is naive at best, punitive to practitioners, and most likely harmful to children.

Equal Support for Implementation

Historically the development phase of an innovation received the bulk of the resources, time, and attention. In order for implementation to be successful, there must be a balance in the allocation of resources, time, and attention. Development and implementation must be recognized and supported in terms of what they really require and cost. This will mean, of necessity, that we cannot do as much. However, by now the track record is clear that trying to do everything at once has resulted in little being accomplished. If we shift in the way we think about policy, and its importance by acknowledging the criticality of implementation, then we will have to develop more systemic ways of approaching change. When we do, we will be able to think more dramatically and differently about what schools will need to be like for the Twenty-first Century.

Imagine on a Large Scale

At the present time we tend to think in too limited ways about change and improvement of schools. The last decade ended with a so-called 'reform movement'. This decade began with a 'restructuring movement'. In neither case have we really broken the structures and limitations of our traditional models of schools, and, in the USA, we have kept the worst features of the one-room school house. We have kept the self-contained classroom, with one teacher, thirty children, a chalkboard, four walls, and rows of seats. We have let go multi-age grouping, community involvement, children teaching children, integrated curriculum, etc. An analysis of the various 'movements' in education would indicate a clinging to the worst features of the one-room school house. There is a difference between 'talking', 'tinkering', and 'transforming'.

Too much of the effort in the US emphasizes talking, we are doing very little tinkering, and nearly no transforming. An emerging case of these differences in set breaking can be seen by contrasting the NSTA's chapter *Scope, Sequence, and Coordination of Secondary School Science* drafts with that of *Project 2061*. In the *Scope, Sequence and Coordination* work there is an adherence to traditional subjects (talking?). In *Project 2061* there is a proposal for using major themes or key ideas (tinkering?). Neither group ventures beyond the contemporary boundaries of mathematics and science teaching, for example, to suggest new and different configurations such as the integration of science and mathematics with social studies, or to suggest that instead of reading for reading, curriculum could be organized with reading in the disciplines (transforming?). Exciting examples of transforming curriculum are described in the television series (e.g., 'Connections') by James Burke. During the 1990s it is going to be critical that we stop dabbling and start thinking seriously about different ways of doing schooling. This will require a new level of imagination, an adventuresome nature and a willingness to think in multivariate ways. To get transforming ideas implemented, we would be well advised to look closely at Van den Berg and Vandenberghe's (1983) *Concept of Large Scale Innovations*.

There Needs to be Trust of All by All

This brings us back around to the very important point that has been brought up in several ways. We have to shift from the vertical to the horizontal playing field. There is a gradual increase in awareness, as is reflected in some of the authors cited here, that all of us are in it together. We must begin to trust in each other. Practitioners have to trust policy makers and policy makers have to trust practitioners. It would be nice if both could trust researchers. Curriculum developers are a key bridge to both ends and play an integrative part in the implementation of policy into practice.

In the next section, this is developed further at the interface between social and technological change for implementation and school improvement.

The Transforming Role of Technology in Education

In a recent paper Henry Kelly of the Office of Technology Assessment in the United States made the observation that we do not have even an adequate vocabulary to describe the nature of the huge socio-economic and technological transformation that is underway, the nature of which has been to sharply increase the demand for education (Kelly, 1991). He also notes, with respect to the USA, that the nation's educational system has been slow to react to changes unless they are forced upon it by external demand factors, and that education seems to be isolated from the sources of innovation that have driven productivity growth. Kelly (p. 11) argues that three things are needed to correct this which are located in:

- a source of innovations in teaching and learning strategies;
- an efficient way to communicate these innovations; and
- and an incentive system that rewards productive innovations and quickly eliminates bad ideas.

The significance of the latent power embodied in accessing and using information in education has been developing and accelerating over the course of the last two decades and is well recognized, if not universally addressed, by schools and school systems. Following the shift from industrial-based to technological-based economies, within a global information society, those who can access information, transform information and create information are substantially advantaged by all the indices of success in the post-industrialized state, while those who cannot create and transform information are increasingly dependent on those who can. Over a quarter of a century ago Marshall McCluhan pointed out that new technologies construct a totally new environment and that this radically alters the way we use our senses and thus the way we act and react to things. On this basis, the restructuring that necessarily occurs as a consequence of introducing new technology enters practically every facet of our lives. Changes come, therefore, because of the application of new technologies and it does not matter so much about the details of the content. The medium is the message. The inevitable transition to a computer-based classroom offers major challenges and new opportunities for teaching and learning, empowering us to break the lock of structures and the inertia of tradition that has tended to constrain change managers to accept these as givens in their efforts to reform schools and education systems.

Developments in technology provide the opportunity to improve existing services at the school and system level as well as providing special types of educational services which could exploit the special features of emergent technologies for improvement and change. These are becoming well recognized but still operate in a piecemeal, disjointed and incremental way, rather than functioning in a truly integrative fashion in supporting and managing curriculum, pedagogy and assessment in an information-dependent environment — and thereby changing it to one that is information-rich. The lead time between envisioning the transformation to information-rich environments and their realization in practice, however, is proving to be inordinately long in the area of education which is naturally information-oriented and information-dependent.

The intellectual tools to support school administration and the operation of the curriculum through the type of information management needed to guide and inform data-based decision-making are already becoming available at affordable prices. Sophisticated Instructional Management Systems (IMS's) which combine administrative functions with a range of others that lie at the heart of schooling, such as curriculum development, teaching, evaluation and assessment, allow for the formation of the information-rich environments with the sort of transformative potential mentioned above (Carter, in press).

Information Overload is a Health Hazard

Creating a curriculum now and for the next century requires us to think about the transformation of schools in seeking justifiable ends based on a vision of the future or alternative futures that we currently hold. The potential use of technology to assist in realizing alternative futures in education seems to have been addressed in a somewhat fragmentary manner in debates concerning current educational reforms. While not wishing to underplay the complexities involved in managing the change process, or to presume that information management is an exclusive consideration in school improvement and change, a number of indicators suggest that information overload is likely to be a health hazard to those who manage and populate schools in the process of their transformation. Diagnosis and treatment *requires* the application of new information technology to bring the current overload back to manageable and human proportions so that relevant and timely information, affecting a particular issue or problem of immediate practical concern, can be utilized in arriving at decisions on behalf of students (Carter and Burger, 1994).

There are two ways of using technology to achieve 'information-rich' environments. One is for the purpose of *automating*: the other for *informing*. While there are some who clearly seek to use technology for the former purpose, it tends to become mechanistic and to isolate the human element from the process itself. Automating then is *not* a satisfactory means for supporting teachers and administrators and for educational problem-solving. To 'informate', however, is to empower educators as professionals. It is in this context that instructional leaders can work with staff in order to resolve the question of what information has to be readily available and easily accessible for them to both understand and execute certain educational processes and curricular events.

From the viewpoint of the practitioner charged with the implementation of change and innovation the swamping effects of extensive information provision following in the wake of centrally driven reform efforts, has, in fact, resulted in a bottleneck, militating against the intentions of change planners, rather than acting in support of the change process. The latent power of technology to assist in reducing information overload seems to be conspicuously absent in much of the contemporary debate about effecting the reform and restructuring of schools and education systems. Where statements about the nature and role of technology *do* feature in the management of teaching and learning, they tend to be focused on the outcomes of the educational process rather than being conceived in terms of the process itself.

The computer serves as a contemporary eolith in magnifying human capacities, and, through its intelligent use to aid thinking about their professional practice, teachers, curriculum developers and administrators may retain more of a sense of control over the side effects of information overload which seemingly envelop them in order to concentrate on managing and facilitating the change process itself. At the school level, for example, information-management systems facilitate the design, development, evolution and alignment of curricula. They provide the means for monitoring which curriculum elements are included in daily lesson plans; student-grouping practices; 'at risk' students; the development of teacher-made learning materials; the management of material resources; the configuration of assessment programmes across different time spans and subject areas, and curriculum alignment to external references, benchmarks and standards on a continuous, routine and substantially unobtrusive basis.

Through the total integration of *all* school functions they represent a marked departure from those Management Information Systems (MISs) currently used essentially for administrative regulation and accessible only to a restricted range of administrative staff. In this regard, it is useful to distinguish between technology specifically designed for educational tasks, such as Computer Assisted Instruction (CAI) packages, and the use of technology to make education possible. Information-management technology referred to here is a case of the latter.

Designing and developing curricula in contemporary and future-oriented educational environments requires not only thinking about how to do things better, but also how to do them differently in realizing alternative futures. This implies a reconceptualization of current practice in the light of past experience and accumulated understanding about the change process itself, but in so doing, the complexity and difficulties attendant to realizing this end should not be underestimated. Fullan notes:

> The process of educational change in modern society is so complex that the greatest initial need is to comprehend its dynamics. Paradoxically, the road to understanding complex social phenomena is through simple and concrete explanations since the main criterion for *understood complexity* is the extent to which it is meaningful. (Fullan, 1991, p. 16)

This is of fundamental importance in seeking educationally justifiable ends based on a vision of the future or alternative futures that we now hold. Many of the recent reforms have spawned an immense amount of information, codified in policy documents, reports, guidelines syllabuses, texts and multi-media formats, which, in sum, has far exceeded human capacities to read, let alone implement on the sort of time scale that change managers have sought. Bringing information attendant to the change process within the ambit of human capacities has been elusive to date with much of it being regarded as 'noise' and simply ignored at the level of the school and classroom (Carter, 1986; Carter and Hacker, 1988). Where and when this has occurred the basic criterion of 'understood complexity' has not been met.

Suggestions for Research on Implementation in the 1990s

Without any claims for comprehensiveness a number of trends and themes, developed elsewhere in this book, suggest areas where more research is needed in the light of our current understanding of the change process, providing both potential insights and promising lines of inquiry.

Unresearched: One Big Change versus Many Little Changes

Although there is a great deal of strongly held opinion, we have little systematic data about the relative merits of launching one major change versus a steady stream of little changes. Some will argue that little changes are less disrupting and gradually accumulate in effects. Others will argue that nothing gets accomplished, or little really changes, when you approach change in small steps and that the only way to succeed is to have large upheavals. Scholars and advocates can be found on both sides of this issue; however, we have no systematic analyses and study of the comparison. As with most questions this one will probably not have a dichotomous answer, once again the answer will probably depend on the local context.

Analysis of Implementation Success: European versus US Educational Policy Initiatives

Reference has been made, in Chapter 7, to the differences in policy approach to educational change in some European countries, notably The Netherlands and Belgium. To push this a little further, it appears that these European countries not only approach their change efforts with a different time perspective (i.e., eight to ten years versus the US one to two years), the design and architecture of the policy initiatives are different. In the US, educational-policy initiatives tend to be undefined sloganized processes, such as 'career ladder', 'longer school year', 'mainstreaming', 'testing', 'choice', 'reform', 'alternative certification', 'standards', 'restructuring', and 'systemic reform'. Each of these initiatives offers few clear descriptions of what would go on in schools, and there is little explanation of the causal linkage between the labelled innovation(s) and the desired effects. Many US policy initiatives represent open-ended exclamations with little follow-through or grounding in practice. Many do not provide tangible mechanisms or structures for doing something at the school and classroom sites.

The European-policy initiatives provide more of an architecture or structure for doing something different in schools. For example, in the Renewed Primary School initiative in Belgium, the change effort entails merging the kindergarten classroom with the primary-grade classrooms and the development of a smoother transition from the child's point of view. In this initiative, the schools have had to shift their expectations in curriculum, roles of adults, and children. A set of outside change facilitators have been hired and trained to support schools in accomplishing this structural shift. A similar set of policy statements, support mechanisms, and architecture has been put into place around the MAVO project and the Relatively Autonomous Secondary Schools in The Netherlands. In each of these initiatives the change architecture is described in policy *and* supports. There is a multi-year time line. External-change facilitators are prepared and put into place to help school staffs in implementing the new approach. Researchers are contracted to analyse and inform the ongoing process. There is contracted evaluation of the policy and its implementation during the *life* of the initiative with the study findings being used by policy and proactive participants.

In contrast, US policies tend to proclaim a more open-ended and sloganized change, without local site operational definition, and without putting into place specialized implementation support for *all* sites. The change itself is not clear, implementation is not supported, and the systemic connections are not addressed. Factors such as external-change facilitators, multi-year perspective, and shifts in other policies, rules and regulations to accommodate the new initiatives are not made. Rather there is the single variable pronouncement, the setting of a deadline and the assumption that all is done. In addition, there are few if any *in-process* studies to inform policy makers and practitioners. Instead there may be a *post hoc* 'policy study', such as the earlier Rand Change

Agent Study. In general, there are not ongoing instructive exchanges amongst all the players as the process unfolds. One developing exception in the US is the work of Marsh and Odden (1991) who have been conducting implementation studies of various initiatives in California. For this case there is an emerging partnership between the researchers, policy makers, and implementors.

At any rate, the proposal here is that there is an important area of research that could be initiated to examine and contrast the architecture and design of large-scale change educational policy in such countries as The Netherlands and Belgium, in contrast to the nominal policy initiatives here in the US. The form, perspective, intent and process of the policies are strikingly different, and these lead to major differences in implementation processes and outcomes.

The Educational System Does not Change in Lock-step Progression

We need to abandon the implicit assumption/expectation that all teachers, classrooms, and schools will develop as one. We behave as if our expectation is that all the schools in this country will move in a controlled flow, just as spectators do in making the human wave around a football stadium. We should keep in mind, that even with enthusiastic fans, there is an unevenness to the human wave in the football stadium, and often the wave motion is washed out! The same is true with our schools. There are individual differences and individual rates of change, whether we are talking about individual teachers or individual schools. Our change efforts need to take into consideration the individuality of the system. There is no such thing as one uniform massive movement to our schools. There are no indications in history of a tidal wave of change in schools. A combination of policy and implementation research initiatives could be launched to examine more closely how it is that the motion of change in our system of schooling in fact does unfold. This work would be of great help in the shaping of policy, as well as of great assistance to schools as they are involved in the details of implementation.

Some Concluding Thoughts on Innovative Practice

The various chapters in this book and its companion volume have assembled sufficient material to illustrate and provide further insight into the change process at many different levels and from a multiplicity of perspectives. There is an inherent tendency in human nature and agency to seek homeostasis and to resist or otherwise be pessimistic about change. An optimistic view of human nature, recognizes that there *is* something called the change process, which we can discern, anticipate, and, as its phases unfold, facilitate. In so doing, it acknowledges that change, in spite of it increasing workloads and states of anxiety, also provides us with new opportunities for growth and regeneration. To avail ourselves of the opportunities which it affords, however, it must be fully recognized, and acted upon accordingly, *that change is a process which takes time and effort and necessarily makes demands on human and material resources.* Change does not come cheaply!

Generally speaking, there is little argument among professionals that helping people learn, grow, and develop in order to realize their full potential lies at the heart of schooling and is what a good education (and school improvement) is about. How well this is achieved in the context of national goals depends on how well teachers are motivated to work for constant improvement, and are themselves provided with the resources and incentives to grow and develop as learners concerning their own professional practice. Sarason (1990) makes an observation to the effect that if teachers as *learners* do not perceive that the appropriate conditions for their own growth obtain, they cannot create and sustain them for their students. From this point of view, student learning is also a function of teacher learning, development and growth. The exercise of high-quality leadership at all levels in structuring environments in support of schools as learning communities is of paramount importance in achieving this set of conditions viewed dynamically (Carter, Glass and Hord, 1993).

As already asserted in this epilogue, and developed as one of its main themes, the latent power of a new generation of information technology, when allied to human capacities and a vision of the future that we hold, has great transformative potential. Its creative utilization by all concerned with implementation and school improvement may help us break the lock of those constraints that have previously inhibited us in making a significant difference on a scale that is noticeable in its cumulative effects. Realizing this will also require the exercise of high-quality leadership as well as political courage.

In addition to establishing and communicating vision and creating a climate for change, leaders also need to understand what is going on in their organizations, how current practices leverage or inhibit the organization's mission (Carter, Glass and Hord, 1993), and, from an informed base, what changes are most likely to produce the results they are seeking.

As students of their own professional practice, if teachers and other educators in general do not access, interpret and use information requisite and/or related to their own practice; if they do not understand the intimacies and complexities of data they and their clients generate as a matter of course; and if they fail to develop and use professional skills because their actions do not, germinate, emanate and mature in informed environments, it is unlikely that reforms will engage the deep structures of the school in even the most dynamic of school systems. If this dimension of educational reform is not addressed at the level of the practitioner, and backward-mapped where it can be shared on an equal footing with policy makers and developers, the type of reform to which we inevitably gravitate will be that of 'endlessly trying new things'.

References

ADLER, M. (1993) *An Alternative Approach to Parental Choice*, NCE Briefing No. 13.

AINLEY, P. (1988) 'From school to YTS', *Education and Training in England and Wales, 1944–1987*, Milton Keynes, Open University Press.

AMERICAN ASSOCIATION FOR THE ADVANCEMENT OF SCIENCE (1989) *Science for All Americans A Project 2061 Report on Literacy Goals in Science, Mathematics and Technology* (AAAS Publication 89-OIS), Washington, DC, American Association for the Advancement of Science.

ANDRICH, D. (1989) *Upper Secondary Certification and Tertiary Entrance: Review of Upper Secondary Certification and Tertiary Entrance Procedures*, Perth, Western Australia, WA Ministry of Education.

APPLE, M. (1992) 'The politics of official knowledge: Does a National Curriculum make sense', *The Politics of Official Knowledge*, New York, Routledge.

AUSTRALIAN EDUCATION COUNCIL (1987) *Proceedings of the Inaugural Joint Conference of the Australian Education Council and the Education Commission of the States*, Brisbane, Australian Education Council.

AUSTRALIAN EDUCATION COUNCIL (1988) *Mapping the Australian Curriculum*, Canberra, AEC.

AUSTRALIAN EDUCATIONAL REVIEW COMMITTEE (1991) *Young People's Participation in Post-Compulsory Education and Training* (The Finn Report), Australian Government Publishing Service, Canberra.

BAILEY, S.K. (1970) 'The office of education and the Education Act of 1965', in KIRST, M.W. (Ed) *The Politics of Education at the Local, State, and Federal Levels*, Berkeley, CA, McCutchan, pp. 57–383.

BATES, R. (1991) 'Who Owns the Curriculum?', Paper presented to the New Zealand Post Primary Teachers' Association Conference, Christchurch, New Zealand, May.

BEARE, H. (1986) 'Shared meanings about education. The economic paradigm considered', The 1986 Buntine Oration, Joint national conference of ACE and ACEA, Adelaide.

BEEBY, C.E. (1992) *The Biography of an Idea: Beeby on Education*, Wellington, NZCER.

BENNETT, W. (1988) *American Education — Making it Work*, Washington, DC, US Government Printing Office.

BENNETT, S.N., WRAGG, E.C., CARRÉ, C.G. and CARTER, D.S.G. (1992) 'A longitudinal study of primary teachers' competence in, and concerns about, National Curriculum implementation', *Research Papers in Education*, 7, 1, pp. 53–78.

BERGER, P.L. and LUCKMAN, T. (1966) *The Social Construction of Reality*, New York, Doubleday.

BIRCH, I. and SMART, D. (1990) 'Economic rationalism and the politics of education in Australia', in MITCHELL, D.E. and GOERTZ, M.E. (Eds) *Education Politics for the New Century*, London, Falmer Press, pp. 137–51.

BJORK, L.G. (1993, May) 'Effective schools — effective superintendents: The emerging instructional leadership role', *Journal of School Leadership*, 3, 3, pp. 246–59.

BLACK, P. (1992) 'The Shifting Scenery of the National Curriculum', British Association Conference Paper (also reprinted in Chitty and Simon).

BLANDY, R. (1988) 'Reforming Tertiary Education in New Zealand,' Research paper commissioned by the New Zealand Business Roundtable, Wellington.

BLOKKER, B. (1991) *Managing the Change to the 21st Century*, Professional Development Institute, Education Service Center, Region 13, April.

BLOOM, A.S. (1987) *The Closing of the American Mind: How Higher Education has Failed Democracy and Impoverished the Souls of Today's Students*, New York, Simon and Schuster.

BOSTON, J. (1991) 'The theoretical underpinnings of public sector restructuring in New Zealand', in BOSTON, J., MARTIN, J., PALLOT, J. and WALSH, P. (Eds), *Reshaping the State*, Auckland, Oxford University Press.

BOYD, V. (1992) 'Creating a context for change', *Issues . . . About Change*, 2, 2, pp. 1–10.

BOYD, W.L. (1987) 'Public education's last hurrah: Schizophrenia, amnesia, and ignorance in school politics', *Educational Evaluation and Policy Analysis*, 9, 2, pp. 85–100.

BROADFOOT, P. (1985) 'Towards conformity: Educational control and the growth of corporate management in England and France', in LAUGLO, J. and MCLEAN, M. (Eds) *The Control of Education*, London, Heinemann.

BROWN, M. (1992) 'Elaborate nonsense? The muddled tale of SATs in mathematics at Key Stage 3', in GIPPS, C. (Ed), *Developing Assessment for the National Curriculum*, Bedford Way Series, ULIE/Kogan Page.

BUSH, R.N. (1984) Effective staff development, *Making Our Schools More Effective: Proceedings of Three State Conferences*, San Francisco, Far West Laboratory for Educational Research and Development.

BUSHNELL, P. and SCOTT, S. (1988) 'From an economic perspective', in MARTIN, J. and HARPER, J. (Eds), *Devolution and Accountability*, Wellington, GP Books.

CAPPER, P. (1992) 'Curriculum 1991', *New Zealand Annual Review of Education*, 1, pp. 15–27.

CARNOY, M. and LEVIN, H. (1976) *The Limits of Educational Reform*, New York, David McKay Company Inc.

CARRÉ, C. and CARTER, D.S.G. (1990) 'Primary teachers' self-perceptions concerning implementation of the National Curriculum for science in the U.K.', *International Journal of Science Education*, **12**, 4, pp. 327–41.

CARTER, D.S.G. (1986) 'Examining the implementation of a curriculum innovation: A centre periphery example', *Curriculum Perspectives*, **6**, 1, pp. 1–6.

CARTER, D.S.G. (1993a) 'Structural reform and curriculum implementation in an Australian education system', *The International Journal of Educational Reform* **2**, 1, pp. 56–67.

CARTER, D.S.G. (1993b) 'An integrative approach to curriculum management using new information technology', *Education Research and Perspectives*, **20**, 2, pp. 33–45.

CARTER, D.S.G. (In press) 'New information technology and the transformation of schools', *Planning and Changing: An Educational Leadership and Policy Journal*, **25**.

CARTER, D.S.G. and BEDNALL, J. (1986) 'W(h)ither non-sexist curricula? Nine years on . . .', *Educational Research and Perspectives*, **13**, 1, pp. 64–73.

CARTER, D.S.G. and BURGER, M. (1994) 'Curriculum management, instructional leadership and new information technology', *School Organisation*, **14**, 2, pp. 153–68.

CARTER, D.S.G. and HACKER, R.G. (1988) 'A study of the efficacy of a centre-periphery curriculum implementation strategy', *Journal of Curriculum Studies*, **20**, 6, pp. 249–52.

CARTER, D.S.G., GLASS, T. and HORD, S.M. (1993) *Selecting, Preparing and Developing the School District Superintendent*, London, Falmer Press.

CATTELL, D. and NORTON, P. (1987) 'TVEI — is there an effective alternative?' *The Vocational Aspect of Education*, **29**, 102, pp. 9–14.

CHIN, R. and BENNE, K.D. (1969) 'General strategies for effecting change in human systems', in BENNIS, W.G., BENNE, K.D. and CHIN, R. (Eds) *The Planning of Change* (2nd ed.), Holt, Rinehart and Winston.

CHITTY, C. (1988) 'Two models of a national curriculum: Origins and interpretation', in LAWTON, D. and CHITTY, C. (Eds) *The National Curriculum*, London, University of London Institute of Education.

CHITTY, C. (1989) *Towards a New Education System: The Victory of the New Right*, London, Falmer Press.

CHITTY, C. and SIMON, B. (Eds) (1993) *Education Answers Back: Critical Responses to Government Policy*, Lawrence and Wishart.

CHUBB, J.E. and MOE, T.M. (1990) *Politics, Markets and America's Schools*, Brookings Institute, Washington.

CIBULKA, J.G. (1990) 'Educational accountability reforms: Performance information and political power', in FUHRMAN, S. and MALEN, B. (Eds) *The Politics of Curriculum and Testing*, New York, Falmer, pp. 181–201.

CIBULKA, J.G. and KRITEK, W.J. (Eds) (In press) *Connecting Schools, Families, and Communities: Prospects for Educational Reform*, New York, State University of New York, Albany Press.

CLUNE, W. (1993) 'The best path to systemic educational policy: Standard/centralized or differentiated/decentralized', *Educational Evaluation and policy Analysis*, **15**, 3, pp. 233–54.

CODD, J. (1990) 'Education policy and the crisis of the New Zealand state', in MIDDLETON, S., CODD, J. and JONES, A. (Eds) *New Zealand Educational Policy Today: Critical Perspectives*, Wellington, Allen and Unwin.

COLEMAN, J.S., KILGORE, S. and HOFFER, T. (1982) *High School Achievement: Public, Catholic, and Private Schools Compared*, New York, Basic Books.

COMMITTEE ON ECONOMIC DEVELOPMENT (1987) *Children in Need: Investment Strategies for the Educationally Disadvantaged: A Statement*, New York, Research and Policy Committee of the Committee on Economic Development.

COMMONWEALTH SCHOOLS COMMISSION (1987) *In the National Interest: Secondary Education and Youth Policy in Australia*, Canberra, The Commission.

COMMONWEALTH SCHOOLS COMMISSION (1987) *The National Policy for the Education of Girls in Australian Schools*, Canberra, The Commission.

COOMBS, P. (1985) *The World Crisis in Education — The View From the Eighties*, Oxford, Oxford University Press.

COX, C.B. and BOYSON, R. (1975) (Eds) *Black Papers*, London, Dent.

COX, C.B. and DYSON, A.E. (Eds) (1969a) *Fight for Education: A Black Paper*, London, Critical Quarterly Society.

COX, C.B. and DYSON, A.E. (1969b) *Black Paper Two*, London, Critical Quarterly Society.

CRANDALL, D. and ASSOCIATES (1982) *People, Policies, and Practices: Examining the Chain of School Improvement*, Andover, MA, The NETWORK.

CROCROMBE, G., ENRIGHT, M. and PORTER, M. (1991) *Upgrading New Zealand's Competitive Advantage*, Auckland, Oxford University Press.

CROHN, L., HAGANS, R. and OLSON, T.A. (1989) *Building Statewide Commitment to Leadership Development: A Review of the Literature*, Portland, Oregon, Northwest Regional Educational Laboratory.

CROWSON, R.L. and BOYD, W.L. (1993) 'Coordinated services for children: Designing arks for storms and seas unknown', *American Journal of Education*, **101**, 2, pp. 140–79.

CUBAN, L. (1988) 'A fundamental puzzle of school reform', *Phi Delta Kappan*, **70**, 5, pp. 341–4.

CUBAN, L. (1990) 'Reforming again, again and again', *Educational Researcher*, **19**, 1, pp. 3–13.

CUBAN, L. (1990) 'Cycles of history: Equity v. excellence: Why do some reforms persist?', in BACHARACH, S.B. (Ed) *Education Reform: Making Sense of it All*, Boston, Allyn-Bacon, pp. 135–40.

CUMMING, I. and CUMMING, A. (1978) *History of State Education in New Zealand 1840–1975*, Wellington, Pitman.

CURRICULUM DEVELOPMENT CENTRE (1980) *Core Curriculum for Australian Schools*, Canberra, CDC.

CURRICULUM REVIEW (1986) *A Draft Report Prepared by the Committee to Review the Curriculum for Schools*, Wellington, Department of Education.

DALE, R. (1985a) 'Introduction', in DALE, R. (Ed) *Education, Training and Employment*, Oxford, Pergamon Press, pp. 1–8.

DALE, R. (1985b) 'The background and inception of the Technical and Vocational Education Initiative', in DALE, R. (Ed) *Education, Training and Employment*, Oxford, Pergamon Press, pp. 41–56.

DARLING-HAMMOND, L. (1990, Fall) 'Instructional policy into practice: The power of the bottom over the top', *Educational Evaluation and Policy Analysis*, **2**, 3, pp. 339–47.

DARLING-HAMMOND, L. (1993, June) 'Reframing the school reform agenda', *Phi Delta Kappan*, **74**, 10, pp. 753–61.

DATTA, L. (1980) 'Changing times: The study of federal programs supporting educational change and the case for local problem solving', *Teachers College Record*, **2**, 1, pp. 101–16.

DAVIDSON, J. (1984) *The Prehistory of New Zealand*, Auckland, Longman Paul.

DAWKINS, J. (1987) *Skills for Australia*, Canberra, Australian Government Publishing Service.

DAWKINS, J. (1988) *Strengthening Australia's Schools*, Canberra, Australian Government Publishing Service.

DEAL, T.E. and PETERSON, K.D. (1990) *The Principal's Role in Shaping School Culture*, Washington, DC, US Department of Education, OERI.

DEAL, T. and PETERSON, K.D. (1992) 'The principal's role in change: Technical and symbolic aspects of school improvement', Occasional paper, National Center for Effective School Research and Development, Madison, Wisconsin.

DEARING, R. (1993) *The National Curriculum and its Assessment*, Final Report, London, School Curriculum and Assessment Authority.

DEL VALLE, C. (1993) 'From high schools to high skills', *Business Week*, 26 April, pp. 110–2.

DEPARTMENT FOR EDUCATION (1992) *Choice and Diversity*, London, HMSO.

DEPARTMENT FOR EDUCATION (1992) *Education (Individual Students' Achievements) (Information) Regulations*, Circular 14/92 DfE 11/12/92.

DEPARTMENT OF EDUCATION AND SCIENCE (1975) *A Language for Life: The Bullock Report*, London, HMSO.

DEPARTMENT OF EDUCATION AND SCIENCE (1984) *Records of Achievement: A Statement of Policy*, London, HMSO.

DEPARTMENT OF EDUCATION AND SCIENCE (1985) *Better Schools*, London, HMSO.

DEPARTMENT OF EDUCATION AND SCIENCE (1987) *The National Curriculum 5–16: A Consultation Document*, DES/Welsh Office.

DEPARTMENT OF EDUCATION AND SCIENCE (1988) *National Curriculum: Task Group on Assessment and Testing: A Report*, DES/Welsh Office.

DEPARTMENT OF EDUCATION AND SCIENCE (1990) *Records of Achievement*, 10/7/90, Circular 8/90, London, HMSO.

DEPARTMENT OF EDUCATION AND SCIENCE (1990) *ERA 1988: The Education (National Curriculum) (Assessment Arrangements for English Mathematics and Science) Order 1990*, Circular 9/90, 23/7/90.

DEPARTMENT OF EDUCATION AND SCIENCE (1991) *Education and Training for the 21st Century*, Volume 1, London, HMSO.

DEPARTMENT OF EDUCATION AND SCIENCE (1992) *The Parent's Charter: Publication of Information about School Performance in 1992*, Circular 7/92, London, HMSO.

DOUGLAS, R. (1989) 'The Politics of Successful Reform', Paper presented to the Mt. Perelin Society.

DYE, T. (1992) *Understanding Public Policy*, (7th ed.), Englewood Cliffs, NJ, Prentice-Hall.

EDUCATION REVIEW OFFICE (1992) *Annual Report*, Wellington, ERO.

EDUCATION DEPARTMENT OF TASMANIA (1987) *Secondary Education: The Future*, Hobart, The Department of Education.

EDWARDS, D. (1991) 'A study in conflict: Inside the Porter Project', *NZ Listener and TV Times*, September 23, pp. 39–42.

ELTIS, K. (1989) 'The quest for quality in the curriculum', Paper prepared as part of the National Seminar on Improving the Quality of Australian Schools, Melbourne, April 1989.

EMPLOYMENT SKILLS FORMATION COUNCIL (1992) *The Australian Vocational Certificate Training System* (The Carmichael Report), National Board for Employment, Education and Training, Canberra.

EMRICK, J.A., PETERSON, S.M. and AGARWALA-ROGERS, R. (1977) *Evaluation of the National Diffusion Network*, Vol. I and II, Menlo Park, CA, Stanford Research Institute.

FINN, B. (1991) *Young People's Participation in Post-compulsory Education and Training*, Report of the Australian Education Council Review Committee, Canberra, Australian Government Publishing Service.

FINN, B. (1992) *Report of the Committee to Advise the AEC and MOVEET on Employment-Related Key Competencies for Postcompulsory Education and Training*, Canberra, Australian Government Publishing Service.

FOWLER, F. (in press) 'The neo liberal value shift and its implications for federal aid policy under Clinton', *Educational Administration Quarterly*, **31**, 2.

FULLAN, M. (1985, January) 'Change processes and strategies at the local level', *The Elementary School Journal*, **85**, 3, pp. 391–422.

FULLAN, M. (1991) *The New Meaning of Educational Change* (2nd ed.), New York, Teachers College Press.

FULLER, F.F. (1969) 'Concerns of teachers: A developmental conceptualization', *American Educational Research Journal*, **6**, 2, pp. 207–26.

GALLAGHER, J.J. (1967) 'Teacher variation in concept presentation in BSCS curriculum programs', *BSCS Newsletter*, **30**.

GAMBLE, A. (1988) *The Free Economy and the Strong State*, London, Macmillan.

GEORGE, A.A. (1978) *Measuring Self, Task, and Impact Concerns: A Manual for Use of the Teacher Concerns Questionnaire*, Austin, TX, The Research and Development Center for Teacher Education, University of Texas at Austin.

GILMOUR, I. (1992) *Dancing With Dogma: Britain Under Thatcherism*, Simon and Schuster.

GINSBURG, M., COOPER, S., RAGHU, R. and ZEGARRA, H. (1990) 'National and world-system explanations of educational reform', *Comparative Education Review*, **34**, 4, pp. 474–99.

GIPPS, C. (1992) 'National assessment: A research agenda', *British Educational Research Journal*, **18**, 3, pp. 227–86.

GIPPS, C. (1993) 'Pupil Assessment in the United Kingdom', Research working paper for the International Centre for Research on Assessment.

GIPPS, C. (1993) 'Reliability, validity and manageability in large scale performance assessment', in TORRANCE, H. (Ed), *Evaluating Authentic Assessment*, Milton Keynes, Open University Press.

GIPPS, C., McCALLUM, B., McALISTER, S. and BROWN, M. (1992) 'National assessment at 7: Some emerging themes', in GIPPS, C. (Ed) *Developing Assessment for the National Curriculum*, Bedford Way Series, ULIE/Kogan Page.

GIPPS, C. and STOBART, G. (1993) *Assessment: A Teacher's Guide to the Issues*, London, Hodder and Stoughton.

GIROUX, H. (1988) 'Educational reform in the age of Reagan', *The Educational Digest*, September, pp. 3–6.

GLENNERSTER, H. (1991) 'Quasi markets for education?', *Economic Journal*, **101**, pp. 1268–76.

GORDON, L. (1992a) 'The state, devolution and educational reform in New Zealand', *Journal of Education Policy*, **7**, 2, pp. 187–205.

GORDON, L. (1992b) 'The bulk funding of teachers' salaries: A case study in education policy', *New Zealand Annual Review of Education*, **1**, pp. 28–58.

GORDON, L. and CODD, J. (1992) 'Education policy and the changing role of the state', *Delta Studies in Education*, Massey University, pp. 81–98.

GORDON, L. and SNOOK, I. (1992) 'Education, 'skills' and technological change: The politics of the 'new economy', *NZ Journal of Industrial Relations*, **17**, pp. 85–94.

GRAHAM, D. and TYTLER, D. (1993) *A Lesson for Us All: The Making of the National Curriculum*, London, Routledge.

GRUBB, W. (1992) 'Giving high schools an occupational focus', *Educational Leadership*, **49**, 6, pp. 36–43.

GUSFIELD, J.R. (1968) 'Social movements II: The study of social movements', in SILLS, D.L. (Ed) *International Encyclopaedia of the Social Sciences*, New York, Macmillan, pp. 445–52.

GUTHRIE, J., GARMS, W. and PIERCE, L. (1987) *School Finance: The Economics and Politics of Federalism*, Englewood Cliffs, NJ, Prentice-Hall.

HALL, G.E. (1992) 'Characteristics of change facilitator teams: Keys to implementation success', *Educational Research and Perspectives*, **19**, 1, pp. 95–110.

HALL, G.E. and GALLUZZO, G. (1991) 'Site-based decision making: Changing policy into practice', Prepared for the Policy and Planning Center of the Appalachia Educational Laboratory, Charleston, WV.

HALL, G.E. and GEORGE, A.A. (1988) 'Development of a Framework and Measure for Assessing Principal Change Facilitator Style', Paper prepared for the Annual Meeting of the American Educational Research Association, New Orleans LA.

HALL, G.E. and HORD, S.M. (1987) *Change in Schools: Facilitating the Process*, Albany, State University of New York Press.

HALL, G.E. and LOUCKS, S.F. (1977, Summer) 'A developmental model for determining whether the treatment is actually implemented', *American Educational Research Journal*, **4**, 3, pp. 263–76.

HALL, G.E. and LOUCKS, S.F. (1978) *Innovation Configurations: Analyzing the Adaptations of Innovations* (Report No. 3049), Austin, TX, The University of Texas at Austin, Research and Development Center for Teacher Education.

HALL, G.E., LOUCKS, S.F., RUTHERFORD, W.L. and NEWLOVE, B.W. (1975, Spring) 'Levels of use of the innovation: A framework for analyzing innovation adoption', *Journal of Teacher Education*, **26**, 1, pp. 5–9.

HALL, G.E. and RUTHERFORD, W.L. (1976) 'Concerns of teachers about implementing team teaching', *Educational Leadership*, **14**, 3, pp. 227–33.

HALL, G.E., RUTHERFORD, W.L., HORD, S.M. and HULING-AUSTIN, L.L. (1984, February) 'Effects of three principal styles on school improvement', *Educational Leadership*, **I**, 5, pp. 22–9.

HALL, G.E., WALLACE, R.C.J.R. and DOSSETT, W.A. (1973) *A Developmental Conceptualization of the Adoption Process within Educational Institutions* (Report No. 3006), Austin, TX, The University of Texas at Austin, Research and Development Center for Teacher Education (ERIC Document Reproduction Service No. ED 095 126).

HANSARD, (1988) *Debates*, United Kingdom, House of Lords, Vol. 495, pp. 1263–4.

HARLEN, W., GIPPS, C., BROADFOOT, P. and NUTTALL, D. (1992) 'Assessment and the improvement of education', *The Curriculum Journal*, **3**, 3, pp. 215–30.

HAVELOCK, R.G. (1971) *Planning for Innovation Through Dissemination and Utilization of Knowledge*, Ann Arbor, MI, Institute for Social Research, University of Michigan.

HAVILAND, J. (Ed) (1988) *Take Care, Mr Baker!*, London, Fourth Estate.

HAWKE REPORT (1988) *Report of the Working Group on Post-Compulsory Education and Training*, Government Printer, Wellington.

HAYES, C., GRIPPE, P. and HALL, G. (In press) 'Capacity-building for site-based leadership', *Journal of Staff Development*.

HAZEN, R.M. and TREFIL, J. (1990) *Science Matters: Achieving Scientific Literacy*, New York, Doubleday.

HEBERLE, R. (1951) *Social Movements: An Introduction to Political Sociology*, New York, Appleton Smith.

HECK, S., STIEGELBAUER, S.M., HALL, G.E. and LOUCKS, S.F. (1981) *Measuring Innovation Configurations: Procedures and Applications* (Report No. 3108),

Austin, TX, The University of Texas at Austin, Research and Development Center for Teacher Education (ERIC Document Reproduction Service No. ED 204 147).

HILL, P.T., WISE, A.E. and SHAPIRO, L. (1989) *Educational Progress: Cities Mobilize to Improve Their Schools*, Santa Monica, CA, Rand Center for the Study of the Teaching Profession.

HIRSCH, E.D. (1988) *Cultural Literacy: What Every American Needs to Know*, New York, Vintage Books, Random House.

HIRSCH, F. (1977) *Social Limits to Growth*, London, RKP.

HORD, S.M. (1987) *Evaluating Educational Innovation*, London, Croom Helm.

HORD, S.M. (1992) *Facilitative Leadership: The Imperative for Change*, Austin, TX, Southwest Educational Development Laboratory.

HORD, S.M., RUTHERFORD, W.L., HULING-AUSTIN, L.L. and HALL, G.E. (1987) *Taking Charge of Change*, Alexandria, VA, ASCD.

HUBERMAN, M. (1992) 'Critical introduction', in FULLAN, M.S. *Successful School Improvement*, Philadelphia, PA, Open University Press.

HUBERMAN, A.M. and MILES, M. (1986) 'Rethinking the quest for school improvement: Some findings from the DESSI Study', in LIEBERMAN, A. (Ed) *Rethinking School Improvement*, New York, Teachers College Press.

JAMES, R.K. and HALL, G.E. (1981) 'A study of the concerns of science teachers regarding an implementation of ISCS', *Journal of Research in Science Teaching*, **8**, 6, pp. 479–87.

JENNINGS, A. (1992) 'Seeing the wood for the trees: The assessment of science at Key Stage 3', in GIPPS, C. (Ed) *Developing Assessment for the National Curriculum*, Bedford Way Series, ULIE/Kogan Page.

JENNINGS, J. (1987) 'The sputnik of the eighties', *Phi Delta Kappan*, **69**, 2, pp. 104–9.

KALANTZIS, M. and COPE, W. (1987) 'Cultural Differences, Gender Differences: Social Literacy and Inclusive Curriculum', *Curriculum Perspectives*, **7**, 1, pp. 64–9.

KEAT, R. and ABERCROMBIE, N. (Eds) (1991) *Enterprise Culture*, London, Routledge.

KEATING, J. (1993) *Education and Training for 16–18 Year Olds: Some Reflections from Europe*, Canberra, Australian Government Publishing Service.

KELLY, H. (1991) 'Technology and the transformation of American education', *Curriculum Perspectives*, Newsletter Edition, pp. 9–12.

KENNEDY, K.J. (1988) 'The policy context of curriculum reform in Australia in the 1980s', *Australian Journal of Education*, **32**, 3, pp. 357–74.

KENNEDY, K., CUMMING, J. and CATTS, R. (1993) 'Vocational Education in Secondary Schools — A Review of the Literature', Paper prepared for the Curriculum Corporation's Vocational Education in Secondary Schools Project, November.

KINGDON, J. (1984) *Employment Related Competencies: A Proposal for Consultation*, Mayer Committee, Melbourne.

KISSINGER, H.A. (1994) *Diplomacy*, New York, Simon Schuster.

KNIGHT, C. (1990) *The Making of Tory Education Policy in Post-war Britain 1950–1986*, London, Falmer Press.

LAWTON, D. (1989) *Education, Culture and the National Curriculum*, London, Hodder and Stoughton.

LAWTON, D. (1992) *Education and Politics in the 1990s*, London, Falmer Press.

LAWTON, D. (1994) 'The national curriculum and assessment', *Forum*, **36**, 1, pp. 7–8.

LESLEY, B.A. (1993, May) 'Do they hear what we say? Understanding school restructuring initiatives', Texas, *ASCD Newsletter*.

LEVIN, H. and RUMBERGER, R. (1989) 'Education, work and employment: Present issues and future challenges in developed countries, in CAILLODS, F. (Ed) *The Prospects for Educational Planning*, Paris, UNESCO, International Institute for Educational Planning.

LEWIS, A.C. (1993, May) 'Using research to improve Clinton's education bill', *Phi Delta Kappan*, **74**, 9, pp. 670–1.

LINGARD, R. (1991) 'Policy-making for Australian schooling: The new corporate federalism', *Journal of Education Policy*, **6**, 1, pp. 85–90.

LINGARD, R., O'BRIEN, P. and KNIGHT, J. (1993) 'Strengthening Australia's schools through corporate federalism?', *Australian Journal of Education*, **37**, 3, pp. 231–47.

LINN, R., BAKER, E. and DUNBAR, S. (1991) 'Complex, performance-based assessment: Expectations and validation criteria', *Educational Research*, November, pp. 15–21.

LOUCKS, S.F. (1975) 'A study of the relationship between teacher level of use of the innovation of individualized instruction and student achievement', Unpublished Doctoral dissertation, Austin, TX, The University of Texas at Austin.

LOUIS, K.S. and MILES, M.B. (1990) *Improving the Urban High School, What Works and Why*, New York, Teachers College Press.

LOWHAM, J.R. (1994) 'Evolving Intentions of an Education Policy from State Development to Teacher Implementation', Unpublished Doctoral dissertation, Greeley, CO, The University of Northern Colorado.

MACLURE, S. (1988) *Education Re-formed*, London, Hodder and Stoughton.

MACPHERSON, R.J.S. (1993) *Curriculum Perspectives — Newsletter Edition*, November, pp. 31–6.

MALEN, B. and OGAWA, R.T. (1988) 'Professional-patron influence on site-level governance councils: A confounding case study', *Educational Evaluation and Policy Analysis*, **10**, pp. 251–70.

MARGINSON, S. (1991) 'Education after Finn', Address to the Annual Conference of the Australian Teachers Union (ACT Branch), Canberra, 9 November.

MARSH, D.D. and ODDEN, A.R. (Eds) (1991) *Educational Policy Implementation*, New York, State University of New York Press.

MARSHALL, J. (1992) 'Principles and the National Curriculum: Centralised "Development"', Unpublished paper.

MARSHALL, J., PETERS, M. and SMITH, G. (1991) 'The business round table and the privatisation of education: Individualism and the attack on Maori', in MAYER, E. (1992) *Employment Related Key Competencies: A Proposal For Consultation*, Melbourne, The Mayer Committee.

McCREDDIN, R. (1993) 'The draft "student outcome statements" in Western Australia', *Curriculum Perspectives — Newsletter Edition*, November, pp. 28–31.

McCULLOUGH, G. (1990) 'The ideology of educational reform: An historical perspective', in MIDDLETON, S. CODD, J. and JONES, A. (Eds) *New Zealand Educational Policy Today: Critical Perspectives*, Wellington, Allen and Unwin.

McDONNELL, L. and ELMORE, R. (1987) 'Getting the job done: Alternative policy instruments', *Educational Evaluation and Policy Analysis*, **9**, 2, pp. 132–52.

McGAW, B. (1984) *Assessment in Upper Secondary Schools in Western Australia*, Perth, Government Printer.

McLAUGHLIN, M.W. (1987) 'Learning from experience: Lessons from policy implementation', *Educational Evaluation and Policy Analysis*, **9**, 2, pp. 171–8.

McLAUGHLIN, M.W. (1990, December) 'The Rand Change Agent Study Revisited: Macro perspectives and micro realities', *Educational Researcher*, **19**, 9, pp. 11–16.

McLEAN, M. (1988) 'The conservative education policy in comparative perspective: Return to an English golden age or harbinger of international political change?', *British Journal of Education Studies*, **36**, 3, pp. 200–17.

McLURE, S. (1991) *Missing Links: The Challenges to Further Education*, London, Policy Studies Institute.

McQUEEN, H. (1990) *The Ninth Floor: Inside the Prime Minister's Office — a Political Experience*, Auckland, Penguin.

MENDEZ-MORSE, S. (1993, Summer) 'Vision, leadership, and change', *Issues . . . about Change*, **2**, 3, pp. 1–8.

MERRITT, R. and COOMBS, F. (1977) 'Politics and educational reform', *Comparative Educational Review*, **21**, 10, pp. 247–73.

MIDDLEMAS, K. (1979) 'Politics in Industrial Society: The Experience of the British System since 1911', London, Andre Deutsch, cited in SULLIVAN (1988), The political theory of neo-corporatism, in COX, A. and SULLIVAN, N. (Eds) *The Corporate State*, Cambridge, Edward Elgar.

MILLER, P. (1989) 'Historiography of compulsory schooling: What is the problem?', *History of Education*, **18**, 2, pp. 123–44.

MINISTER OF EDUCATION (1988) *Tomorrow's Schools*, Wellington, Government Printer.

MINISTER OF EDUCATION (1991) *Education Policy: Investing in People, Our Greatest Asset*, Wellington, Government Printer.

MINISTER OF FINANCE (1991) *Budget 1991*, Wellington, Government Printer.

MINISTRY OF EDUCATION (1990) *Today's Schools*, The Lough Report, Wellington, GP Books.

MINISTRY OF EDUCATION (1991) *The National Curriculum of New Zealand: A Discussion Document*, Wellington, Learning Media.

MORGANTHAU, H. (1956) *Politics Among Nations*, (2nd ed.), New York, Knopf.

MORRIS, P. (1991) 'Freeing the spirit of enterprise: The genesis and development of the concept of enterprise culture', in KEAT, R. and ABERCROMBIE, N. (Eds) *Enterprise Culture*, London, Routledge.

MORT, (1953) 'Educational adaptability', *The School Executive*, **71**, pp. 1–23.

MUNGER, F.J. and FENNO, R.F. (Jr) (1962) *National Politics and Federal Aid to Education*, New York, Syracuse University Press.

MUNN, P. (1991) 'School boards, accountability and control', *British Journal of Educational Studies*, **39**, 2, pp. 173–89.

MURPHY, C. (1992, November) 'Study groups foster schoolwide learning', *Educational Leadership*, **50**, 3, pp. 71–4.

MURPHY, J. (1991) *Restructuring Schools: Capturing and Assessing the Phenomena*, New York, Teachers College Press.

MURPHY, J. and HALLINGER, P. (1986, Summer) 'The superintendent as instructional leader: Findings from effective school districts', *The Journal of Educational Administration*, **24**, 2, pp. 213–31.

MURPHY, J., HALLINGER, P. and PETERSON, K.D. (1985) 'Supervising and evaluating principals: Lessons from effective districts', *Educational Leadership*, **43**, 2, pp. 78–82.

NATIONAL DIFFUSION NETWORK (1988) *Educational Programs that Work*, Department of Education, San Francisco, Far West Laboratory of Educational Research.

NATIONAL FOUNDATION FOR EDUCATIONAL RESEARCH (1992, September) *An Evaluation of the 1992 National Curriculum Assessment at Key Stage One*, Slough, Berkshire, NFER.

NATIONAL GOVERNORS' ASSOCIATION (1987) *Results-Education 1987*, Washington DC, The Authors.

NATIONAL LEADERSHIP STUDY GROUP ON RESTRUCTURING (1993) *Toward Quality in Education: The Leader's Odyssey*, Austin, TX, Texas Association of School Administrators.

NATIONAL SCIENCE TEACHERS ASSOCIATION (1991) Scope Sequence, and Co-ordination of Secondary School Science The Content Core A Guide for Curriculum Designers (Draft).

NAYLOR, M. (1986) *Granting Academic Credit for Vocational Education: Overview*, ERIC Digest No. 57.

NEW ZEALAND QUALIFICATIONS AUTHORITY (1991) *Designing the Framework*, Wellington, NZQA.

NUTTALL, D. and STOBART, G. (1994) 'National Curriculum Assessment in the UK', *Educational Measurement: Issues and Practice*, pp. 24–7.

ODDEN, A.R. (1991) 'Policy implementation and current curriculum reform: An analysis of implementation of the California mathematics and science curriculum frameworks', in MARSH, D.D. and ODDEN, A.R. *Educational Implementation*, New York, SUNY Press.

OECD (1989) *Education and the Economy in a Changing Society*, Paris, Organisation for Economic Cooperation and Development.

PAULU, N. (1988) *Experiences in School Improvement: The Story of 16 American Districts*, Washington, DC, US Department of Education, Office of Educational Research and Improvement.

PETERS, M. (1992a) 'A Critique of the User-pays Philosophy in University Education and the Democratic Alternative', Paper presented to the New Zealand University Students' Association Conference, University of Canterbury, May.

PETERS, M. (1992b, May) 'A critique of the Porter report', *Delta*, **46**, pp. 3–14.

PETERS, M. (1992c) 'Starship education: Enterprise culture in New Zealand', *Access*, **11**, 1, pp. 1–10.

PETERS, M. and MARSHALL, J. (1988a) 'Social policy and the move to community', *The April Report*, Vol. **3**, 2, *Future Directions*, Royal Commission on Social Policy, Wellington, Government Printer, pp. 655–76.

PETERS, M. and MARSHALL, J. (1988b) 'Social policy and the move to community: Practical implications for service delivery', *The April Report*, Vol. **3**, 2, *Future Directions*, Royal Commission on Social Policy, Wellington, Government Printer, pp. 677–702.

PETERS, M.A., PETERS, M.C. and FREEMAN-MOIR, J. (1992) 'The 1991 budget and tertiary education: Promises, promises . . .', *New Zealand Annual Review of Education*, **1**, 1991, pp. 133–46.

PETERSON, P.E. (1967) *School Politics: Chicago Style*, Chicago, University of Chicago Press.

PHILPOTT, B. (1991) *Review of Upgrading New Zealand's Competitive Advantage*, New Zealand Economic Papers, **25**, 2, pp. 275–82.

PICOT REPORT (1987) *Administering for Excellence*, Report of the Taskforce to Review Education Administration, Wellington, Government Printer.

PIPER, K. (1989) 'National Curriculum: Prospects and Possibilities', Unpublished paper presented to the Australian Curriculum Studies Association Curriculum '89 Conference, Canberra, ACT, 6–9 July 1989.

PIPHO, C. (1987) 'The States are bullish on education', *Phi Delta Kappan*, **68**, 7, pp. 494–5.

POWELL, A.G., FARRAR, E. and COHEN, D.K. (1985) *The Shopping Mall High School: Winners and Losers in the Educational Marketplace*, Boston, Houghton-Mifflin.

PRAIS, S. and WAGNER, K. (1983) *Schooling Standards in Britain and Germany*, London, National Institute for Economic and Social Research.

PRING, R. (1986) 'The curriculum and new vocationalism', *British Journal of Education and Work*, **1**, 3, pp. 133–48.

QUALITY OF EDUCATION REVIEW COMMISSION REPORT (1985) *The Quality of Education in Australia*, Canberra, The Australian Government Publishing Service.

RAND CHANGE AGENT STUDY: FEDERAL PROGRAMS SUPPORTING EDUCATIONAL CHANGE:

Vol. I, BERMAN, P. and MCLAUGHLIN, M.W. (1974, September) *A Model of Educational Change*, R-158911-HEW.

Vol. II, BERMAN, P. and PAULY, E.W. (1975a, April) *Factors Affecting Change Agent Projects*, R-158912-HEW.

Vol. III, GREENWOOD, P.W., MANN, D. and MCLAUGHLIN, M.W. (1975b, April) *The Process of Change*, R-158913-HEW.

Vol. IV, BERMAN, P. and MCLAUGHLIN, M.W. (1975c, April) *The Findings in Review*, R-158914-HEW.

Vol. V, BERMAN, P., GREENWOOD, P.W., MCLAUGHLIN, M.W. and PINCUS, J. (1975, April) *Executive Summary*, R-158915-HEW.

Vol. VI, SUMMER, G. and ZELIMAN, G. (1977, January) *Implementing and Sustaining Title VII Bilingual Projects*, Title VII, R-158916-HEW.

Vol. VII, BERMAN, P. and MCLAUGHLIN, M.W. (1977, April) *Factors Affecting Implementation and Continuation*, R-158917-HEW.

Vol. VIII, BERMAN, P. and MCLAUGHLIN, M.W. (1978, May) *Implementing and Sustaining Innovations*, R-158918-HEW.

RAYWID, M.A. (1990) 'The evolving effort to improve schools: Pseudo-reforms, incremental reform, and restructuring', *Phi Delta Kappan*, **72**, 2, pp. 139–43.

REICH, R.B. (1994) 'The fracturing of the middle class', *The New York Times*, Op-Ed page, A13.

REYNOLDS, J. and SKILBECK, M. (1976) *Culture and the Classroom*, London, Open Books.

RICHARDSON, R. (1991) *Budget Speech*, Minister for Finance.

ROGERS, C.R. (1969) *Freedom to Learn*, Columbus, OH, Charles Merrill.

ROGERS, E.M. and SHOEMAKER, F.F. (1971) *Communication of Innovations: A Cross Cultural Approach*, (2nd ed.), New York, Free Press.

RUST, V. and BLAKEMORE, K. (1990) 'Educational reform in Norway and in England and Wales: A corporatist interpretation', *Comparitive Education Review*, **34**, 4, pp. 500–22.

SARASON, S.B. (1990) *The Predictable Failure of Educational Reform*, CA, Jossey-Bass Inc.

SASHKIN, M. and EGERMEIER, J. (1992) 'School change models and processes: A review of research and practice', Paper presented at the Annual Meeting of the American Educational Research Association, San Francisco, CA.

SAUNDERS, M. and HALPIN, D. (1990) 'The TVEI and the national curriculum: A cautionary note', *British Journal of Educational Studies*, **28**, 3, pp. 224–36.

SCHILLER, J.M. (1988) 'The primary school principal as an agent of change: The relationship between interventions and implementation of computer education', Unpublished Doctoral thesis, University of Newcastle.

SCHOOL EXAMINATIONS AND ASSESSMENT COUNCIL (1993) *1994 Assessment Arrangements*, Sir Ron Dearing, SCAA.

SCOTTISH OFFICE EDUCATION DEPARTMENT (1992) 'Placing requests in education authority schools', *Statistical Bulletin*, EDN/B6 SOED.

SEXTON, S. (1988) 'No nationalised curriculum', *The Times*, 9 May 1988.

SEXTON, S. (1991) 'New Zealand Schools: An Evaluation of Recent Reforms and Future Directions', Report commissioned by the Business Round Table, Wellington.

SHYMANSKY, J.A., KYLE, W.C.JR. and ALPORT, J.M. (1983) 'The effects of new science curricula on student performance', *Journal of Research in Science Teaching*, **20**, pp. 387–404.

SKILBECK, M. (1987) 'Culture or technology in the curriculum', *Curriculum Exchange*, **5**, 2, pp. 22–35.

SMITH, M.S. and O'DAY, J. (1990) 'Systemic school reform', in FUHRMAN, S. and MALEN, B. (Eds) *The Politics of Curriculum and Testing*, New York, Falmer Press, pp. 233–67.

SPAULL, A. (1987) *A History of the Australian Education Council 1936–1986*, Sydney, Allen and Unwin.

STAKE, R.E. and EASLEY, J.A. (1978) *Case Studies in Science Education*, Vol. I and II, Urbana-Champaign, IL, Center for Instructional Research and Curriculum Evaluation, University of Illinois.

STENHOUSE, L. (1975) *An Introduction to Curriculum Research and Development*, London, Heinemann.

STOBART, G. and BURGESS, T. (1992) 'Assessing English at Key Stage 3: Dilemmas for SAT Developers', in GIPPS C. (Ed) *Developing Assessment for the National Curriculum*, Bedford Way Series, ULIE/Kogan Page.

STRESHLY, W. and BERND, M. (1992, July) 'School reform: Real improvement takes time', *Journal of School Leadership*, **2**, 3, pp. 320–9.

SULLIVAN, N. (1988) 'The political theory of neo-corporatism', in COX, A. and SULLIVAN, N. (Eds) *The Corporate State*, Cambridge, Edward Elgar.

THE MAYER COMMITTEE (1992) *Employment-Related Competencies: A Proposal for Consideration*, Melbourne, p. 313.

THE TREASURY (1984) *Economic Management*, Wellington, Government Printer.

THE TREASURY (1987) *Government Management*, Wellington, Government Printer.

TIMAR, T. and KIRP, D. (1988) *Managing Educational Excellence*, New York, Falmer Press.

TOMKINS, G.S. (Ed) (1979) *The Curriculum in Canada in Historical Perspective*, Vancouver, Canadian Society for the Study of Education.

VAN DEN BERG, R. and VANDENBERGHE, R. (1981) *Onderwiisinnovatie in Verschuivend Perspectief*, Amersterdam, Uitgeverij Zwijsen.

VAN DEN BERG, R. and VANDENBERGHE, R. (1983) *Large-scale Innovation in Education: Two Analyses*, Leuven, Belgium, Centre for Educational Research and Innovation.

VANDENBERGHE, R. (1988) 'Development of a Framework and Measure (in Dutch) for assessing principal change facilitation', Paper presented at the

Annual Meeting of the American Association for Research in Education, New Orleans, LA.

WALSH, P. (1992) 'The employment contracts act', in BOSTON, J. and DALZIEL, P. (Eds) *The Decent Society: Essays in Response to National's Economic and Social Policies*, Auckland, Oxford University Press.

WEILER, H. (1988) 'The politics of reform and non-reform in French education', *Comparative Education Reform*, **32**, 3, pp. 252–65.

WIENER, M.J. (1981) *English Culture and the Decline of the Industrial Spirit, 1850–1980*, Cambridge, Cambridge University Press.

WIJLICK, W. Van (1987) 'The activities of internal change facilitators: An analysis of interventions', in VANDENBERGHE, R. and HALL, G.E. (Eds) *Research on Internal Change Facilitation in Schools*, Leuven, Belgium, Acco (Academic Publishing Company).

WILLMS, J. and ECHOLS, F. (1992) 'Alert and inert clients: The Scottish experience of parental choice of schools', *Economics of Education Review*, **11**, 4, pp. 339–50.

WIRT, F. and HARMAN, G. (Eds) (1986) *Education, the Recession and the World Village: A Comparitive Political Economy of Education*, Philadelphia, Falmer Press.

WYLIE, C. (1990) *The Impact of Tomorrow's Schools in Primary School and Intermediates*, NZCER, Wellington.

YOUNG, M. (1993) 'A curriculum for the 21st century: Towards a new basis for overcoming academic/vocational divisions', *British Journal of Educational Studies*, **41**, 3, pp. 203–22.

Notes on Contributors

Richard Aldrich is chair of the Department of History, Humanities and Philosophy at the Institute of Education, University of London. He is past president of the UK History of Education Society, and currently is a member of the Committee of the International Standing Conference for the History of Education. His international experience has embraced work in many European countries, in Asia and Australia, and in North and South America.

David Carter is a foundation staff member and senior lecturer in educational leadership at the University of Notre Dame, Australia. He is also visiting professor to the Department of Educational Administration at the University of Texas at Austin. His main research interests are in curriculum studies, educational change and innovation, and educational leadership.

James Cibulka is professor of administrative leadership at the University of Wisconsin-Milwaukee. He received his PhD from the University of Chicago, where he studied educational administration and political science. He is currently senior editor of *Educational Administration Quarterly*.

Caroline Gipps is professor of education and dean of research at the University of London Institute of Education. She was president of the British Educational Research Association (BERA) in 1991–3, and is convenor of the BERA Policy Task Group on Assessment. She has published widely on policy and practice in assessment.

Gene E. Hall is a professor of educational leadership and policy studies at the University of Northern Colorado. The central theme in his research continues to be developing new understandings about the change process, especially from the point of view of practitioners engaged in implementation. While at the University of Texas at Austin, he and his colleagues, developed and verified the basic elements of the Concerns Based Adoption Model (CBAM), the results of which are now used worldwide.

Shirley M. Hord is senior research associate at the Southwest Educational Laboratory (SEDL) in Austin, Texas. She is currently researching the 'leadership for change' project at SEDL. She serves as a fellow of the National Center for Effective Schools Research and Development, and as US representative to the Foundation for the International School Improvement Project, an international effort to develop research, training, and policy initiatives that will support local-school improvement practices.

Kerry J. Kennedy is currently director at the Centre for Continuing Education at the Australian National University. He was formerly professor and dean of education at the University of Southern Queensland; assistant director of the National Curriculum Development Centre, and subsequently director of the Federal Government's Curriculum Policy Unit. His research interests include curriculum-policy development and the impact of curriculum policy on educational practice.

Dennis Lawton is a professor of education at the Institute of Education, University of London. He became professor and head of curriculum studies in 1974 and director of the Institute of Education in 1983, returning to curriculum studies in 1989 to concentrate on writing and research. He is a specialist in educational planning and curriculum studies. His 'cultural analysis' approach to curriculum planning has been applied in a number of countries.

Marnie O'Neill is a lecturer in education at the University of Western Australia. She has previously been head of English in Western Australian secondary schools, and education officer in the curriculum branch of the Education Department of Western Australia, and chief and supervising examiner for tertiary entrance examinations in English.

Michael Peters is a senior lecturer in the Education Department at the University of Auckland. His research interests are in the combined areas of educational philosophy and policy. He has been a contributor to a number of edited collections and a wide range of international journals covering a number of areas in the field of education.

Ivan Snook is emeritus professor of education, and prior to his retirement in 1994, he was also the dean of education at Massey University, New Zealand. He is the author and co-author of several books and has published more than 100 articles in philosophical and educational journals.

Index